"Proud, defiant, brave, these are the Muslim women of America. Hear them roar!"　　　　　　　—Asma Gull Hasan, author of *Why I Am a Muslim*

"Looks behind media hype to explore the realities of this misunderstood culture."　　　　　　　　　　　　　　　　　　　—*Publishers Weekly*

"Enlightening. . . . In their diversity, forthrightness, and honesty, the voices of these women ultimately sound more American than anything else—and therein lies the strength of this book."　　　　　　　—*Library Journal*

"A 'five-star read' packed with inspiring stories about the lives of American Muslim women. In view of the crosscultural tensions of our post-9/11 world, this 'must-read' is a powerful reminder that Muslims are Americans, too!"
　　—Jean Sasson, *New York Times* bestselling author of *Princess*

"Sheds light on the lives of Muslim women by way of more than four dozen well-crafted profiles, cutting across cultures and lifestyles."
　　　　　　　　　　　　　　　　　—Mike Conlon, Reuters

"Invaluable. . . . Donn Gehrke-White, a reporter for *The Miami Herald*, has attempted to do for Muslim women what Studs Terkel did for American workers. . . . She has sought to give voice to the women themselves, letting them tell their own stories of belief and practice." —*Louisville Courier-Journal*

"Adds depth and insight to a widely misunderstood picture."
　　　　　　　　　　　　　　　　　　　—*Kansas City Star*

"Successfully incorporates dissenting religious opinion with minimal editorializing."　　　　　　　　　　　　　　　　　—*Nashville Scene*

"One fallacy non-Muslims tend to believe is that Islam promotes the idea of women's inferiority; the proof used to support this myth is the veil. Gehrke-White's book is a vital corrective to this misconception, guiding the reader to a deeper understanding of what the religion actually is and what it means to its practitioners."　　　　　　　　　　　　—*Miami Herald*

"Compelling, edifying and uplifting."
　　—Nathan Katz, professor of religious studies and director of the Center for the Study of Spirituality, Florida International University

"A must-read for women who recognize the heart-to-heart connection among all of us."　　　　　　　—Lisa R. Delman, author of *Dear Mom, I've Always Wanted You to Know . . .*

"Delves beyond the mystery and misconceptions associated with veils to put a personal face on a complex group of women bound by their faith. . . . The stories vary widely—from very successful career women with supportive families who belong to Americanized mosques to women who were oppressed and abused by husbands."　　　　　　　—*St. Louis Post-Dispatch*

THE FACE BEHIND THE VEIL

The Extraordinary Lives
of Muslim Women in America

DONNA GEHRKE-WHITE

CITADEL PRESS
Kensington Publishing Corp.
www.kensingtonbooks.com

CITADEL PRESS BOOKS are published by

Kensington Publishing Corp.
850 Third Avenue
New York, NY 10022

All Kensington titles, imprints, and distributed lines are available at
special quantity discounts for bulk purchases for sales promotions,
premiums, fund-raising, educational, or institutional use. Special book
excerpts or customized printings can also be created to fit specific needs.
For details, write or phone the office of the Kensington special sales
manager: Kensington Publishing Corp., 850 Third Avenue, New York,
NY 10022, attn: Special Sales Department; phone 1-800-221-2647.

First printing: March 2006
First paperback printing: March 2007

10 9 8 7 6 5 4 3 2 1

Printed in the United States of America

Library of Congress Control Number: 2005934014 (hardcover edition)

ISBN-13: 978-0-8065-2722-2
ISBN-10: 0-8065-2722-6

Thanks Tim, Nick and Alex

for being there

Contents

PART V: THE CHANGERS 207

Preface

Like so many other reporters who covered religion, I was asked to write about Muslims after the terrorist attacks of September 11, 2001. Mohammad Shakir, executive director of the Miami-Dade Asian-American Advisory Board, recommended that I examine a trend he had seen: More Muslim women were taking up wearing the traditional Islamic head covering known as a *hijab*—even though in America such apparel is still relatively rare. His own daughter, a law student in Michigan, was one of those "New Traditionalists"—even though her sister and mother didn't wear a covering in public.

I took Mohammad up on his suggestion and became fascinated with the women I met. They were devout Muslims, but also educated career women, including a doctor, medical lab director, social worker, and teacher. For one story in particular, I interviewed a Muslim student at the University of Miami who didn't wear any covering, yet strongly identified with Islam. She and the others who didn't wear a *hijab* had found a way to adapt to those aspects of Islamic tradition that suited them, managing to meld their "old" religion with the high-tech America we live in today.

The spiritual journey these women took fascinated me. It might lead them to different practices but they still prayed to Allah. Many are helping transform the mosque into a place of worship that fully includes women. They are Americanizing it into a place where potluck dinners, Brownie troop meetings, and even self-help sessions can be held—the kinds of programs American churches and synagogues already offer.

Even with anti-Muslim sentiment running higher in the United

States than ever before, these women persist with their faith. They wear their veils despite catcalls; they attend mosque despite being segregated from men. Indeed, Islam is flourishing, with new mosques opening every year. While many American women are pushing for reforms within the mosque, they still don't give up their faith. In Islam, they find solace.

I set out to find out why this is so, and who these women are.

Acknowledgments

This book would never have been written had it not been for the many patient Muslim women who answered my questions. Thank you, ladies, for sharing with me your lives. Special thanks to Anisah David for telling not only her story but her daughter's, but also for helping me find other fascinating *Muslimah* and offering invaluable suggestions as I wrote the book. Sakeena Mirza, Sireen Sawaf, Okolo Rashid, and Deedra Abboud also pitched in to recommend contacts for the book. Zainab Elberry, Ingrid Mattson, and Luby Ismail did that, as well as furnish invaluable background information about Islam and Muslims in America. I also need to thank Zuly Martinez, who shared with me her extraordinary photographs of Muslim women.

Mukit Hossain both recommended likely subjects and helped set up interviews. He also helped me locate important research materials that helped me understand the anxieties of American Muslim women in the wake of the September 11 terrorist attacks, especially those women who had been detained or had their homes searched by federal agents. Mohammad Shakir, executive director of the Miami-Dade Asian-American Advisory Board was also extremely helpful with my research. Jawaad Abdul Rahman of Unity Productions Foundation, Ibrahim Hooper of the Council on American-Islamic Relations, and Helen Samhan, director of the Arab American Institute Foundation were invaluable in recommending fascinating women. Professor John G. Douglass at the University of Richmond School of Law was also helpful in his research on how Muslim charities and private homes became objects of scrutiny by government agents. A book like this could not have been written without these experts' help.

I am also especially indebted to Dr. Ihsan Bagby of the University of Kentucky for his important research on Muslims in America, which I quote throughout the book. Special thanks also to Mohiaddin Mesbahi, an associate professor of International Relations at Florida International University, and Stephen Sapp, chairman of the Religious Studies Department at the University of Miami. Early on, when I was writing my first article on Muslim women for the *Miami Herald*, they helped send me on the right path.

Rosalind Rivera, the executive director of the Arizona Refugee Community Center, opened her doors—and heart—to me. She arranged for me to interview several women and provided excellent interpreters.

It goes without saying a book like this needs a nurturer, and I thank Kensington's editor in chief, Michaela Hamilton, for her excellent suggestions. I want to thank her for sharing my excitement about these fascinating Muslim women and for her patience in working with me as I sorted through my research and interviews.

This book simply wouldn't exist without my agent, Agnes Birnbaum. Everyone should have someone like her in their lives. Thanks, Agnes, for always inspiring me.

Finally, thanks to *Miami Herald* editors Teresa Mears, Joan Chrissos, and Kathy Foster. They not only gave me encouragement but granted me a leave of absence to work on the book. Teresa also kept busy forwarding to me stories on Muslim women and Islamic trends—even giving me computer tips. *Herald* photographer Marsha Halper was a godsend as she helped gather pictures for the book.

For numbers-crunching, the State Department's Amanda D. Rogers-Harper was invaluable in providing data on the latest number of refugees arriving in the United States.

Heartfelt thanks to a patient editor: my husband, Tim White. He helped expunge my foibles out of the book and made it better. Nick and Alex, you were great in overlooking your mom's absent-mindedness during the long months of writing.

Finally, thanks to the many who kept encouraging me to hang in there and finish *The Face Behind the Veil*.

THE FACE BEHIND THE VEIL

INTRODUCTION

A JAPANESE AMERICAN raised in a Louisiana fundamentalist church calls herself a Muslim. So do an award-winning teacher, a former drug-addicted prostitute turned counselor, a New York lawyer, a Nashville feminist, a Florida doctor, and a group of Afghan refugees in Phoenix who are learning to read for the first time.

They are all Muslim women in America, or as they call themselves, the *Muslimah*. They hail from at least seventy-seven countries. Thousands of women in America, from every ethnic group, convert to Islam. Indeed, the United States has the most diverse Muslim population in the world.

Today's American *Muslimah* come from posh Los Angeles suburbs, African refugee camps, rural South Dakota, Beirut high rises, the Iraqi desert, and a city on the Adriatic Sea. Some are learning to use electricity and plumbing for the first time. Others are middle-class, car-pooling moms, or human rights leaders advising the White House.

There are those who stand out. The African immigrants wearing their turban-like headdresses, the Asian Americans in their flowing scarves, the Middle Eastern–born women in their veils, the converts opting for their own styles, some going for the most dramatic — the head-to-toe burqas. Most American *Muslimah*, however, are not so easily spotted. They don't wear any kind of head covering that would identify them as Muslims. They blend into the American fabric.

Who are these women?

Americans know more about the downtrodden *Muslimah* in Iran, Saudi Arabia, Afghanistan, and Europe than they do their own neighbors. Yet American Muslim women have forged their own identity.

You are about to discover these American *Muslimah*. You will meet more than fifty women from this complex, diverse, and engaging group.

They are far from the stereotype of the downtrodden Muslim woman forced to wear a detested veil — although some *are* struggling

1

as refugees while others face domestic violence, polygamy, and child-custody battles. But even the *Muslimah* who face daunting challenges tend to adapt an American can-do, you-go-girl attitude, which in other parts of the world can provoke a stinging critique from those who accuse our *Muslimah* of being so American, so Westernized. Their pluck, though, is helping to create a vibrant Islam, and shows how an age-old faith can fit into a new high-tech age.

You are about to meet:

- The New Traditionalists. Women who wear the veil or a hijab, in some cases taking it up after earlier generations did not. They include career women and full-time mothers.

- The Blenders. Women who don't wear any veil or head covering. They don't look "Muslim" but still consider themselves spiritual. They are mostly immigrants, second-generation Americans, and career women.

- The Converts. A surprising number of American women, of all races and ethnic groups, have converted to Islam. They're among the most enthusiastic about wearing traditional women's attire, some of them adding gloves and long gowns in addition to a veil.

- The Persecuted. Many Muslim women come to America to escape violence and oppression, from such countries as Afghanistan, Iraq, Sudan, Somalia, Bosnia, and India. Some are also fleeing from abuse and applying for asylum to avoid going back to a country where they may be killed by an enraged man.

- The Changers. These women are taking a public stand. Some are running for public office, or starting humanitarian groups and nonprofit social associations that help abused or needy Muslim women. Some are fighting within the mosque for equal rights for women.

Thanks to a worldwide trend among many *Muslimah* who prefer some sort of covering, more veiled women are being seen on American streets these days. Most wear the *hijab*, as it is called in Arabic.

Many Muslim women in the United States, whether covered or not, say they don't like to draw attention to themselves. The reason: They are a religious minority in a country that promises religious freedom but has been at times hostile to those practicing new or "different" faiths.

Yet Islam has been part of America's overall return to the spiritual. The number of Muslims has doubled in a decade, making it one of the fastest-growing religions in the United States. Overall, the nation is more religious than even a couple of decades ago. Witness the phenomenal success of Mel Gibson's film, *The Passion of the Christ*, the tens of thousands who flock to hear the Dalai Lama speak, and the growth in Orthodox Judaism. Even the 2004 presidential election was affected, with "family values" seen as a major issue in voters' minds.

Similarly, many American Muslims say they have become more spiritual in recent years. That's but one of the reasons for a return to some sort of covering.

In the past, though, many Muslim women appear to have not been included in various religious surveys, which skews estimates of how many Muslims live in America. Many U.S. studies base their membership numbers on how many attend weekly services at a house of worship. As many traditional or immigrant Muslim women do not go to mosque, they have been overlooked.

There are now perhaps three million Muslim women in the United States. No one knows for sure. The U.S. census does not ask Americans their religion. The American Religious Identity Survey found the total number of Muslims—1.1 million—had more than doubled from 1990 to 2001. However, the Council of American-Islamic Relations, an advocacy group, believes there are actually six to seven million Muslims living in the United States, an estimate based on the number of mosques in the country.

In Canada, where the government does include religion in its national census, 2 percent are Muslims. If that same percentage would hold true for the United States, then about six million Muslims now call this country home. Indeed, Ihsan Bagby, an associate professor of Islamic Studies at the University of Kentucky, who has conducted surveys on mosques, believes the number of U.S. Muslims is five to six million. If those numbers are correct, there are now more Muslims in America than the two to three million members the Episcopal Church claims in the United States.

Immigration, Dr. Bagby says, is fueling much of that growth. *The New York Times* wrote in February 2005 that for the first time, more Africans—many of whom are Muslim—are arriving on American shores now than during the slave trade. International turmoil is a key factor in immigration patterns. According to government statistics, more than 229,000 Muslim refugees from seventy-seven countries arrived in the United States from 1990 to September 30, 2004. They came from such turbulent countries as Sudan, Bosnia, Iran, Iraq, Afghanistan, and Uzbekistan.

Some of these *Muslimah* refugees are running not only from their country's violence but from arranged marriages or abusive men. One twenty-three-year-old I interviewed might become the victim of an "honor killing" if she returns to her country. Her fiancé remains enraged that she "humiliated" him by leaving for a trip to the United States and refusing to come home. He has gone so far as to attack members of her family who remain in her South Asian country. The United States now allows asylum for such endangered women.

There is also a new generation of *Muslimah*—the grown-up daughters of the newcomers. Most either were born here or came as small children. Many already have families of their own. The second generation also includes the daughters of converts. Some have foreign-born fathers and American mothers who converted to Islam. For others, both of their parents are converts. This new generation of *Muslimah* varies widely. Some went back to a covering their mothers abandoned. Others are the first in their family *not* to wear a *hijab*. Many chafed at the restrictions their parents imposed upon them: They were not allowed to date, for example.

What they have in common is that they tend to be educated. Many hold professional jobs. They also tend to be devout, pray regularly, and observe Ramadan and other Islamic holy times. Many view their local mosque as like a church, part of their social life, not merely a place for weekly prayer service. They go to the mosque for home-schooling clubs, Daisy troops, and canned-good drives to help the poor. In that, they and the converts have helped Americanize the mosque.

Many *Muslimah* want their mosque to reflect how they live in America as equals with men. They want to have access to the same prayer services as men and demand that their spiritual needs be given the same weight. Some are considered radicals. A mixed prayer service was held in March 2005, in New York, in which a woman led the prayers and—even more scandalously to many Muslims—allowed men and women to pray side by side. Change is coming, predicts Ingrid Mattson. She should know: She is the first woman to become vice president of the Islamic Society of North America, the largest Muslim organization on the continent.

Also fueling the change and growth in American Islam are the *Muslimah* converts who, for the most part, are among its most enthusiastic practitioners. Many of these converts say they are relieved to find a faith that finally suits them. Most are former Christians who have had problems accepting the Christian idea of the Holy Trinity (God the Father, Jesus, and the Holy Spirit). Islam, by contrast, recognizes only one God but acknowledges Jesus as a prophet.

Most converts are African Americans, who are resuming what may have been their ancestors' original faith. Historians and religious scholars estimate that up to 30 percent of African slaves who arrived in the New World were Muslim. Ihsan Bagby's latest research indicates that fewer Muslim slaves reached the American colonies than were sold to buyers in the West Indies and Latin America. Still, he says, about 10 percent of the United States' newly arrived slaves were Muslim.

As soon as slaves arrived in America, their new masters brutally suppressed their religion and forced them to become Christians. Hundreds of years later, their descendants reclaimed Islam. Indeed, for decades, Islam has been part of a black movement such as the Nation of Islam. While today most African American Muslims adhere to a more orthodox Islam, Ihsan Bagby estimates about 10,000 are still part of the Nation. (The Nation of Islam does not release its membership numbers.)

Because of a spike in curiosity about Islam after the terrorist attacks of 9/11, more Americans are going to the mosque—and staying. Since 2001, Islam appears to be attracting more whites and Hispanics, and in one study at Detroit mosques Bagby found that whites and

Hispanic Americans now make up 40 percent of the latest converts. In a national 2000 study, just four years earlier, white and Hispanics were only 25 percent of the converts, he says.

The *Muslimah* converts I interviewed are as varied as their immigrant sisters. A white woman in rural South Dakota converted as a college student, collects *hijabs*, and started an Internet matchmaking service for Muslims. A young Mexican American photographer in Texas became one of the first Hispanics at her mosque. Master Zakia Mahasa, who sits on Baltimore's judicial bench, as a Master in Chancery in the Family Division of the Baltimore City Circuit Court, converted as a teenager, has traveled to Mecca on a *hajj*, and now leads a national Muslim charity.

Surprisingly, many of these new members say they were first attracted to Islam by what they perceive as its feminist message.

Despite the message of some leaders in the Muslim world who invoke Islam to suppress women, most Muslim women in the United States see their religion as a liberating force. They say their faith has helped them develop spiritually and intellectually, and they consider themselves feminists. In fact, some of the *Muslimah* I interviewed played prominent roles in the U.S. women's rights movement during the 1960s and 1970s. Today, a new generation of *Muslimah* feel they are the new American feminists, see themselves as part of a sisterhood, and claim they are better able to balance work and family than other working mothers in the United States because their religion requires men to support their children. They also point out that religion's traditional separation of the sexes actually helps women achieve.

Deedra Abboud, former executive director of the Arizona chapter of the Council on American-Islamic Relations, an advocacy group, says Islam is more feminist oriented than the Christianity she grew up with. "I found I liked Islam and what it stood for," she says. Islam has none of the Biblical teachings traditionally used by some Christians to malign women, such as Eve being portrayed in the Book of Genesis as the temptress who cajoles Adam into eating the forbidden fruit.

Interviews and surveys indicated that American *Muslimah* are economically much better off than their European counterparts, who have been traditionally relegated to the lowest level of the workforce. European countries brought in low-skill Muslim workers to do the jobs that their own people would not do. American Muslim immigrants, on the other hand, have until recently tended to be much more highly educated, entering the labor force as engineers, doctors, teachers, or post-graduate students.

Their children, the United States' emerging second generation of Muslims, are becoming equally well-off and educated. Both daughters and sons are encouraged to go to college. Even the refugees who arrive in the United States with only the clothes on their back are striving hard to join the middle class, and if they don't quite make it, many of their children will. The American-born converts to Islam are also relatively comfortable financially, with many of them educated and holding professional or managerial positions. As a whole, American Muslims tend to be affluent. Ihsan Bagby's 2004 Detroit study of 1,298 male and female mosque congregants found that the average Muslim is thirty-four years old, married with children, has at least a bachelor's degree, and earns about $75,000 a year.

Like other American women, many *Muslimah* work outside the home to contribute to their family's income. They are career-focused women who practice law, sell insurance, head nonprofit agencies, and start their own businesses and nonprofit organizations. They run the gamut, from a New York–born attorney who has never worn a veil — and never will — to a veiled Seattle convert who has made a business out of designing clothes for other adherents.

Many of the interviewed younger *Muslimah* moms opt to stay home with their children, at least before the kids are old enough to go to school. Some also home-school their children. They want careers — but later. Their focus is to have a rich family life with well-raised children. They tend to marry early (some before the age of twenty) and have their own children while in their twenties. Then, after their children start school, they pursue a higher education, or go to work.

American *Muslimah* tend to have at least started their college education by the time they marry. The exceptions are the newest refugees, but even these women who were denied the right to read and write in their countries are now eagerly attending classes in the United States for the first time. (They credit the Quranic emphasis on education for their own appetite for learning.)

American *Muslimah* tend to vote Democratic like other American women, according to Mukit Hossain, president of the Muslim American Political Action Committee. They also vote in greater numbers than their Muslim male counterparts: 53 percent as opposed to 47 percent of the men, according to one of the committee's studies. Indeed, more women are becoming politically active and running for office, from the California state assembly to a county office in Virginia.

Many *Muslimah*, however, have traditional family values that are more associated with Republicans. Fewer than 10 percent of the *Muslimah* interviewed have never been married—about half the rate of American women overall. Of the women older than thirty-five, only two *Muslimah* interviewed were childless.

Many of the immigrant women interviewed had marriages arranged by their parents. For the most part, many American *Muslimah*, including those of the second generation and as yet unmarried converts, did not "date" their future husbands in the usual sense. Intriguingly, the converts tend to be the most enthusiastic about following tradition: One woman did not even meet her husband until they were married—an elder at the mosque selected him—and she says he has turned out to be a caring spouse.

Although there are horror stories—one arranged marriage ended in disaster in Miami for a South Asian bride—most American Muslimah report that their traditional marriages have worked out surprisingly well. They and their husbands enjoy mutual respect and affection. The husbands are generally as religious as their wives and treat them well. Sarwat Husain of San Antonio, Texas, says that agreeing to an arranged marriage in her native Pakistan was her ticket to America, as well as to winning a good husband.

"Since the marriages are not based on infatuation, looks, or money, the divorce rate is very low in that part of the world," Sarwat says. "And, indeed, my husband and I were a good match. I call myself a hyperactive person, and my husband is very calm and mature. He has always been there to listen to me and he has encouraged me to do what I wanted to do."

Like other American *Muslimah*, Sarwat is becoming more vocal about civil rights violations in the United States since 9/11. Currently a volunteer with a Muslim civil rights advocacy group, she knows firsthand the need for such groups: She was once followed home and accosted by a group of anti-Muslim men. Another *Muslimah* I spoke with reported that she and her teenage daughter were handcuffed in their Virginia home after federal agents broke down her front door in broad daylight in 2002. They were never charged with any crime.

Most *Muslimah* wearing a *hijab* say they have been harassed in some way, usually with foul language, threats, or an exhortation to "go home." (When one young convert was yelled at by a driver from his Corvette, she replied, "I *am* home!")

American *Muslimah* are also increasingly concerned about helping other Muslim women in the U.S. and internationally. They are forming groups, for example, to help victims of domestic abuse. Muslims have the same rate of abuse as other Americans, yet many are reluctant to discuss the subject publicly, some *Muslimah* say. These women want to be able to talk frankly in their community about abuse—and how to stop it.

Many *Muslimah* also want to be able to provide foster care to Muslim children. Under current policies, Muslim children sometimes have to go to homes where the foster parents are active Christians. One young woman told me she has not been able to see her siblings because they are in a Christian foster home, the same one from which she was expelled because she objected to going to church and eating pork, which Islam prohibits.

One *Muslimah* I spoke with wanted to be able to talk frankly about polygamy, which Islam condones under strict conditions. The great majority of American Muslims practice monogamy but one woman says she was tricked into marriage by a man who already had a wife. She wanted to warn other naive women about men who use Islam as a way to justify having multiple wives.

Another woman says she went back to Christianity because she was concerned that Islam promotes wife abuse, including polygamy and beatings. She is now a minister and has started a mission to help abused Muslim women. "The whole abuse thing—he said I made him do it," adds the woman, who is now known by her pen name, W. L. Cati. "He says it was my fault that he hit me."

Some American Muslim women *are* abused. One woman was brought thousands of miles to Miami in an arranged marriage, only to be repeatedly hit by her husband. Later he would leave her and then report her to police for neglecting their children. She wound up jailed and institutionalized at a mental hospital until outraged Muslims fought for her release. One of those who worked for her freedom worries that a trend may be growing of men who take advantage of immigrant wives who are ignorant of their rights under U.S. laws, abusing them physically, emotionally, and financially, even stealing their dowry or family money.

Still, most of the interviewed *Muslimah* report happy marriages and loving husbands who treat them as equals and support their careers. One Florida Muslim man took care of his two daughters so his wife could go to medical school. Another, an engineer, watched over his son and daughter while his wife earned her doctorate at the University of Chicago. There are also professional partnerships, such as a husband-and-wife medical practice. Happily, these women also say their husbands support them having an equal presence in the mosques.

More than ever before, Muslim women in America are becoming an integral part of the mosque and part of the American Islamic leadership that is creating a new strain of Islam, one that adheres to the Quran and Islam's heritage, as well as adapting to the needs of the Western world.

"I think it is inevitable that as more educated Muslims come out with new interpretations [of the Quran and other religious books] things will change," religious scholar Ishan Bagby says.

Ingrid Mattson, for one, is confident that better times are ahead. "There will always be very conservative mosques," she says. "But they will come to be marginalized."

Muslimah also have had an impact on American society through their open practice of Islam. Clareen Menzies, of Minneapolis–St. Paul, is a convert who remembers how her neighbors from Uganda hid the fact that they were observing Islamic holy days and praying the required five times a day while attending services at a church that sponsored them as immigrants.

Emma Al-Aghbhary, of the Chicago suburbs, finds the United States a better place to practice Islam than her native New Zealand. In her opinion, Americans are more tolerant than New Zealanders, even in spite of incidents of harassment in the wake of 9/11 and the wars in Iraq and Afghanistan.

"I have worn the *hijab*, including modest clothing and *abaya* [the outer garment that is long, loose and modest] since the beginning of 2002," she says. "People's reactions have not been bad in Chicago. In New Zealand many people don't quite know how to react. Some say rude remarks or give rude gestures. Here in America, people usually mind their own business."

Muslims, she says, are "treated like anybody else." And that's just what the *Muslimah* want: to be part of the American fabric. "They are very desirous of becoming involved in society," Ihsan Bagby says.

Still, many do not find it easy. Areej Abdallah struggled for nine months to find work as a software engineer. She had her three children soon after her marriage, and studied for her computer science degree afterward. When she was ready to graduate, she discovered that major U.S. companies would interview her on campus at Arizona State University in Tempe, but she never heard back from them. She kept trying, though.

"I thought to myself, it's my *hijab*," she remembers. "That's why I can't find a job."

When Boeing offered her a job, Areej remembers accepting excitedly before the offer from the airplane manufacturer was rescinded. "I thought I was going to collapse," she now admits with a laugh.

Other *Muslimah* say they face struggles in the American judicial system, claiming that their children were taken away from them by judges who viewed with suspicion their practice of Islam. Says one Muslim convert, a Native American who now lives in New Jersey: "The court system gave custody to [my daughter's] father after a nasty custody battle in which my religion played, it seemed, a major role in the decision of the judge. I had custody of her all her life before the judge turned her over to her father." Still, she would not consider leaving Islam. It has meant too much for her. It is her spiritual home; it gives her strength to confront her many problems.

She and the others, then, offer insight into what has perplexed other Americans: How would women in free-spirited America remain a part of—or convert to—Islam, a religion that supposedly discriminates against women?

Their answer: Look at us. We are better for being Muslim.

PART I

⋙

The New Traditionalists

Ask Sahar Shaikh about her *hijab* and the twenty-something says it's all about identity. By wearing it, she says, "I found out who I am."

More and more American *Muslimah* are donning some sort of covering as part of their spiritual journey, from a head scarf to a veil that covers most of the face. Unlike others in the West, they don't see the covering as a symbol of female inferiority. Indeed, many *hijab*-wearing American women are highly educated: They practice law, teach at universities, develop software, or treat the ill.

As a social worker, Sahar wears a *hijab* and long gown when she sees elderly clients. She wants to clear up what she says is a common misperception. Muslim women wear a *hijab* because they want to, not because their husbands or fathers force them. "It makes me feel more at peace with God," Sahar says. "It also makes me aware of time management: I ask what should I be doing, what is His purpose?"

Sahar grew up in suburban Miami with blue jeans, Girl Scouts, and rock and roll. But she felt something was missing in her life. She found it on a tennis court in her freshman year at the University of Florida in Gainesville, surrounded by her Muslim friends. They were wearing their *hijabs*, even while running to lob the ball and then having to pat their head covering back in place. She was the only one bareheaded. "Look who is the outcast now," they gently teased her.

"It was a revelation to me," Sahar says. "I was trying so hard to fit in with the rest of the world." So despite being afraid of being labeled

13

"different" from the other university students, Sahar donned a *hijab*. And she says she discovered the warm intimacy of such a shared culture.

Mohiaddin Mesbahi, an associate professor of international relations at Florida International University, offered some insights on this developing trend among American Muslim women while I was working on a *Miami Herald* story. "They are returning to their identities, to spirituality, but they are feminists," Mesbahi said. "It's difficult for Western people to understand, but a woman putting on a *hijab* is not a sign of repression, like what they see on television with the women in Afghanistan. Although there is no data available, a significant number of American women are doing so."

These veiled feminists believe Islamic traditions have benefited women. Passages in the Quran, for example, promote educating women, emphasizing education over physical looks, says Stephen Sapp, chairman of the Department of Religious Studies at the University of Miami. "Islam, from the very beginning, emphasized the importance of having women be economically secure in their own right," he adds. "The Quran gives them the right to own and manage their own property. That is spelled out in great detail."

Indeed, the veil, or some sort of head covering for a woman, predates Islam. Ancient Greeks, Jews, and early Christians included head coverings as part of a woman's wardrobe. In some ancient societies it was a status symbol: Only slaves and prostitutes didn't wear them.

Today, it is true, many women wearing their Islamic covering believe they pay a heavy price for their spirituality. Many of the youngest feel lonely as the only girls to wear head scarves in middle or high school. (More *Muslimah* tend to wear some sort of covering in college.) Meanwhile, many older women who wear the *hijab* feel they are discriminated against at their work place. Others say they are singled out for harassment on the streets or in the mall, in misguided retaliation for the terrorists who kill in the name of Islam. As a result, some avoid going out in public, except to go to work or the mosque.

Still, most say such harassment could be much worse—and *is*—in other countries. France, for example, bans school girls from wearing a *hijab*. For the most part, *Muslimah* say Americans are accommodating, even curious about Islam.

Sakeena Mirza found that she is more comfortable in the United States than her father's native Pakistan. She now lives in Las Vegas. Meanwhile, her older sister, Haseena Mirza, discovered that she could wear her *hijab* while working at a predominantly Orthodox Jewish facility and be accepted. The American *Muslimah* feel so at home that they have developed their own couture with a "Western feel," says designer Michaela Corning of Seattle who caters to the growing number of women wearing the *hijab* and other traditional Muslim women's clothing. Indeed, if you look beyond the exotic apparel, you'll find the New Traditionalists, profiled in the following pages, could be your next-door neighbor, your doctor, or your lawyer. ⌒

❦ 1 ❧

Zarinah: An Islamic-Style High School Queen

WE ALL HAVE FELT the terror of being alone in a crowded school hallway, of somehow being *different*. We've felt the humiliation of not fitting into the tribe, of being uncool, whether it was for a few hours or our whole school career.

Imagine the plight of Zarinah Nadir, a second-generation Muslim who wore the hijab in school when no one else did. Zarinah was one of the relatively few African Americans in the overwhelmingly white state of Arizona. In addition, she had to wear an odd-looking scarf—years before 9/11 at a time when there wasn't much awareness of Muslims in America.

Now twenty-four years old, she recalls, "I was the only one in my elementary school through high school to wear the hijab. I have worn the hijab since sixth grade. I knew I looked different."

Other Muslim girls have bewailed this kind of experience. Zarinah's mother, Aneesah Nadir, for her doctoral dissertation, interviewed some girls who were traumatized during their public school years when their parents, many of them immigrants and unfamiliar with American customs, sent them to school wearing the required scarf, a symbol of Muslim female modesty. "I had a very difficult time," one girl told Aneesha. "I was the oldest in my family so I didn't have anyone to show me around. I didn't know what to expect. My parents didn't know what it was like for me. They're from a different culture. They've never been in my situation. They had sympathy but not empathy."

Zarinah didn't have an easy time, either. She didn't want to be the

17

only one wearing a hijab. Occasionally, she was called names and singled out for being "different." On the other hand, though, she didn't want to turn her back on her faith. She could *not* wear her scarf. Naturally outgoing, and proud that her parents converted to Islam, she decided to tough it out. She concentrated on what she had in common with the other kids at school. "I wore jeans like everyone else," she says. Plus, everyone wants to have fun, right? To have loyal friends? "I saw it as an opportunity. I didn't walk around with my head held down. I had lots of non-Muslim friends and we had common ground. I enjoyed having fun with them. We went to the movies. I wasn't able to do all the things they did—I didn't drink, I wasn't able to go to parties where there would be both boys and girls present. They respected that.

"But, to be honest," she adds, "there sometimes *were* difficult times." Some guy would make a dumb remark. A girl would stare at her.

In response, Zarinah and some other Muslim girls from the mosque started their own group. "For example, we started our own graduation party," Zarinah says. "Our philosophy is: We can do it—but in an Islamic way. I have my kicks, my fun. I didn't go to the high school prom or to pool parties or barbeques. I did, though, go to the homecoming football game—just not the prom."

Then she corrects herself. She did, indeed, go to a high school dance. Once.

It turns out that some of her friends nominated her as a candidate to be Junior Class Coronation Queen. Coronation was the last big dance before prom. Zarinah was touched but asked her friends to nominate someone who attends dances.

"But," she says, "they wouldn't hear of it, and a couple of days later I heard my name mentioned among other nominees. I wound up participating in the Coronation assembly during school hours."

The assembly turned out to be a highlight for Zarinah, who acknowledges she "was not the slender, blond cheerleader type." Then she had to grapple with whether she would be allowed to go to the dance. She and her mother came to the same conclusion: She *could*, but only to hear the election results. Still, what would she wear?

"I often dressed up in prom-like gowns for our ladies-only parties, but I never attended a mixed-gender formal. This was one of the hardest shopping trips I had ever taken!"

She ended up finding a cool—but modest—evening gown.

Zarinah asked her older brother to escort her to the dance, as Muslim boys and girls do not date. He had graduated from the same high school a year before, and thought it would be fun to return to his alma matter and see old friends.

"But, this being high school," Zarinah adds drolly, "the inevitable was bound to happen. The rumor spread that I would be going to the dance with my older brother. When friends came to me to check out what they heard, I confirmed it without hesitation."

So Zarinah went serenely to her first high school dance—with *hijab* and brother. Unusual to say the least but, then, Zarinah had adapted to being different.

It was almost an anticlimax when Zarinah was announced Coronation Queen, the school's first *hijab*-wearing queen—and, no doubt, its first to wear a gown buttoned to the neck.

"I believe that this event serves as a testament to my life and what I stand for. While there were some days, as the only *'hijabbed'* Muslim girl in school, I felt noticeably different, for the most part I used it as an opportunity to build bridges and form bonds—from cheerleaders and football players and those in the band to all students in between."

In retrospect, she feels her experiences forced her to mature, to tough out difficult situations. She now attributes her poise and confidence to overcoming the fear of being different.

"I had, fortunately, what other girls didn't have: a focus."

Some years later, Zarinah was accepted as a law student at Arizona State University, where she started the Muslim Law Students Association as an anchor for young Muslims trying to make it through law school. She has since worked in a family law office and wants to work as an intern in immigration court. She's not timid about trying out various legal areas until she finds her niche.

She feels her other *Muslimah* friends are equally strong and goal-oriented. One, she predicts, will break into broadcast journalism—*hijab* and all—and anchor a newscast. Another, she feels, could become a United States senator.

"The sky is the limit," she says. "We are coming of age. I see good things. I see hope." She believes there has been a disconnect between how Muslim women are treated in predominantly Muslim countries and how they once were. "Muslim women were once teachers, scholars, leaders on the battleground, and naval commanders. I feel our generation and the next generation will be reclaiming that history," Zarinah says.

Living in the United States, Zarinah feels she has enjoyed the best of both worlds. She's an American woman—with all the freedom that permits—and she's part of a closely knit Muslim community.

"I love this sense of community that Islam gives," she says. "Everyone is included. We address each other as brother or sister. If they are elders, they are aunties or uncles. We have this strong bond as a family. My extended family doesn't live in the same area I do. That's kind of hard. But we have built kind of an adopted family through our being Muslims—our own aunties and uncles who have seen me grow up and who have been to all of my special events.

"I appreciate the boundaries that Islam sets," she adds. "I believe in a higher power. Believing in that power really frees you from the burdens of the world. Oftentimes, people judge one another, and people make their own lives difficult by worrying what others think. But the weight goes off your shoulders if you remember that you are judged only by your Lord. No one can take that away. If God has not written something for my life, then it was not to be. That frees me from any burden. I try as hard as I can but if, for example, I don't get that job, then I don't worry."

"I am a second-generation Muslim," she continues. "I love that I am a link between American culture and Islamic culture, that they can coexist within me. Our parents didn't go through what we did. We were raised strictly on American soil. Second-generation Muslims, the children of immigrants, have a connection to America our parents don't have."

Zarinah feels a distinction between Muslim African Americans and the children of Muslim immigrants. The latter know where they come from, she says; they have a sense of their history. African Americans know, of course, that their forebears came from Africa, but most don't know anything more beyond that. Slavery took away much of their past, their heritage, she observes.

It has been estimated that from 10 to 30 percent of slaves brought to the Americas were Muslim. Although slaveholders suppressed Islam, some slaves refused to give up their faith. They carried the words of the Quran in their heads and secretly wrote down the holy passages in Arabic once they were in their slave quarters.

"Fortunately," Zarinah says, "now we are having our history unveiled. We need to carry on, to continue to explore our legacy. It helps when individuals know their history, that African Americans severed from their history learn about their legacy. We came to America as educated princes, as scholars."

Zarinah herself wants to become as educated as she can.

"I like law school at ASU," she adds. "I know it has a reputation as a party school, but it's a small and close-knit community. All the activists know each other."

Still, she admits, there have been some scary incidents, one of which involved her and a friend shortly after 9/11. "A guy tried to run over one of my friends with his bike," Zarinah says. "We were walking on the sidewalk. I pulled her out of the way. 'Do you want to die?' he shouted at her. "Can you believe that? We didn't believe it at the time. Someone reported it as a hate crime."

Zarinah was relieved that the police took this and subsequent incidents seriously. Her mosque was attacked in 2004 as the war in Iraq continued; a swastika was painted on the front door. In response, Tempe, Arizona, police scheduled a joint press conference with the Council of American-Islamic Relations to denounce the hate crime. The media covered it, and a suspect was swiftly arrested—a man who sported a swastika tattoo.

Those incidents don't stop Zarinah from going about her normal life. Nor has she considered moving to a safer community.

Vandalism would not deter Zarinah from staying in Arizona. "I am more resolved. I feel invested in this community," she says. "We have a large Muslim population here and it's growing. I would like to improve the conditions in Arizona. Of course, everything depends on my future career or when I get married. But I feel Arizona is my home base. I would love to see our community advance."

She adds, "When people ask me if I would ever consider removing my scarf or leaving my faith, I think about the time I was crowned

Coronation Queen in full Muslim regalia, and I think that if I were to succumb to such pressures, to denounce my faith, I would be betraying my friends who were not Muslim and were of other faiths, who loved me, cared for me, and defended me."

Not wearing her scarf, something she believes in, would be a betrayal of herself, she adds.

"And *that*," she says, "is the ultimate betrayal."

❧ 2 ❧

WHY SIREEN'S SCARF
MEANS SO MUCH

SIREEN SAWAF'S UNCLE was a taxi driver starting an early shift, just after five in the morning in sleepy West Covina, California, a mere two days after his forty-ninth birthday. Like so many other Syrian Muslims who emigrated to the United States in hopes of a better life for himself and his family, he worked wherever and whenever he could. He didn't care how many hours he worked; he just wanted to provide for his five children, the youngest only a year old. But his shift had hardly started before it ended. He was murdered, shot in the back and in the head.

More than a year later, his family—which includes Syrian Americans, Mexican Americans, African Americans, and Anglos—still grieves at the loss and cannot understand why anyone would have killed him.

For his niece, Sireen, twenty-three at the time, the murder was a shocking eye-opener, a reminder how precious and brief life is. She made up her mind to do the things that were important to her, no matter how inconvenient or hard they appeared to be.

"I didn't want to live with regrets," she said. "I realized that silly excuses and procrastination should never stand in the way of actions driven by understanding and deep conviction."

At her uncle's funeral, Sireen decided to don a *hijab* over her luxuriant hair, something she had been wanting to do but somehow had always found an excuse not to. One of the things that had kept her from wearing a scarf was the tendency of other Muslims to use it as a litmus test for piety. In the end, she says, "I realized that people's standards and expectations were irrelevant in the broader scheme of things." More than a year afterward, she could say proudly, "I've adopted it as part of my attire ever since."

Some of her family objected—or at least questioned why she kept wearing it. Many women in her extended family do not wear any head covering.

"They thought I was being emotional and subconsciously reacting to my uncle's tragic death. They thought I was going through a phase. They didn't realize I had been seriously considering making it part of my daily routine in an attempt to enhance my modesty and to support a concept of feminism through my actions. But I had already shared my thoughts with my mother."

Sireen's mother, who wears a head cap in public with her bangs showing—her own adaptation of a *hijab*—supported Sireen's decision.

So did her fiancé. "He had the best response," she said. " 'Sireen,' he said, 'if you do [wear *hijab*], I would be your number-one supporter, and if you don't I would still be your number-one supporter.' "

Despite the September 11 terrorist attacks and all the adverse publicity to Muslims, Sireen finds herself every day putting on an item of clothing that clearly marks her as a Muslim. She hasn't noticed too many hostile reactions except for the stares on the train as she goes to work at the Los Angeles office of the Muslim Public Affairs Council.

"I try to keep to myself but I do notice a lot of people staring," she says. "One man kept staring at me, so after trying unsuccessfully to generate a smile from him, I ended up staring back."

She has only had one comment—and thankfully she didn't hear it. She was going up in an elevator when a man mumbled, "My God, she's got a bomb." Another man on board, a Latino, reproved him, saying, "Look, man, that's not appropriate to say." Sireen had to ask him what the other man had said. She was grateful that the Latino stood up for her on an occasion when she missed the chance to do so for herself.

Sireen was born in Tokyo, where her Syrian-born father was working at the time as an importer and exporter. By the time she was two, her family had moved to southern California, where she, her older brother, and her younger sister grew up.

On weekends, they went to a special school to learn about Islam and the Quran, and to learn Arabic. Her parents wanted to make sure they were formally educated about their culture and religion. During one of her last classes, Sireen remembers learning the special rhythm and grammatical rules of reading the Quran.

During the week, they went to a public school where Sireen acknowledges, "I didn't exactly fit into the cookie-cutter social environment." She had to adapt in a popular culture foreign to her parents. Although she had a lot of friends, she couldn't always do what they did. For example, she could not attend the prom. In some traditional households, Muslim teens aren't allowed to go to co-ed social events such as dances. Sireen's parents expected her to follow their rules: No dating, no proms, no clubbing.

"At that age, I definitely felt left out," Sireen now says. "At the same time I was able to go out with friends when my parents felt it was a clean environment. I wasn't necessarily deprived but I wasn't able to do everything I wanted to do."

Today she looks back on her high school experience from a different perspective. In college she became immersed in politics and human rights causes. She made friends who shared her desire to strive for social justice and equality for all individuals. Her high school concerns now seem superficial. "I didn't miss out much," she admits.

Sireen says she watches out for her little sister, not wanting her to fall under the wrong influence or succumb to peer pressure. She once came across her sister building a website with a song that included a racy video: half-naked women in erotic poses, singing as they pretended to be using a jackhammer and other tools at a construction site. "The video completely sexualized women in an offensive manner. Their breasts were hanging out and their shorts were showing half their behinds," Sireen says. "Their breasts were bouncing as they moved back and forth in sexual motions."

When she tried to explain why the video was offensive and degrading to women, her little sister looked at her blankly. She didn't understand the fuss. Her girlfriends had shown it to her and they had gotten a big laugh over it. Sireen tried to explain how the women on the video were being used like "pieces of meat," and suggesting that one of her friends had probably gotten the video from the guys at school who most likely had been ogling the scantily clad women.

Sireen was relieved when her sister understood.

She makes it a point to tell her younger sister how pretty she is, and that her body is perfect the way it is. Sireen doesn't want her sister to feel compelled to diet unsafely, to hate her body the way some other girls in this country do.

Sireen feels blessed that she has managed to avoid such lethal attitudes. Indeed, in donning the hijab, Sireen has discovered that it protects her from obsessively worrying about her physical beauty. She says she is free from most of the "beauty" pressure that so many other young American women face. "My *hijab* sends the message that I reject conforming to being sexualized, to valuing my outer appearance exclusively." Her fiancé—who is now her husband—is supportive and doesn't want her to conform either. "He always says to me, 'There's no one quite like you.' "

Also a child of Syrian parents, he appreciates her as a strong woman who is passionate about politics and social justice. They met while working on political causes in college, but they didn't date the American way. Instead, he went to her father and announced he would like to get to know Sireen better—for possible marriage. Her father agreed to the courtship. He was allowed to call Sireen—they would talk for hours—and go out as long as others went with them. Their love blossomed and Sireen is confident that he is her soul mate. They were married in May 2005.

Sireen is engrossed in her work as an American Muslim advocate, a calling she first answered while in college, when she conducted research to help Muslims secure their civil rights in America. In some ways she says her work before 9/11 was an eerie prelude to the ongoing protest over the USA Patriot Act, which she believes deprives Muslims and others of their constitutional rights to privacy and due process. Sireen was preparing research to show that about two dozen individuals, most of them from the Middle East, had been improperly charged with being terrorists or affiliated with terrorist groups. The government refused to turn over what its investigation showed about those indicted because prosecutors claimed it needed to be kept secret for reasons of national security.

"They were being prosecuted on the basis of secret evidence,"

Sireen says. "Many of those charged, along with their attorneys, were unaware of their charges until they were in court."

Sireen was helping prepare what she considered a strong case to convince California lawmakers to vote for a bill that would have forbidden such tactics. "Then 9/11 occurred, and these efforts were placed on the back burner," she says. Instead there was *more* pressure to hunt down terrorists, increase wire taps, comb through once confidential records (including computer use at a public library), and to stage raids on homes and businesses.

Sireen believes the government does need to go after those who hurt her fellow Americans and innocent civilians around the world, regardless of who the oppressor is. But she also believes that civil liberties do not need to be compromised to maintain national security.

Sireen goes to schools, law enforcement training sessions, and public forums to help educate others about Islam and Muslims and to address misconceptions. She is there to assure them that American Muslims are peaceful and law-abiding. She also talks to these groups about Muslim customs and religious beliefs and explains how Islam shares many beliefs with Judaism and Christianity. Invariably, she is asked by the participants: Are Muslim women oppressed? Why do women have to wear a headscarf? Now wearing her own scarf, Sireen can answer confidently.

"The more I talked about it as an empowering tool, the more my conviction developed," she says.

❦ 3 ❧

MICHAELA'S MUSLIMAH
HIGH-FASHION DESIGNS

A COUPLE OF CENTURIES AGO, American women waited for ships to dock to see the latest fashions from far away—silk dresses from Paris, fancy hats from London. Now Muslim women in America are only a click away on their computers from the silk scarves and flowing gowns available from their own favorite cyber-ports, as far-flung as, say, Kuwait or Saudi Arabia.

Then again, they may prefer their own American designs. Michaela Corning, from the Seattle area, provides both.

Both on e-Bay and at her own Yahoo website, Michaela sells the latest styles from the Middle East as well as her own American-style clothes for Muslim women. They are far from the dreary head-to-toe heavy black wool burqas that Afghan women were forced to wear under the Taliban. Nor are they the plain black—and distinctly unattractive—*hijabs* Americans see worn by some Iraqi women on their nightly television news. Michaela offers what she describes as modern *Muslimah* couture. After all, Muslim women have a fashion sense, too. It just fits in with their faith.

Take a silken charcoal black-and-white wrap scarf Michaela recently offered on e-Bay for a starting bid of $4.99. "The scarf is excellent for the sophisticated, professional *Muslimah*," she advises.

If a woman doesn't like dark hijabs, Michaela offers a cobalt-blue fringe scarf or a peachy-pink floral wrap scarf. Or how about a golden-yellow hijab for a special occasion? For the truly experimental there's a light pink-and-orange-stripe silk scarf perfect for America's warmer regions. Michaela also offers several *hijabs* with the fringe that she is fond of.

Then there are Michaela's flowing Saudi-style caftans embellished with intricate embroidery, in colors from forest green to silvery white. Or the pantsuits she makes herself with super-wide legs and a matching tunic.

"I have created a few fashion trends in my area—and through e-Bay as well," she says. "I have ladies all the way in Kansas who prefer my sewn *abayas* to the traditional Arab imports."

She also advises her customers on the latest fashions from the Middle East. Although bright colors are "in," she also recommends basic black.

"I think there is a misconception that black is boring or there is no fashion behind it. This is contrary to reality," Michaela says. "Women in countries like Kuwait and Oman, where black is very popular (or even in Saudi Arabia, where black clothing is mandated) choose black as a fashion statement because it is thought of as 'elegant,' not dreary. When I traveled to Kuwait this was the general sense I got from many women who wear black. They think it is much more sophisticated looking. There are one million choices in black, from different cuts to different embroideries, beads, sequins, and fringe. Even the Khaliji [Gulf] *abaya* that the Iraqi women (and also many Kuwaiti women) wear can be fashionable. In Iraq it is probably chosen out of ease of wear and for economic reasons, but in Kuwait there are also many choices in this style (and a huge array in prices)."

Michaela is happy to provide such clothes—and her own expertise—to her Muslim customers in the United States. She knows how Islam has helped her emerge from confusion. And as a young Muslim woman she understands the need for fashion, soft fabrics, and attractive colors.

She is a twenty-nine-year-old who was introduced to Islam as a child and first considered becoming a Muslim while in college. She dearly loves her family but she admits to becoming confused and unhappy after her parents divorced. Islam helped her find her meaning in life.

As she tells it:

"I was born in 1975 to an upper-middle-class Christian family living in the farmlands of eastern Washington. I led a very happy care-free childhood . . . full of more leisure than worship, as I barely remember going to church. My understanding of God was limited to experiences such as a few Easters spent looking for money in haystacks at the country club, and ripping through piles of presents stacked around the Christmas tree. It was not until many years later that I even realized what the religious reasoning was behind such holidays.

"In 1982, my reality abruptly fell apart when my parents divorced. The world I had known became a thing of the past, and I spent a lot of time crying and feeling angry. It felt as if my parents had deceived me, and I became very unsure about life."

Big changes followed the divorce: new town, new schoolmates, new neighborhood, even a new stepfather, and a new home on an island off the coast of Washington. But some good came, too: Michaela met a brother and sister who became good friends with her and her sister.

"Since Mariam was my age and her younger brother, Adam, was my sister's age, we spent many afternoons after school playing in the woods and digging for sea life on the rocky beaches of the north end," Michaela says. "I remember Mariam showing me her Quran and explaining to me what it meant to be Muslim. Even at the age of ten, I found it fascinating, as I have always been very intrigued by other cultures and religions. She also told me cool stories about her dad's life as a Sonics basketball player."

When Michaela's family moved to another part of the island, she became friends with a different group of kids, and didn't see Mariam as often.

"I still considered her a friend, though, and would often defend her when immature kids would make rude comments about her *hijab* and other Islamic customs. I prided myself on understanding her beliefs, although I did not know them extensively."

She says she began associating with teenagers she shouldn't have—the risk takers, who drank, smoked, and some took drugs. Although she avoided their vices, she was still caught up in their clique of protest—from rebelling against their parents to joining in with protests they knew nothing about. Michaela remembers walking out of school in 1990 with these new friends when the United States declared war against Iraq. "I knew nothing of the politics of the war and demonstrated in the streets in protest against our involvement in it. I knew nothing of the heinous crimes committed against the Kuwaiti people. I was merely going along with the crowd. God was always in the back of my mind, but I lost myself in my own selfishness and bottled-up hurt from my parents' breakup."

At seventeen, Michaela ended up living with her father in Bellingham, a move that helped her start over, and she credits her father for helping her escape the clique and turn her life around. *"Hemd' Allah* [thank God] that he was there to support me and heal some of those emotional wounds," Michaela says.

That fall, she entered Whatcom Community College, where one of her classes was Middle Eastern History.

"I wrote a lengthy research paper on ancient Egyptian civilization and learned the truth about many stereotypes and falsehoods relating to Islam and Muslims. The idea behind men as the head of the household and women being modest to avoid the strong sexual desires of men really made sense to me. I also learned from an American Muslim man who lectured in the class that Muslims believed in Jesus but did not say that he was the 'Son of God,' as Christians do. The fact that Muslims believe that Allah is above the mortal qualities of having children really clicked with me."

For all her attraction to Islam, she didn't commit to it, and, indeed, from late 1992 to 1998, had little if any encounters with Muslims. Then she met a Kuwaiti named Saleh at her gym through her personal trainer.

"I thought he was handsome and friendly, but he seemed too good to be true and I automatically labeled him as a player," she ruefully remembers. "When I found out he was Muslim, I became even more turned off. Even though I had more knowledge about Islam at that time than most Americans, I was still blinded by my prejudices."

As she got to know Saleh better as a friend, she realized how truly caring and unselfish he was. He began talking to her about Islam and telling stories about the Prophet Muhammad.

"He even prayed in front of me until I felt comfortable to talk openly about my misconceptions of Islam, especially the role of women," Michaela says. "I began to realize that all the time I worried about partying, drinking, and hanging out with my supposed 'guy friends' was all a waste. None of these things were going to get me any closer to feeling happy about myself and about life as a whole." Michaela quotes from Quran 3:185: "As for the life of this world, it is nothing but a merchandise of vanity."

"It might be very difficult for non-Muslims to accept that I chose Islam and was not forced to or persuaded to by my friend, Saleh," Michaela insists. "My acceptance of Islam was not a prerequisite of our friendship. I did not automatically believe everything I heard or read. It was a slow process of learning, and Saleh was perfect about telling me the right thing at the right time. Some of the hardest things for me to accept included Islamic attire for men and women, polygamy, and the prohibition of alcohol. Not to mention I wanted proof—logical proof and reasoning to understand why Saleh felt obligated to pray, fast, and abstain from drinking and sex. At first I saw it as so many don'ts and so few do's."

"My hardest internal struggle was about revealing these ideas to my parents and family," she continues. "The number-one idea I had to rid my family of is the incorrect belief that women have a subservient role to men in Islam. From an American perspective, these ideas are easily confused with reality, especially since many Muslim countries have gone astray in inhibiting women's education or right to work.

"I always relate the story of the Prophet's first wife, Khadija. She was a rich woman who not only owned her own business but successfully raised her children. So many seem to skip over this fact—including Muslims. People also forget or misunderstand the acceptance of polygamy. This is not a preferred way a life according to Allah's word, but an *option*. The Quran reiterates this, stating that it is impossible to treat multiple wives equally, and unless you can, then marry only one woman. Before I understood Islam, I always assumed that having multiple wives was the suggested way of life according to the teachings of Islam, and relying on media influences made me blind to the truth. What really hit it home for me was that the Prophet was married to a much older woman for twenty-five years, and it wasn't until after she died that he remarried. He was allowed more than four wives in order to teach people how to treat different wives, whether much older, much younger, Jewish or Christian. He showed us that marrying women of other religions was accepted and that marrying women of other ethnicities or ages was good in the eyes of God. Far too many men today refuse to marry women of different colors and cultures. Prophet Muhammad showed us that these prejudices should be avoided. Furthermore, he married a couple of these women because their husbands had died in war, and he wanted to provide means and a father figure for their children. Marriage was not based on sexual desires."

Her family peppered her with questions: Is Saleh going to have a harem of wives? What if he steals your children? What if you move to Kuwait and you're held captive there?

"It took so much explaining to even justify why I liked a Muslim man as a friend, let alone explaining to them why I have become Muslim," she says. "*Insha'Allah* [God willing], Islam will bring me closer to my family, as I have seen it helping me mend my friendship with my sister. She has been a Christian for years, and now that I believe in one God, Allah, we have many religious and spiritual discussions about God. It seems we have more in common now than ever before."

She admits it was much harder to tell her father about wearing the *hijab* than converting to Islam. He knew of her interest in Islam. This did not upset him. He had a few questions, but they were resolved. The *hijab*, however, did concern him. His reasoning: His daughters are beautiful, he's proud of them, and they should be proud of themselves.

"He doesn't understand that I still feel good about myself, but my purpose has changed. I do things differently now, and wearing my *hijab* is something I do to bring me closer to my purpose—worshipping Allah," Michaela says.

Like most American fathers, she adds, "he could not fathom me accepting a religion that allows polygamy. I told him that Islam did not invent this and gave him the facts from the Bible and the pre-Islamic world. I told him that it works for some but would not for me. I believe it is an option, but I don't have to live in that type of a marriage. He understood that; it just needed a little clarity."

Now that he understands why Michaela converted, he can concentrate on her other accomplishments: school, work, languages, and artistic ability. Indeed, Michaela's father and sister get offended if people stare at her in her *hijab*. Nevertheless, that doesn't mean he isn't still trying to convince her to drop the scarf. Sometimes, when he has been watching an Arabic television station at her house, he'll say something like, "I saw women on such-and-such channel who do not cover." Michaela simply reminds him that she considers her *hijab* obligatory.

In many ways her mother has the hardest time coping with Michaela's conversion. While spending a lot of time together sewing and crafting—"Luckily I inherited her and my father's creative genes"—they avoid talking about religion.

"But," Michaela says, "my mother has made a lot of accommodations for me. She is, for example, very careful not to serve pork or pork by-products. She has done this completely on her own. I told her not to go out of her way, because I can make do, but she has been very supportive in this regard."

Meanwhile, Michaela's sister remains supportive, but admits the conversion hasn't been easy to accept. She is in her third year of medical school at the University of Washington and has had contact with several Muslims locally as well as travelers from abroad.

"This has helped us bridge the gap," Michaela says. "In public she can get pretty lippy with people who stare at me. I tell her to relax, but she is adamant about it. I must be used to it, because I don't usually notice it anymore unless it is very blatant. Once, in Nordstrom, I was shopping and an older couple was looking around in the same section. The husband was just standing there, staring at me as if I were a ghost or alien. His wife got right up in his face and said very firmly, 'She is a person, you know!' Wow! Did he get scolded! I felt bad for the guy. He probably did not realize what he was doing."

Michaela's paternal grandmother, who is eighty-five and a devout Catholic, has been among the most supportive family members. She sent an e-mail to Michaela—"pretty nifty for a granny," Michaela says as an aside—to report that when she told her priest that Michaela had become a Muslim, he said, "At least she believes in God."

"She is always sending me Ramadan cards and e-mails," Michaela adds. "She asked me, 'Is it Merry Ramadan or Happy Ramadan?' I told her it is 'Ramadan Mabruk', so any English rendition is fine.

"Once, I was talking to her on the phone, and she was going on and on about misplacing some photo of her as a child. She asked me to say a prayer for her. I told her okay. Then she said she thought it should go something like this: 'Oh Allah! Please help Grandma Corning find her photo.' I was so shocked she said Allah instead of God. She does that every once in a while. She is also very supportive of my eating requirements and likes my *hijab*. She has told me she likes how Muslims dress because she is tired of seeing everyone's cleavage. I think my grandma really understands the human need for religion, especially a religion with rules and traditions. Like me, she also wakes up very early to say her prayers—only she has her rosary and Hail Marys."

Michaela's family is happy to see her use her creative skills. As a designer for Muslim women, she creates pullover *abayas* as well as hooded ones and others with mandarin collars. She loves to pick out the fabrics, from lightweight chiffons to brocade tapestry fabrics, "for the woman who wants something that looks very exotic."

"American converts want their own style that fits the Islamic dress code but also has a Western feel," she says. "Whether they are African American, Caucasian, or Hispanic converts to Islam, these women are still Americans. They do *not* convert to a different culture. Some of us feel that we look ridiculous in *shawar kameez* [the traditional pant and long shirt worn by many Pakistani women]. Putting a scarf on your head already makes you look like a foreigner (and not just a Muslim), so those of us who are not immigrants do not want to look like we come from another country.

"Don't get me wrong," she adds, "I wear just about every type of Muslim dress from a variety of countries, but when I go into the office, I don't want to look like anything other than a Muslim who is also an American. This is my culture."

It is her faith, not her nationality, that has changed, she says.

It has been five years since Michaela converted, four years since she told her family, and three and a half years since she started wearing the *hijab*. And she feels more strongly drawn to Islam than ever.

"Sometimes, I have small, insignificant doubts, but they quickly pass," Michaela says.

❧ 4 ❧

MARIA'S NIGHTMARE OF AN ARRANGED MARRIAGE

THE GROOM'S FAMILY was from Europe, a prosperous cosmopolitan Muslim family who had lived in the United States and had a business in South America. They had come all the way to South Asia to arrange a marriage for their twenty-nine-year-old son. They had heard about Maria, a lovely liquid-eyed nineteen-year-old going to college. She was a proper young woman from a well-regarded family.

"They came to our house to see me," remembers the bride.

She wants to tell what happened to her, but the young woman called here "Maria" is embarrassed. More important, she wants to protect her children, whom she fears she will not see again, from knowing the true circumstances of what their mother endured.

Maria and her family thought nothing amiss when they invited the prospective groom's family into their home. In their country many parents arrange marriages for their children. The practice is not so much a Muslim custom as a cultural one, thousands of years old. Besides, the family seemed so pleasant.

Maria's mother and father listened to the other parents' proposal. First, they said, they liked Maria and they liked the idea of their son marrying a proper young Muslim woman. It was time for him to settle down with a wife and children. For Maria it was almost a dream come true. She would be marrying a suave European Muslim who would take her to America where he operated part of the family business. They would live in Miami, which has a subtropical climate similar to

36

what she was used to. The family had businesses in South America so Miami, the gateway to Latin America, made sense as their home. The groom's family seemed prosperous and able to give Maria a good life. And, above all, they seemed warm and personable.

Some parents arrange marriages without allowing their children to meet until the day of the wedding. Maria got to meet her future in-laws and husband. However, she stresses she barely was introduced to him before she was whisked down the aisle.

Thus, with Maria's consent, her parents agreed to the proposal and Maria married him in a ceremony in her hometown before traveling across the world to Miami.

At the time, Maria didn't think anything about her new husband being ten years older than she—a difference that to a nineteen-year-old can seem vast. As Maria had traveled little, he seemed very much a man of the world.

She wore the *hijab*—and still does. She wouldn't think of leaving the home without her hair covered. She came from a family rooted in centuries of tradition—not worldly like her future husband and his family.

"I didn't know anything about marriage," Maria adds. But in retrospect, she feels that such a gap in age and experience between her and her husband should have been a warning.

As soon as they moved to Miami, their marriage quickly degenerated. Maria found out that her husband had had a girlfriend, an American. While his parents wanted him to marry a more traditional—and Muslim—woman, he was unable to give up this previous romance.

He began losing his temper and hitting Maria. The beatings began early on in the marriage. "He would be drinking and get mad," she says. He had total control over her, doling out money for groceries, barely enough for her to live on. He was just as miserly after they had children. And he hit them, too.

She tried to tell her family about her problems. They told her not to complain. "They would tell me: Have patience," she says. They would also tell her that such conduct is "normal in a marriage." It was almost as if this was the fate of women, an attitude Maria attributes to their living in a "backward country. That's how we are."

Three years ago, her husband left her for his old girlfriend. He had gotten her pregnant and, Maria says, "We had a fight over that and he went with her."

At the time, she felt relief. At least she would be left in peace. But that was not to be.

Even though by then she had been in the United States for about five years, she still didn't understand much about American life, as he had controlled where and when she went out of the home. Now, though, he left her alone to fend for herself, with no job or family, in what to her was still a strange country. Maria tried to count her blessings: He still gave her money, but she barely had enough to feed herself and their children.

He had kept a key to their home and was able to come and go whenever he wanted. One day, he decided he didn't like what he saw and accused Maria of being an unfit mother: He complained that the children were making marks on the walls. Maria tried to point out that she had put paper up on the walls for the children to paint on. He complained that she was sloppy and unclean. A child had spilled juice that she hadn't cleaned up. Maria protested that she was keeping her home neat according to the traditions of her homeland.

"I am clean—but my ways are different," she adds.

While taking care of two small children, "I wasn't able to clean all the time," she admits. Sometimes she was too tired.

A group of Miami Muslims who found out about her situation, and who ultimately rescued her, thinks Maria was also too depressed to cope with everyday matters. It is common for abused women to have low self-esteem. Maria found it hard to talk to anyone about what was happening to her. With her parents telling her to accept her situation, it was all she could do to keep her marital problems quiet.

Her husband saw things differently. He went to the police to report that Maria was neglecting the children. The next thing Maria knew, her home was being invaded by police officers, who had believed her husband's story.

Maria tried to tell them that actually it was her husband who was the abuser. He had hit the children, she told them. They didn't believe her, and took her children away. She was handcuffed and jailed. Shaking and terrified, she tried to tell her side of the story. Still the authorities didn't listen.

Thus began her ordeal in the United States judicial system.

According to Mohammad Shakir, executive director of the Miami-Dade Asian American Advisory Board, Maria was first locked up in jail, and subsequently committed to a mental institution for being unstable. "She was detained for almost four weeks," he says. "She was put in with hardened criminals. When she came out, she was petrified."

Such abuse of young married women from traditional cultures is occurring with increasing frequency in the Miami area, he adds, where Muslim or Hindu men more savvy than their immigrant wives use the American legal system to get out of marriages, in some instances absconding with the woman's dowry or family money. The women do not know how to protect themselves, and for that reason, Shakir is helping start a group to help these women.

In Maria's case, there was worse to come: She was assigned a public defender and agreed to plead to a reduced charge of child neglect and receive probation. But she was unable to comply with the court's order to see a psychologist and obey the treatment plan. "I didn't have money for gasoline," she says. "I didn't have money for medicine either." So she was picked up again for violating her probation. That meant more time in jail.

When assistant public defender Rebecca Cox saw her new client, she was shocked. "Her hair was dirty and greasy; she was totally unkempt and uncommunicative," Cox says. Maria's eyes were downcast and she would barely look up at Cox, to whom she was deferential and very meek.

What saved her client, Cox adds, was that a group of Muslims led by Shakir discovered her situation, intervened in her behalf, and agreed to take her into their homes and provide shelter and care. They attended every court proceeding, and there were many because the case was repeatedly postponed.

"These incredible people jumped through hoop after hoop, in an attempt to satisfy the judge's concerns and obtain her release," Cox says. Never had Cox seen strangers offer such support.

Outraged at what had happened to Maria, Shakir had felt compelled to intervene. He and his wife Shahida agreed to house the young woman as they sorted out her problems. Nearly catatonic when she first came to them, she opened up to them little by little, talking about her abuse and her legal problems.

She's still not sure what happened at her court hearings, how her husband was able to divorce her and obtain custody of their children. "I didn't know much about the American system," she admits.

The Shakirs treated her like a daughter, making sure she had plenty of sleep and nutritious food. Slowly, she began to recover. Months later she seemed on the rebound; her eyes were sparkling. Maria was even able to go to a party. She dressed in a loosely flowing pantsuit and *hijab* and looked lovely.

Her depression returned three months later. She became weary and was unable to imagine her life getting any better. As a result, she decided to go home. Her newfound friends objected but they couldn't persuade her to stay in America. The best they could do was to pool money for Maria's one-way plane ticket home to her native country. She says she has no intentions of returning to the United States. And in any event, she can't: She violated her probation by leaving the country. She was even warned by her probation officer that if she left before her probation ends, the United States will never let her reenter. But Maria saw no hope—or point—in staying.

Her husband now has custody of her children in South America, she says. He took them while she was in jail. In retrospect, she says, he probably had planned this all along. She is resigned to the fact that it's unlikely she will ever see her children again.

She tries not to grieve. She tries to tell herself that he loves his children and will take care of them. She tries not to remember his past abuse of them, nor the recent pictures he gave her of their children during a visit when she was in the mental ward. "They don't look happy," she repeatedly says. "They don't look happy."

Still, there is nothing she can do. He has them and they are a continent away. She is what some would consider a criminal and certainly not to be trusted. She admits she doesn't know what she will do in the country she hasn't seen in eight years. She is trying to be grateful: "Thank Allah, I am healthy, I am okay," she says.

The Shakirs, though, believe it is a tragedy that she was compelled to go home.

Before she left, she wanted to pass on advice to other young women so they never end up in the nightmare she endured.

The most important thing, Maria says, is not to agree to an arranged marriage. "Don't get married without knowing the man," she says. Furthermore: "Don't get married so early. I was too young." Finally, she advises, Don't marry an older man, who may want you young and naive for a reason—so he can control you.

❦ 5 ❧

AYSHA: THE PERILS OF
BEING A MUSLIMAH

IT WAS MID-MORNING on a day in March 2002, and a new refrigerator had just been delivered to the suburban home of Aysha Nudrat Unus. When she heard a loud boom she thought the delivery men had somehow dropped the old refrigerator they had taken out.

Imagine her surprise—and terror—when she spotted a group of men in black at her front door. They banged on her front door, not even bothering with the doorbell. "Open the door!" one of them barked. She saw a man brandishing a gun. "He was close to the door," she says. She remembers being so stunned that all she could do was stand and gasp. "I couldn't go to the door, I was so paralyzed," she remembers. Her eighteen-year-old daughter managed to run to a phone to call 911 for help.

But it was too late.

The men knocked down the front door. "They called out in a very loud voice, which made them all the more scary," Aysha says. "I never thought police would yell like that." But she says, it is a different world after September 11, 2001. These strange men, towering above Aysha (who is at most five feet tall, and weighs 100 pounds), identified themselves as federal agents, and forced Aysha and her daughter to sit on the floor of their own home and hold their hands behind them.

"They handcuffed both of us," she says. "They didn't explain anything."

Nor did they read the women their rights—an event made familiar by American television but not part of Aysha's experience. The agents began searching the house, tearing through rooms and cupboards, ransacking desks and files.

The local police had no knowledge of the raid. Two officers responded to the 911 call and thought a robbery was in progress. They were told of the federal investigation by one of the agents as the officers tried to enter the house. It turned out that the agents were raiding Muslim organizations and households in Virginia and Georgia—from the offices of charities to Aysha's home—as part of an investigation into possible financial ties to terrorists. No charges have ever been filed. No apologies have ever been given.

The following day, the Washington-based Council on American-Islamic Relations strongly condemned the raids as a "fishing expedition" that used "McCarthy-like tactics in search of evidence of wrongdoing that does not exist." Aysha appeared at the press conference to try to spread the word of what was being done to Muslims.

John G. Douglass, a former prosecutor and now professor at the University of Richmond School of Law, says he is troubled that information on raids was leaked to the media and that well-regarded Islamic institutions and individuals had been tainted by the barrage of publicity.

"One of the most troubling aspects of the March 2002 searches is that the government chose to use search warrants at all," Douglass wrote in 2003 in the *Journal of Law and Religion.* "In an investigation targeting financial transactions, the government has other means for obtaining the records necessary to trace money and identify its sources. The simplest, of course, is just to ask for the information. Another is to subpoena it. In the vast run of financial investigations, the government obtains most of its information through these means rather than through search warrants."

That issue of the *Journal* also included clinical social worker Meredith McEver's analysis of how Aysha and other women had suffered from the raids.

McEver reported that one woman (she did not list names) couldn't get the memories out of her mind, and that whenever she heard a knock on the door she thought the raid was beginning all over again. "Another woman, awakened in her bed at 10:30 A.M. by ten large men pointing rifles at her, now will coincidently look at her clock at 10:30 every morning and memories of the raid will overwhelm her," McEver wrote.

Most of the women had symptoms of post-traumatic stress syndrome and many, she said, suffered physical reactions from the raids.

"Some had trouble with their hearts racing," she reported. "To varying degrees, they had trouble sleeping, were irritable, had angry outbursts and had difficulty concentrating. One woman said that she went to work and people thought she was working, but she wasn't. No matter what she did she couldn't concentrate so she just sat there. The women reported being hyper-alert, always on watch for the next raid."

One woman told McEver that she didn't bother to fix her broken door because "the FBI would just break it down again the next time they came."

The quiet and soft-spoken Aysha says she is still in shock over the raid into her home. Born in Pakistan, she is a housewife who has been in the United States for thirty-three years. "I was raised in Catholic schools," she says. "I had a coed education." She eventually got a master's degree and came to the United States as a newlywed. She and her husband have been American citizens for years.

A devout Muslim, she wears a *hijab*. On the day of the raid she felt violated as the agents would not allow her to cover her hair in their presence. She and her daughter were handcuffed for two and a half hours with their hands behind their back. When the pain became too much, the agents allowed them to wear the handcuffs in front. In all, they spent four hours handcuffed.

Aysha says she and her teenaged daughter were not told why the federal agents had picked their home or what they were looking for. When her daughter protested, one of the agents angrily said, "We are treating you better than your own police!" He apparently assumed that she had been born in a Middle Eastern country under a dictatorship.

The girl was stunned. "Which police?" she asked in disbelief. She had been born in Indianapolis.

The local police officers, though, were helpful and eventually persuaded the agents to let the women wear their scarves, and allow them to pray as part of Islam's five-prayer daily routine.

As the feds' investigation stretched into the afternoon, the agents told the two women that they could leave the house and come back, but only after the agents had left. However, Aysha, understandably, did not want to leave her home.

After the agents had gone—about 2:30 P.M.—she and her daughter were able to walk freely around their own home. They examined the wreckage caused by the agents, and imagined the cleanup that was before them.

Since that March day, they have not been visited again. Nor have they been told anything more about the reasons for this raid.

The family's attorney is looking into the situation. Aysha hopes no other woman will have to go through what she and her daughter did. "We have been treated unfairly," she says.

The raid has galvanized local Muslims into becoming politically involved. They started their own Platform for Active Civil Empowerment to contribute to political candidates who will be sympathetic to Muslims. They have already had success with more Muslims running for office, and they are getting more media coverage. The raid "was the defining moment," says Mukit Hossain, one of the organizers. Never will Muslims be in such a weak position again, he promises.

❧ 6 ❧

AREEJ: WEARING A HIJAB INTO THE WORKING WORLD

LIKE MANY OTHER MOMS returning to the workforce after taking time off to raise three children, Areej Abdallah fretted over what prospective employers might think. She was about to finish her computer-science degree and was eager to put it to use. She was ready to be part of an office and some exciting projects. The question was: Were U.S. companies ready for her?

Areej is a Palestinian who grew up in Kuwait and studied and worked in Jordan after she married her husband, who is also a Palestinian. They came to the United States as a young couple in the late 1980s, and currently live in Arizona. She wears a head covering as part of her Islamic faith. At first she was afraid to wear her *hijab* to job interviews, knowing that it would identify herself as a Muslim. Even before 9/11 there were stereotypes about battered, subservient Muslim women, and this was hardly the image Areej wanted to project as a former stay-at-home mom entering the computer-science field, a predominantly male preserve. But she couldn't give up her hijab, which she sees as an extension of herself. This is who she was, and she prayed a good company would accept her.

She steeled herself to the interviewing process, but the going wasn't smooth. Major U.S. companies interviewed her on campus at Arizona State University in Tempe but Areej would never hear back from them. She kept trying, presenting her résumé with its list of impressive grades and academic achievements. The telephone stayed silent. "I was applying for jobs for nine months," she says. "Oh, I thought to myself, it's my *hijab*. That's why I can't find a job."

Then she met with a representative from Boeing, the airplane manufacturer. The company needed software engineers. Areej thought, "It's not going to happen." Still, she had researched the company and went to the job interview prepared.

"I didn't have high hopes," she remembers. "But, I got a call two to three days later."

During that call, which came through on a Friday, a Human Resources officer asked her one question: When would Areej like to start? Areej blurted out, "Monday!"

The HR worker told her not to worry, she didn't have to start that soon.

But Areej insisted, "No, no, I will start Monday."

As she tells the story, she is grinning. "I thought she was going to take back the job!" she says. "It was a happy moment. I was so happy I thought I was going to collapse."

Three days later, despite her nervousness, she indeed went to work at Boeing as a software engineer—her luxuriant, henna-enriched brown hair tucked under her *hijab*—and has been employed there ever since.

Besides working with computers at Boeing, Areej has discovered she has other skills. She has helped lead the company's diversity classes, four-hour sessions in which she discusses her faith and the clothing related to it. As the class progresses, she can see participants noticeably relax and become more friendly as she regales them with jokes, anecdotes, and facts about Islam. Weeks, even months later, she still finds employees coming up to her to thank her for the classes.

Boeing has turned out to be an understanding company that even allows Areej private time to pray the required five times a day. A boss helped cajole HR into allowing Areej to pray in a room normally reserved for breast-feeding moms. "I have been surrounded by great people," she says.

She remembers that one of her bosses came up to her after 9/11, and suggested that she come to him if she had any problems with harassment. She didn't need to, she says, "but he was so nice."

She also has enjoyed flexibility in scheduling her work, sometimes alternating between part-time and full-time. Boeing allows her to work part-time during the month of Ramadan so she can leave early to prepare the dinner feasts for her family. The company has also held sessions on educating employees about achieving their goals. These have made a big impact on Areej, who explains, "It helps me decide what I want to do."

Both Areej and her thirteen-year-old daughter Aseel find, though, that they have to gird themselves to patiently rebut stereotypes about Islamic women.

For example, her daughter reports that when she enrolled in a public high school and started wearing her *hijab*, other students—intending to be friendly and sympathetic—said, "I would hate to have that religion." They wrongly believe that Aseel would prefer a religion with fewer strict rules, and that she doesn't want to wear clothes that set her apart from the other teens.

As Aseel says, "They think I am pressured. I am not."

Wearing the *hijab* is a way of keeping a spiritual life, she says. It's also a reminder that she has crossed into womanhood. Once Muslim girls reach puberty they are expected to cover their hair, although many in the United States opt not to wear it until they graduate from high school or college—or maybe not ever. Some increasingly do not see their faith linked to covering their hair. But Areej and Aseel do. Both view the *hijab* as holy. They also like the Muslim prayers and holidays which reinforce their spirituality.

Take Ramadan, the month-long holiday that requires Muslims to fast from sunup to sundown. Aseel is glad that she is able to fast like the adults. She and her Muslim friends bypass the pizza and burgers in the school cafeteria to use their lunchtime to talk and hang out. Ramadan is also a time for reading the Quran and thinking about God, she points out.

She and her mother feel they can be both devout Muslims and achieving women.

Aseel, for example, has decided she is going to try out for her high school's girls' soccer team—wearing her hijab and long pants. (She can wear gym shorts during practice, when only other girls are around, but during actual games when both sexes are present she must cover herself. She is undeterred when told that an Orlando, Florida, college student decided to quit her basketball team when she felt she was becoming the focus of a media circus. A controversy broke out over whether the young player could wear her *hijab* on the basketball court during games. Across the country, in suburban Phoenix, Aseel doesn't think that she will have to face that issue. "I'm sure they will let us," she says.

As a high school freshman, she is already committed to doing volunteer work in her community. "Anything to help," she says.

She also is considering what she wants to do in her life. Like her mother, she wants to have both a career and a family. "I used to want to be a teacher," she says. "Then I wanted to be a pediatrician. Now I am thinking of something different—becoming a makeup artist or a chef. It would be so much fun."

Her mother loves to be creative in the kitchen. During one recent Ramadan she was making lamb, stuffed zucchini, and Middle Eastern–style chopped salad in the large kitchen of their comfortable suburban home. Her hungry children—the two oldest having fasted from sunrise to sunset—lingered nearby until she announced dinner. Then, with long contented silences, the high schoolers politely wolfed down the delicious dinner. Areej excused herself to pray then returned to the dinner table to help herself to the stuffed zucchini and salad.

Areej claims her specialty is elaborately concocted desserts—gourmet sweets from around the world. She's especially known for her pastries, from baklava to tarts. She has always dreamed of opening her own dessert shop, and in 2005 she decided to act on her dream, snagging the last available location in an upscale shopping center being constructed near her home.

The excitement and joy of being an entrepreneur keeps her occupied. It also deflects her sad thoughts about her homeland and the never-ending violence there. Areej was born in Palestine but grew up in Kuwait. The family had no choice but to relocate: Her Palestinian father was banished from his strawberry and flower fields because the newly organized state of Israel learned that he was supplying munitions to fellow Arabs. Luckily, Areej's half-siblings were allowed to keep the family land—"I think how beautiful it is when we go there"— that remains within Israel's borders.

Today, Areej's family—three brothers and five sisters—are separated. Two half-brothers remain on the family land in Israel, two sisters live in the Palestinian area, and the others are in Jordan. The half-brothers have not seen their siblings in Jordan for years since they are not allowed to enter that country. Areej is grateful that she has an American passport. It allows her to visit both Jordan and Israel—and all her brothers and sisters.

Areej and her husband have thought about going back to Jordan to live and work. In some ways life would be easier there, but they cannot do it, Areej says, because their children are Americans with their own dreams to establish careers here. Her oldest son, Saith, a high school junior, is directing a film based on his own screenplay. "He's very dedicated," says his proud sister, who helps him with the makeup for the actors, who are among their friends.

The family likes the American Southwest. They often go horseback riding and biking. They enjoy the red and peach–colored sunsets and blue-tinged mountains. They also like taking drives on some of the rural Arizona highways—the ones where there are more cacti than people. "Arizona is so gorgeous," Areej says.

The family also feels they "fit in." After all, their ancestors lived in a desert land. "We love Arizona. It is so much like where we come from, from where we grew up in the Middle East." The peace she and her family have found here, she says, is priceless.

Areej's Baklava

(or as she calls it, *baqlawa*)

What is needed:

12 × 16-inch baking pan
2 cups unsalted butter
Filo dough which can be bought in grocery store
4 cups ground walnuts mixed with ¼ cup of sugar
½ cup of ground pistachios
2 cups syrup (instructions below)

1. Melt butter in a saucepan over low heat.
2. Butter the pan.
3. A package of filo dough has 16 sheets. Place 8 sheets on the greased pan.
4. Spread melted butter on the sheets.
5. Put the mixed walnuts with sugar on the sheets.
6. Put the rest of the sheets on top of the walnuts.
7. Cut baklava into desired pieces before baking.
8. Bake at 350 degrees for a half hour. Raise oven temperature to 450 degrees and bake for an additional 10 minutes until it becomes a golden color.
9. Take the pan out and cover baklava with the syrup.
10. Sprinkle the ground pistachio in the center of each piece.

Syrup:

Mix 2 cups of sugar and 1½ cups of water in a small saucepan. Bring to a boil, remove from heat, and let cool.

❧ 7 ❧

SAKEENA: FINDING HER WAY
HOME TO AMERICA

AMERICAN-BORN SAKEENA MIRZA went to Pakistan with her husband and small son to help out during a family emergency. "We didn't know how long it would take to sort out the problem and were prepared to stay in Pakistan long-term," she says. Indeed, they were thinking of settling there. In a sense, both Sakeena and her husband would be going "home." He still had younger brothers and sisters in Pakistan and Sakeena's father had long ago emigrated to the United States, where Sakeena had grown up hearing his stories about the old country.

"I have always thought of myself as an American but my Pakistani heritage has also been a big part of me," Sakeena says.

During her months in Pakistan the twenty-something Sakeena discovered how much she treasured the richness of Pakistan's culture. She loved feeling that she fit in, and that she was not the only woman on the street wearing a *hijab*.

But she discovered something else, something that stunned her: She missed the American way of life, with its cultural diversity, so much that she wanted to go home. In Pakistan, she says, "everyone seemed the same," not like the people of the Los Angeles area where she had grown up. "I missed Mexican food—that was funny," she says. Although her family in Pakistan tried to make her understand that many people there were just trying to survive and didn't have the time for the "bigger" questions in life, Sakeena missed the particularly American "can-do" attitude, that if you don't like it, you can do something about it.

Many Pakistanis would have traded places with her in a nanosecond: to be able to live and work in America, to have the kind of opportunity one finds there. "It made me feel grateful," she says, to be an American, and so she decided not to fight against her homesickness. She and her husband returned to the United States.

After a time in California, Sakeena and her husband are now establishing roots in rapidly growing Las Vegas, Nevada. Soon, Sakeena's older sister and her family are planning to move to Las Vegas from their home in northern Arizona. Sakeena appreciates Las Vegas's diversity. It's a young city where many feel comfortable, regardless of their ethnic or racial background. "That's one of the reasons I like Las Vegas," she says.

Five months after moving there, Sakeena finds herself in the middle of the Nevada desert's rainy season. The irony of this amuses her. She is getting more rain now than she ever experienced while growing up in the Los Angeles area.

She is part of a small group of young Muslim women who meet at an apartment complex's recreational center to discuss the Quran. They're all newcomers to Las Vegas: Amanda, who converted to Islam, is originally from Arkansas. Myta was born in Indonesia but grew up in Washington, DC. Sakeena's older sister Haseena also joins them from time to time. They laugh as they gather the news of what they've been doing.

Sometimes, Myta jokes, while driving her four-year-old daughter to preschool or running a quick errand, she realizes that she forgot to put on her *hijab*. It has not been a regular habit for her to wear one, nor the flowing white scarf that completely covers her thick black hair.

Indeed, her mother didn't wear one either, and when Myta visits her native Indonesia, she notices how many women in her predominantly Muslim country no longer wear the traditional head coverings and modest long-sleeved clothing. But Myta feels a spiritual rebirth in going back to her Muslim roots, in praying every day. "It's become part of my daily routine," she says. As a result, she feels more serene, more giving. Wearing the *hijab* in public, she maintains, only adds to that well-being. "I've become more open-minded."

Unlike some Americans who have converted to Islam, Amanda has not encountered much discrimination. Instead, she has won praise from others who tell her that they find her modest clothing refreshing in an era when many women dress provocatively.

All in the group say they can practice Islam freely in America. Sakeena wants to be part of her mosque's efforts to help the homeless and those with AIDS. She admires the Muslim woman who have set up a food program on Sunday mornings. Muslims, Sakeena adds with pride, have also come together to establish charter schools. "This is the kind of thing that we as Muslims should be doing—that we *are* doing as we become more fully established."

As a young girl growing up Muslim in southern California, she was always bothered that while she heard a lot of talk about helping the poor, as the Quran requires, she saw little action. Her Pakistani father and American-born mother, who also converted to Islam, emphasized a Muslim way of life. They socialized with other Muslims who read the Quran and tried to pass on their traditions to their children.

"But when I looked around, Muslims weren't actually *doing* anything," she says. "That lack of helping out disillusioned me."

Now she realizes that there were relatively few Muslims in her community at the time and that they weren't sufficiently organized to help. But all that is changing as the growing Islamic community in the Las Vegas area reaches out to help others, from providing turkeys at Thanksgiving to preparing banquets for the poor at the end of Ramadan.

As a child, Sakeena says she wasn't bothered that she was part of a religious minority. True, she sang Christmas carols at school. "But my parents did a good job of passing on Islamic traditions at home."

Sakeena is close to her family. She is glad that Haseena, her older sister, is joining her in Las Vegas. Growing up as the eldest of five girls, they are close. Now they are young, educated mothers raising their children in an Islamic way, comfortable wearing their *hijabs* in public, and raising their children to be good Muslims. "There are certain guidelines God has given us," says Sakeena. "God created peace and order and our mission is to fulfill our role in serving God."

One day, she says, that might include going back to Pakistan.

"I think there will always be a pull to be there with the rest of the family," she says. "My husband has younger siblings in Pakistan, and since his mother passed away four years ago, in the back of our minds is always the question of whether or not we should be there to support them."

But, she knows, she'll go there thinking and feeling like an American.

Her sojourn in Pakistan, she concludes, "emphasized for me that my Americanness—if that's a word—overshadows the cultural heritage handed down by my parents."

❧ 8 ❧

HASEENA'S LESSON IN DIVERSITY

HASEENA MIRZA needed to do an internship to finish her graduate studies. But her placement at one facility did cause her to blink: She — a young Muslim woman wearing the *hijab* — was being sent to a rehabilitation unit in New York City run by Orthodox Jews. Even though this occurred before militant Palestinians had started their Intifada against Israel, tensions were running high. Haseena, the sister of Sakeena (see chapter 7), worried about the assignment but felt she had no choice: She needed the internship to graduate. So Haseena showed up — scarf and all — for her work in using exercise to facilitate cardiac rehab.

The insight Haseena gained from the experience was quite different from that of her sister, who had traveled to their father's native Pakistan only to discover she was more American than she thought. Haseena found that Americans are primarily, Americans. Tensions in the Middle East didn't cause American Jews to refuse care from an American Muslim.

To be sure, she found *some* anxiety — and friction. Many of the patients, after all, had family in Israel or knew of someone living there. Most, however, welcomed her help. They soon depended on her. "I found them very friendly, very welcoming," she says.

She also discovered at the rehab center that for all the fighting in the Middle East, traditionalists in both religions were remarkably similar. "They were pretty strict," she remembers. Just like many Muslims, she adds. Men and women had separate waiting rooms,

56

treatment centers and classes, as some Muslims would do, she points out. Also, Hasidic women were expected to dress modestly much like traditional Muslims are. Haseena felt surprisingly at home wearing her long sleeves and modest pants.

One of the elderly patients even told her, "You know what? I respect you." That was a compliment, for sure.

Haseena saw clearly how Americans could come together to reach a common goal, even though in other countries, their religious counterparts were bitter enemies. She has taken that lesson to heart as she finished her course work, married, and returned to the West.

Haseena now lives in a small city near the Nevada border in northern Arizona but is in the process of moving to Las Vegas with her husband and two small sons. She is preparing to enroll for her second master's degree, in preparation to be a physician's assistant. Her graduate work, she says, will be something akin to a condensed medical school training. As a P.A. she will be able to see patients and prescribe medication. After her experience in New York she is confident that her patients will accept her—*hijab* and all—regardless of their faith.

Haseena continues to wear her *hijab* in public, and doesn't care that she might not fit in. Nor does it bother her to be part of a religious minority in the United States. She is raising her two preschool-age sons, four and two and a half years old, to be proud of their faith, and has found no difficulties so far.

Sometimes the older boy points out women who don't dress as his mother does. "I just explain that they aren't Muslim. They are nice people," she says. "When he gets older, I will explain and discuss it."

❧ 9 ❧

DR. AMENA HAQ:
A STETHOSCOPE AND A HIJAB

THE GUARD at the gated community of mobile homes was transfixed by Amena Haq.

It wasn't because she was a Muslim woman wearing her silken scarf in a predominantly Jewish section of Broward County in southern Florida. No, he said in awe: He couldn't get over that she was making a house call. "You don't see that anymore," the guard said.

Amena—that is, *Doctor* Amena Haq—chuckled at the guard's amazement and smiled serenely as he lifted the gate for her to drive through. At fifty years of age, Amena is an admittedly old-fashioned M.D. who still makes house calls to check on patients who can't come into her office. She feels she's become a more caring person after a spiritual awakening caused her to go on a pilgrimage to Mecca and then, for the first time in her life to don the *hijab*. However, her newly awakened spirituality hasn't been without risk, especially after the 9/11 terrorist attacks and the wars in Iraq and Afghanistan.

Her routine follows a narrow path: home to office, office to home. She allows herself once-a-week visits to the mosque, maybe a quick lunch at a "safe" restaurant, run by other Muslims. She says she doesn't feel particularly safe appearing anywhere else in a *hijab*. She's stopped shopping in malls, she says, where people stare at her. They didn't before 9/11. (During a trip to Washington, D.C., one woman who saw Amena on the street without any provocation called her a bitch.)

Her patients, most of them elderly Jewish and Christian women, have stuck by her. Only a few would-be patients balked when they spotted Amena in her scarf. She is bewildered by this hostility. In addition, she is sometimes angry over what she perceives as ignorance about her faith.

Still, she tries to practice what she considers the proper Islam: a religion based on love and consideration for others. She shares a medical practice in a suburb about a half hour northwest of Fort Lauderdale, with her husband, who looks after the male patients. Both trained as physicians in their native India, the Haqs came to the United States as twenty-somethings drawn to the better healthcare system here.

"She is a good doctor," attests one elderly patient while waiting to be transported from the office in her wheelchair. She's been going to see Amena for about six years. Other longtime patients say they don't even notice her head covering anymore. What they care about is that she is a conscientious doctor whom they can trust. "She's very thorough — she looks into everything," says one. She is so caring that many patients frequently ask her for nonmedical advice. Sometimes, Amena takes them to her favorite Indian restaurants to chat about their problems over lunch.

"None of my patients go to psychiatrists," she joked. "They just come to me."

Her patients are protective, sometimes voicing worries that she is still wearing her Muslim head scarf in public despite the tensions that arose after 9/11. She does not wear the drab garment that Americans often associate with Muslim women. Hers are colorful, silken creations. Amena, after all, flies home to her native India on vacations and buys fabric in an out-of-the-way, high-fashion boutique that actress Jennifer Lopez is said to frequent. Still, patients worry that her scarves draw attention to her Islamic faith. Although her manner is gentle, Amena can be blunt. She thanks them for their concerns but tells them, "I would rather die with my scarf on than live without it."

Amena's head covering constantly reminds her of her Islamic spiritual life, something that means a great deal to her. Her faith, she claims, has made her a better person, reminding her, for example, to bite her tongue before saying an unkind thing, and to care for others who can't take care of themselves.

Amena decided to wear her *hijab* full-time—even in the office—
about ten years ago. While on the hajj, the required pilgrimage to
Mecca, she donned the required *hijab* to pray at the sacred sites. "The
tradition [of the *hijab*] can be liberating—not dressing for men's ap-
proval but for who we are," Haq added. The trip, she says, was life
changing. "I found so much peace," she said. She decided to follow all
the commandments to be a good Muslim, as these would ensure her
newfound tranquility. It was a time in her life when she needed serenity most: Her mother and sister had recently died of cancer. Her father
had died years earlier. She's grateful to her faith for sustaining her during her grief.

Amena also finds that Islam makes her life easier as a woman. For
example, she says she doesn't feel pressured to earn money the way
many other American women are. The Quran requires Muslim men to
be responsible and support their families. She works part-time, so she
can spend plenty of time with her children. She doesn't come home exhausted every night like other American women who work long
hours—and even overtime—for a bigger paycheck.

Still, working gives Amena the opportunity be in a stimulating environment. The Quran, she believes, gives her the best of both worlds:
a close family and an interesting, challenging career.

Islam is partly misunderstood in the United States, because, as she
puts it, "Islam is more than a religion. It's a way of life. It's very family oriented."

It hurts that her faith agitates some Americans. Merely a symbol
of Islam, such as her hijab can make some people nervous. But her
loyal patients make up for those who can't see beyond the scarf. At
Amena's request, one patient, a retired judge who is Jewish, came to
the aid of a Muslim woman trying to obtain a divorce from an abusive
husband. (Amena dotes on the young woman, encouraging her to be
independent, while also watching over the woman's young son. She
also looks after the daughter of her housekeeper, who supports her
family since her husband was disabled at work.)

In the southern Florida Muslim community, Amena is affectionately nicknamed Apu—"big sister"—the one who sees that things get
done, and that people get the help they need.

In 2004, when Hurricane Charley devastated Punta Gorda and

other Gulf Coast communities in Florida, Amena helped lead a fund-raising drive at her mosque to deliver carloads of supplies and about a hundred $25 gift certificates to buy groceries. "Everyone pitched in $1,000," she is pleased to report. Helping others allowed the doctor to forget her own family's hurricane troubles. The downed tree branches from Hurricane Frances—the second of four hurricanes to hit Florida earlier that year—filled her backyard; a tree had toppled the patio screen over the family's pool. Nevertheless, Amena was up at five in the morning to prepare that night's dinner—proud of her skill as gourmet cook, she won't let her family touch fast food—so she could be on the road by seven to take part in the Helping Hurricane Charley caravan. She faced the six-hour round trip without hesitation, because as she succinctly expressed it, "People need help."

She regularly welcomes new Muslim families arriving in southern Florida. She recommended an obstetrician for one new arrival who was nine months pregnant. She helped sponsor a baby shower for the family, then delivered a week's worth of hot meals after the infant was born.

"That's her role in the community," one such newcomer, Salma, says affectionately. Salma herself was amazed when Amena showed up at her doorstep to welcome her, even though she had moved into a neighborhood far from the doctor's. Now, Salma says, "I consider her my friend, my sister, my mother." Besides Salma, Amena has a cadre of young women who are appreciative of her mentoring. "She has taken each and everyone of us in," agrees another friend, Nusrat.

Patients, too, become part of Apu's large extended family. In addition to making home visits to a ninety-one-year-old woman named Mildred when she became terminally ill, Amena also introduced Mildred to many of her friends. That way, she could make sure that Mildred, who would otherwise be alone, had companions during her last days when she was in hospice care.

Mildred "became everyone's friend," says Nusrat.

Before Mildred passed away, she became sufficiently curious about Islam to ask her doctor for a copy of the Quran. After work, Amena would go and talk to her about the holy book, much the way she has taught about the Quran at her mosque. Usually, though,

Amena's faith doesn't come up as a topic in the doctor's office — she believes in respecting her patients' privacy. Amena learned from her parents to be considerate of others.

Amena comes from a close-knit family of eight children. Her father was an English-educated professor who returned to India to teach. Education was emphasized and "piety was instilled in us." Amena remembers herself being a mischievous child, not exempt from getting a spanking from her exasperated mother. But, unlike today's kids, Amena says she accepted the punishment. "I was a naughty girl and she disciplined me," she says.

She outgrew her rebellion by her teenage years. At sixteen she was already in college preparing to become a doctor, and it was at her Indian medical school that she met her future husband, Saleem.

She did not date him, as such. She was never allowed to be alone with him. They didn't go to dinner or the movies as a couple unchaperoned. Yet she decided he was the one for her — as long as her parents liked him. She said she would not have married him unless they approved and gave her permission to wed him — and they did. Her two daughters and son think this quaint custom is something they themselves would never tolerate. But Amena sees the practicality in it: Her parents were merely looking out for her interests. And the tradition has worked out. The Haqs have been married for nearly thirty years. While other American couples with two stressful careers have seen their marriages crumble, theirs has flourished, through moves from India to South Carolina to Chicago to South Florida. They have had three children and frequently travel to India to keep in touch with their families.

Amena's husband has always encouraged her to achieve. She was, after all, a top medical school student who earned three first-place gold medals. And as her three brothers were already doctors, her family quite naturally expected her to excel. Amena first came to the United States in the mid-1970s to be with her father, who was in South Carolina to have a lung removed. One of her brothers had arranged for the operation near where he had a practice. As a full-fledged doctor, Amena decided she would join her father while he was recuperating.

"I was a daddy's girl," she said, "and he wanted me to be close to him."

After beginning a residency in South Carolina with an Indian-born cardiovascular surgeon, Amena surprised herself by how much she liked and appreciated the American medical system. She saw that patients were treated with respect, and that kind of medicine appealed to her. She decided to accept another residency at the University of Illinois hospital in Chicago where her new husband, Saleem, also could complete a residency.

At first, she specialized in pediatrics. Big mistake, she soon realized. "I just couldn't deal with really sick kids," she said.

She switched to the emergency room and discovered her passion. She liked the drama of life-or-death situations that brought out her quick thinking to save lives. "I loved saving people right in front of your eyes," she said. "It was the best thing that ever happened to me." But the long shifts and overnight hours weren't good for family life. After she had three children, and the family had moved to South Florida, she went into private practice with her husband.

Amena still remembers the magical sensation of moving to an area they had once visited as tourists enamored by the palms, the sea, and the balmy subtropical weather. While house-hunting, they came across the same wooded North Broward community they had admired years ago. Years later, it was as if a genie granted her wish: The one house on sale in the neighborhood was on that same lot, and the Haqs snapped it up. It has become their refuge, with its bubbling brook and fountain, and, a stand of oaks and palm trees.

In the years since 9/11, Amena has come to understand Americans' revulsion for Arab extremist terrorists, and she shares their disgust. In her opinion, the men who hijacked the planes and flew two of them into the World Trade Center were unspeakably evil. It sickens her that they killed in the name of Islam—a faith that for her remains peaceful and life-affirming. It is not, she says firmly, a religion that promotes terrorism. Nor were those men of the faith. "They showed them in nightclubs drinking [in later footage shown on television]," she said, "but Muslims do not drink."

Neither can she accept that the Allah-invoking terrorists who held hostage the Russian schoolchildren, parents, and teachers in the summer of 2004 were true Muslims. No religious person, she says, would have sponsored a mass kidnapping that led to the tragedy of more than

300 dead, including many children. A mass killing, to her mind, is an act of barbarity no religion would condone.

The terrorist killings in Iraq add to her sorrow. These are times no one can understand, she has observed. Nevertheless, she and others will continue to do good to offset the evil that has inflicted so much pain in the world.

❧ 10 ❧

THE ENTERPRISE OF EDINA

JUST FIVE YEARS AGO, Edina Lekovic was applying for a job in southern California as a broadcast television journalist. As editor in chief of UCLA's student newspaper she certainly possessed the journalistic credentials. She was stunned when one TV news boss told her bluntly, "You should give up the idea of being in front of a camera. It's just not going to happen."

The reason: "I was wearing a head scarf," Edina says.

This exchange occurred before 9/11, but discrimination against Muslims was already in play, to the extent that the television executive felt comfortable telling Edina that as a Muslim woman wearing a *hijah* she would never land a job on TV.

For Edina, to be told such a thing was a blow. But what she soon learned was even worse: He was right.

Despite interview after interview, she couldn't land a reporting job. She ended up a school teacher, then an editor for a Muslim magazine, and now the communications director of the Muslim Public Affairs Council, a national policy institution with offices in Washington, D.C., and Los Angeles. At twenty-seven, she feels fulfilled in her position at the council. It's the perfect blend of all her interests—journalism, education, Islam, international affairs—and it allows her to advocate for people with unique stories (and these days, in her opinion, Muslims are especially vulnerable).

Nevertheless, it rankles Edina that this *is* America, the land where one can realize one's dreams, and Edina finds it hard to accept the fact that religion might hold someone like herself back. Her own parents had flourished here when they had arrived as immigrants from what was then called Yugoslavia.

The irony is that she probably could have landed a broadcast television job had she been willing to forgo the *hijab,* which she hadn't worn for that long anyway. Edina and her sister had decided to wear it after meeting some other Muslims — for the first time — on the UCLA campus.

"But to take off the scarf — it wasn't even a consideration," Edina says, adding, "I have no misgivings. I am not willing to settle in order to get a job."

It's not that she thinks she is required as a Muslim woman to wear the scarf. It is because her scarf is a constant reminder of what she gained: her faith. And that faith is also something her parents were long denied in the formerly Communist-controlled Yugoslavia. The post–World War II government, led by Tito, did away with religion — or tried to — including Islam and Christianity. As the so-called ethnic cleansing in the Balkans would later show, the old Yugoslavia remained ethnically and religiously diverse long after Tito's demise.

Edina and her sister grew up in southern California. They looked like stereotypical California girls: blue-eyed and with sandy blond or light-brown hair. "To our friends and the outside world, we were like most any other Becky or Jody," Edina says.

But she and her sister *knew* they were different. They didn't celebrate Christmas like their school chums and other Americans — although on one occasion Edina asked for what she called a "New Year's tree."

"We would go to the mosque for major holidays, for Eid, maybe for some Friday prayers when there was time," Edina remembers.

But how they looked and practiced Islam seemed quite different than what they saw on American television. They knew their family members weren't fanatical Middle Eastern terrorists, and these seemed to be the only kind of Muslims shown on American television. And while her parents were strict, they never required them to cover their hair. Nor did they tell their daughters not to wear shorts in public. In retrospect, Edina feels that during her high school years, "being

Muslim was weird. There were no other Muslims in my high school. I never knew anyone like me. I always felt alone in my religion."

That all changed when she went to UCLA, soon followed by her sister, who transferred there from another school. For one, Edina was stunned to meet on campus an African American who had converted to Islam. "I was dumbfounded that someone would *choose* what I had spent most of my life running away from, or at least distancing myself from."

Piqued by curiosity, Edina picked up a Quran to read for the first time. "It changed my worldview tremendously and my relationship with my God." She started praying five times a day.

She and her sister also happened to pass by a booth on campus run by a Muslim students' association.

"We're like, 'hi'!" remembers Edina.

The young man appeared a bit taken aback by the two young co-eds in shorts and tank tops, but cheerfully asked if he could help them.

The sisters told him they were Muslim and wanted to find out more about the association.

Now the student was *really* taken aback.

"He told us there were prayers on Friday. He was trying to get over his shock," Edina says laughing, "but he was very kind and giving."

The sisters began going to prayer services and Muslim student functions. Edina's sister, in fact, ended up marrying that very Muslim volunteer who turned out to be the son of Egyptian immigrants and a graduate student, and who went on to earn a doctorate.

But Edina has paid a price for her regained faith.

When she was about to be named editor in chief of UCLA's newspaper, there were questions: Could she really do the job? Not that she wasn't competent, but there was skepticism that she could be non-biased. "Even members of my own staff questioned if I could separate my religious beliefs," she says.

Those doubts were a foretaste of what Edina would find in the real world. When she graduated she decided to try to enter "mainstream" journalism—she wanted to be on TV. She had, after all, an impressive résumé. But she encountered resistance at the thought of hiring a woman wearing a *hijab*. The one editor who spoke to her candidly was the exception. Others who interviewed her were polite, but she never got past first base.

"There is still this notion from the old boys' club that no reporter should display outward symbols of his or her religion," she says.

Later, however, the public school system *did* hire her, and she ended up teaching English and history to fifth and sixth graders in Pasadena. "It was a very positive year," she remarks before adding with a laugh, "I think it was the hardest job I have ever done in my life."

Soon afterward, she was offered a job as managing editor for the Muslim magazine *Minaret*. She loved being back in journalism and being able to explore a broad range of issues. Her stint with *Minaret* also allowed Edina to further explore her faith and talk with other Muslims from around the world. In 2003, the country of Malaysia invited her to be part of an international conference of Muslim leaders that included discussions on how Muslims could help stop violence worldwide. Attending was an eye-opener for Edina. Other Muslims from around the world pounced on her to tell how they despised the United States for sending troops to Iraq and causing thousands of deaths of civilians there. Edina took pains to explain that many Americans agreed with them and were against the Bush administration's war policy.

Now that she has joined the Muslim Public Affairs Council in Los Angeles, she is busy with outreach to the community, promoting a positive image of Muslims, and helping to protect against civil rights infractions. "It's been a rough time for the American Muslim community," she says.

But she'll be there to help out.

PART II

The Blenders

In her mid-twenties, Sofia Shakir wears stylish flowing pantsuits to work at the Miami-Dade State Attorney's Office. No *hijab* for her, thank you. Instead, she welcomes new fashions just like any other young American woman. Yet she feels as drawn to her Islamic faith as her younger sister Sadia, who began wearing the *hijab* while in law school in Michigan. "Islam is in my heart," Sofia maintains. "I don't have to wear clothes to show it."

Many other American *Muslimah* feel the same way. They are the Blenders. They fit seamlessly into the American fabric. Indeed, their co-workers and neighbors might be surprised to learn they are Muslim. Scholars believe most *Muslimah* in America are Blenders. They don't wear any head coverings or other clothing traditionally associated with Islam.

Blenders can be first- or second-generation Muslim Americans. They rarely include converts, though. The converts, or reverts as they are called in Muslim circles, tend to be the most enthusiastic about veiling and donning traditional clothes. They also stand out in American society, unlike the Blenders, most of whom prefer anonymity.

"I'm doing fine, living my life, obeying my God and not attracting any attention," says one Blender, an accounting professor in the Chicago area. She says the *hijab* was on its way out in her native Egypt when she was growing up in the 1950s. Her mother did not wear one and she wasn't expected to, either. It was mostly a habit of poor rural women. Now, however, the professor notices the *hijab* is making a comeback. On her yearly trips back to Egypt, she sees chic young women sporting them. In Chicago, she notes the young *Muslimah* donning head scarves. That's fine with her. Just don't expect her to wear one.

She and other Blenders says they are as spiritual as those who do wear some sort of covering. They say they do not need to show their religion with "a bit of cloth." Blenders says they attend mosque services in as great a number as those women who do wear the traditional Islamic head covering. But the Blenders take pains to find a mosque where they will be accepted and not be drawn into any "cloth war." Wearing a *hijab* "is not something that I think shows my faith as a practicing Muslim," Sabrina Hossain maintains. She has an ally: her husband.

Some American *Muslimah* are unwilling blenders. They would like to wear a *hijab* but they fear harassment or discrimination. Indeed, some employers have complained about Muslim refugee women showing up for work wearing *hijabs*, according to a report by the Washington-based Cultural Orientation Resource Center, which receives federal funding to help the refugees. (The refugees' social workers tell the bosses that they must allow the women to wear their scarves.)

Many other Blenders, however, chafe at their fellow Muslims dictating a dress code. "They say, 'You can't do that,' but why?" asks Farrukah "Fay" Peshimam, who grew up in India and now lives in Florida. She opts to go bareheaded. She thinks other women should be able to decide for themselves as well.

As a founder of the Progressive Muslim Union of North America, Sarah Eltantawi strongly agrees. In an article called "Yes or No to Hijab: Not for Men to Answer," she wrote: "I fear that unless Muslim women stand up for the right to make their own decisions about what they are going to wear . . . while they still have the chance, the fundamentalists will have completely succeeded in convincing yet more women that the simple act of wearing what makes them comfortable and adjusted is somehow shameful, traitorous, or *haram*."

She herself doesn't wear one. She says she can still be religious without covering her hair. Many religious scholars support her assertion. "The Quran prescribes some degree of segregation and veiling for the Prophet's wives, but there is nothing in the Quran that requires the veiling of *all* women or their seclusion in a separate part of the house," writes noted religious scholar Karen Armstrong in her book *Islam: A Short History*. "These customs were adopted some three or four generations after the Prophet's death."

Besides, says Nashville feminist Zainab Elberry, "Islam has progressed and changed so much. We have more important issues to tackle than what people should wear." Indeed, she and the other Blenders you will read about are among the most active in their American communities, whether they are volunteering in schools or fighting for women's rights. ⌒◅

❖ 11 ❖

ZAINAB: A PIONEERING
MUSLIMAH FEMINIST

ZAINAB ELBERRY, A POET, young mother, and Egyptian émigré, was attending a Nashville governor's conference in the mid-1970s, listening to a speaker give advice on where women should be looking for work, when insurance was suggested. Zainab, who came from an affluent family in Egypt, was struggling in Nashville just to get by, so a good-paying job in the insurance field sounded great. She liked business. She figured that insurance offered flexible hours, ideal for a working mother.

Little did she know how hard it would be for a foreign-born Muslim woman trying to make it in the white-shoe, good-ol'-boy town of Nashville. "Talk about [glass] ceilings," she now jokes. "I was a woman, an Arab, and Muslim. You learn about frustration."

In 1984 she told a local magazine frankly "When a foreign person, such as an American, is living in the Middle East or Egypt, he is highly regarded, well-paid and receives good treatment. It is the reverse in this country: A foreigner has a handicap—he's foreign; he has an accent. But you have to face the problems and live with it."

Through sheer grit, she ignored jokes made at her expense, slights against her, harassment, and the bad pay. She played by the rules of the game, even though they were tilted against her and other women. She still remembers how carefully she followed the "dress for success" guidelines for women—that is, to dress like a businessman but in a "feminine" way. That translated into wearing skirted suits (never pantsuits) and donning floppy silky bows, the feminine version of a tie.

73

On this score, having been born in the Middle East was an asset: She used her old-world charm to fit in with men who were more comfortable with conventionally feminine Southern women. That charm also helped her convince businesses to buy healthcare insurance from her for their employees.

With 50 million Americans still lacking any health insurance coverage, this is a subject about which Zainab is passionate, and that passion helped her to create her own business, including a "good-ol'-girls" network that has served her well. She helped start Nashville's first business club for women—and some of the members who eventually started their own businesses later became Zainab's clients.

She remembers taking her young son into the office: He played, she worked.

She rose in the ranks to become a representative and underwriter at one Fortune 500 insurance company in Nashville and after a while became a manager and million-dollar-club member at another top national firm, as well as being listed in *Who's Who*. Then, after more than twenty years at the company, she was asked to resign. She joined a class-action discrimination lawsuit that eventually was resolved with the women given a settlement. "It made me sick to my stomach what was done," Zainab says now. Still, she is glad the lawsuit made the company agree to a two-page list of reforms that will benefit its present and future female employees.

Today, after more than two decades in the business, she is president of her own independent insurance brokerage company, PINC Financial. She is married to Moroccan-born economist, Dr. Nour Naciri, who is also a lay authority on Islam. Their son, Nadeam Elshami, is on staff for a U.S. senator after having served as communications director and deputy chief of staff for a congressman.

In Nashville, Zainab is heavily committed to working for the Democratic party, to the extent that a Bill Clinton aide once wrote to her, "Your energy, devotion, commitment and belief in the United States only renews that same spirit in all of us who know you." At her home she displays autographed pictures from former president Clinton and vice president Al Gore, fondly sent to her for her volunteer work. (She became known as the "pie lady" for keeping Gore's staff supplied with pastries during the 2000 election.)

She's also on the board of directors for former representative Paul Findley's Council for the National Interest. "He is my political mentor," Zainab says. "I learned a lot about our democracy from him during the past fifteen years."

Zainab has been a major mover-and-shaker in Nashville where the local newspaper once nicknamed her a "one-person embassy" for her volunteer work helping educate locals about the Middle East and Muslims. (She has produced Muslim fashion shows that highlight apparel from twenty countries, started annual international art, cultural and food festivals, and helped promote such exhibits as "Empire of the Sultans" that highlighted the rich heritage of the Ottoman Empire.)

By all accounts she is a remarkable success. Yet she doesn't rest on her laurels. She still remembers the pains that led to those successes. And, some thirty-five years since arriving here, Zainab says she is still fighting misperceptions, both as an Arab American and a Muslim.

"America is not an easy place to work in," she says. "You have to be strong. It's very hard. It's still a male-dominated world."

She considers herself a feminist—she is on the board of the Women's Fund of the Community Foundation of Middle Tennessee— *and* a devout Muslim. She sees no disconnect between these two aspects of her life. Islam promotes learning for both men and women. Furthermore it's a religion, she says, "that asks you to improve yourself, especially through education and learning."

For Muslim women, that includes handling their own inheritances, charitable giving, and income. Islam also gives a woman the option to keep her maiden name, which Elberry did.

Then there's the *hijab*. Except for a head covering when she goes to mosque and prays, Elberry has never worn one and doesn't plan to.

Americans, she is sad to say, have an "unfortunate image" of perennially veiled Muslim women, that "you *have* to be like that to be a Muslim." It is a notion she considers "insane."

She rejects the idea that the *hijab* allows a woman to get back to the so-called basics of Islam. The religion hasn't changed. The basic tenets remain the same, such as believing in one God, praying five times a day, loving your neighbor, giving to the poor, and forgiving others. "These things will never change," she insists.

The return to the *hijab*, she feels, is a reflection of some women's soul-searching, of their attempts to examine who they are. While Zainab appreciates that certain women feel more spiritual wearing a *hijab*, it's a concept she doesn't share.

The convention of women covering themselves started in Mohammad's time, in seventh-century Mecca, when there was more lawlessness, she adds. "Women," Zainab says, "needed to dress for protection—in case of danger, other Muslims needed to know what they looked like, from their modest clothing and scarf, so they would rescue them if needed."

Today, however, "Islam has progressed and changed so much. We have more important issues to tackle than what people should wear. Islam does not have a 'uniform' although Muslims understand and respect a certain dress code."

She notes that few men are bearded, as tradition dictates. So why should women be held to a different standard? "Should we deem any man without a beard a lesser Muslim?" she adds. "Of course not."

Zainab feels that Americans need to understand that throughout the Muslim world, many women do not wear any head covering. When she was growing up in Cairo, she did not see many women in scarves, at a time when Egypt had a population of two million people in 1950.

"I went to the then-called American College for Girls, the only American school in Cairo, when I was four years old, and finished high school there," she says.

As a young girl she wanted to work for the United Nations and, toward that goal, she learned fluent English and some French. When she began pursuing her master's degree in comparative literature at the American University in Cairo, she focused on playwright Tennessee Williams and his portrayal of Southern women.

"The plight of Southern women comes close to how Muslim women have been treated by their society—*not* by religion," she learned. "They weren't expected to work or be politically involved."

Zainab was uncomfortable in Egypt. The country was still trying to recover from three wars. Egypt's then president, Gamal Abdel Nasser, had been leading his country for years steadily toward socialism. He restricted civil rights; dissent was not tolerated. Phone lines were tapped, letters opened, student leaders followed. "There was brainwashing—kids had to go to camp to learn about socialism," she laments. "Opponents ended up in jails, their families unaware of their whereabouts."

Zainab believed she would feel safer—and freer—in the United States, so she finished her master's degree at Vanderbilt University. Her emigration made a profound impression on her.

"You come here and understand what Americans have," she says. "People have to be free. Tolerance and understanding, is the world's strength."

Now, as Americans become more respectful of diversity, Zainab upholds that standard of respect, freely helping all kinds of groups. When she was asked to organize the annual fundraiser for The Links, an African American civic group, Zainab didn't hesitate—and recruited the help of other Nashville Muslims.

She was thrilled when a friend remarked at her son's wedding reception: "This looks like a U.N. party. Look at all the different foods, costumes, and people."

"He was right," Elberry later wrote in the now defunct *Nashville Banner* newspaper. "When I composed my guest list, it contained a wide mix of last names of both native-born and new Americans, all of whom I consider good friends and family."

Her appreciation of America extends into getting involved in politics. Like most Muslim women, she is a loyal Democrat. A particular fan of Tennessee native son, Al Gore, she threw herself into his 2000 campaign and was a stalwart volunteer at his national campaign headquarters in Nashville.

In 2002, after volunteering in a gubernatorial campaign, she affectionately wrote a tribute to political campaign workers and their 24/7 way of life:

The countdown calendar is in a prominent place. Sometimes the countdown days have slogans and pictures of the opponents or their campaign staff: "Woozy Eyes Sally," "Dumb Jo," "We'll whip your . . . , Don," etc. All in good fun, not always politically savvy, but it satisfies the purpose of cheering. When the last days come near and the Day of Reckoning is upon the campaign the whole picture takes a dramatic turn.

There are signs that a finale is near: A black velvet dress with silver beads hangs on a staffer's door—hopefully to be worn at a victory celebration. A Mexican piñata with all kinds of goodies dangles for a month and will be hit hard. A bottle of bubbly is stored in view on a filing cabinet. . . .

She still has trouble accepting that Gore did not get to go to the White House even though he won the popular vote. But she tries to be philosophical and accept reality.

In that spirit, she was part of a panel in Nashville to discuss *Unconstitutional,* a film that explores how Muslim and Middle Easterners' rights had been violated after the U.S. Congress passed the Patriot Act. She also has joined rallies in Nashville to protest the Iraq war. As she put it in a poem, "We are afraid," but we must not allow ourselves to simply "go on about our / business . . . / ignoring the reality of our humanity."

❧ 12 ❧

LUBY TEACHES AMERICANS
ABOUT ISLAM

LOBNA "LUBY" ISMAIL is a wife, mother, daughter, entrepreneur, business owner, cross-cultural trainer, PTA volunteer, first-generation American, Muslim, former Floridian, college grad, nature lover, former Miss Softball America player, homemaker, and suburbanite who happens to have multiple sclerosis, a new baby (at age forty-two), and a home in the Maryland woods.

Her life—and the lives of all Muslim women, she points out—amounts to much more than whether or not she wears a scarf to cover her hair. As all Muslim women do, Luby covers her hair when at prayer and at certain religious or cultural events. But she does not make it a habit to wear a scarf at all public outings. Unlike some other women, she does not see the scarf as integral to her faith. To her, differences in attitude toward the veil are part of the diversity and rich tapestry of Muslim life that sometimes is not well understood.

Traditionally, Christian women also have worn some sort of head covering. It is written in the Bible for Christian women to cover themselves and, indeed, until the 1960s Catholic women did so when attending Mass. And Orthodox Jewish women still cover their real hair with wigs.

But, Luby says, only Muslim women are defined and measured by whether or not they cover their hair.

She points to an article by Mona Eltahawy, another Muslim woman, entitled "Boxed in by a Bit of Cloth." In it, she mourns that when Iranian lawyer Shirin Ebadi became the first Muslim woman to win a Nobel Peace Prize in 2003, every news story made the point that she did not wear a head scarf.

"I long for the day," Eltahawy writes, "when . . . a Muslim woman is neither the sum or the absence of a head scarf."

Luby couldn't agree more. "It's the pressure, the labels, the assumptions for Muslim women [that restrict us]," Luby adds, remarking on how the *hijab* reflects the diversity of Muslims. "We're not one monolithic group and there are various interpretations of practice."

Indeed, today, only two out of the world's more than fifty predominantly Muslim countries mandate what women wear in public: Saudi Arabia and Iran. The rest leave it up to the women, although there may be strong social pressure for women to wear the *hijab*, especially in rural areas. Some secular governments, such as in Turkey, encourage women *not* to wear any sort of veil.

"Islam talks about the diversity of people, of the different nations and tribes," Luby adds. It is something she knows firsthand.

She is a first-generation Arab American. Her parents are Egyptians who came to the United States to study for their doctorates. Because Luby's maternal grandmother in Egypt insisted that her daughters get college educations, Luby's mother pursued her Ph.D. studies despite the barriers against advanced education for women that existed in the United States at that time in the 1960s.

Luby's parents decided to stay in the United States after they finished their education because of the wars and unrest in Egypt. Her father became a research scientist for the state of Florida. Indeed, he was the state's top citrus expert for what is now a billion-dollar industry, and eventually director of the Citrus Experiment Center. Luby grew up in the state's citrus farm belt—the state's wide middle swath, about thirty minutes from the water-skiing pleasures of Cypress Gardens, a location Luby calls "great."

She and her family were the only Arabs—and Muslims—in the mostly rural area, and so they could not attend a mosque. However, Luby's parents taught their faith to their children. With their unusual ethnicity, Luby's family became a novelty in the community. She remembers her parents speaking at women's clubs, churches, and at other civic meetings. "It was very positive," Luby remembers. Her family immersed themselves in American culture, enjoying the

Fourth of July picnics, annual county fairs, and trick-or-treating on Halloween.

Still, there were some awkward moments. Luby went to grade school at a time when desegregation was beginning in earnest and a "big issue," as she calls it, arose: What "color" was she?

"I'm Egyptian," she would tell them. "I'm not black, nor am I white."

She did not feel different from her other classmates until she became a teenager. That's when her faith and parents' cultural traditions started to set her apart from the rest of the kids. She wasn't allowed to date, go to dances, drink beer, or eat the pepperoni on pizza (as Muslims are forbidden to eat pork).

"The difficult high school years. . . . ," she now muses. "Suddenly all the girls had boyfriends and were able to go to parties. I didn't fit in."

Her solution: She befriended evangelical Christians. When her mom and dad became alarmed, Luby assured them it was okay. Evangelical Christians shared the same values — They loved God, and didn't date, drink, or take drugs.

"I could go to their youth group events," Luby says. "There was a real connection. As I look back on them, they were true to their faith and belief in God."

So she joined their prayer meetings in the band room. They read the Bible, she the Quran.

This was how she became interested in interfaith dialogue and how people from different backgrounds could find common ground.

She even became fast friends with the PKs — the preachers' kids — and the only activity of theirs she drew the line on was that she wouldn't go "evangelizing" with them. To this day she has pleasant memories and respect for evangelical Christians.

She believes they and Muslims have much in common. For example, they are both against gambling, they encourage modesty, and value sex within marriage. Both faiths can help their congregations inoculate themselves against the societal pressures of today.

To Luby, the irony is that Americans look "at the poor Muslim women as being oppressed." But what about the oppression and pressure many American girls feel to be a certain size or have a particular "look" — to be sexually active, wear provocative clothes, and engage in behavior that compromises their values and their intellect? Luby now feels gratitude that her parents set boundaries that protected her from those kinds of pressures. She is just as grateful that they encouraged her to obtain an education.

Luby attended American University in Washington, D.C., where she would earn her bachelor's degree and where she met her husband, Alexander Kronemer, now a film producer and a converted Muslim. (He has gone on to be one of the producers of the PBS documentary *Muhammad: Legacy of a Prophet.*)

They re-connected when Alex went to Harvard's Divinity School and Luby was pursuing a graduate degree in intercultural relations at Leslie College in Cambridge.

Islam, Luby explains, helped her husband integrate the disparate threads of his background. He was raised a Christian. His parents were divorced and his mother had taken him to church as a youngster. But his father was Jewish. Islam combines both faiths, Luby says, by including teachings from both Jesus and the Torah.

After their marriage, Alex agreed to go back with her to Washington so she could be an adviser to international students at American University. She was swamped with work during her first two years. Then she became pregnant with their first son, who was born in 1990.

Suddenly, Luby had a dilemma. She wanted to continue her career but she also wanted to spend time with her son. She couldn't see how she would work all the hours required and still have enough time for her family. All the same, Luby wanted both. "Just because I am committed to my family doesn't mean I don't want a career."

So she resigned and decided to form her own company, Connecting Cultures, that would reflect her desire to promote intercultural understanding. Her company's mission, she says, is also her passion: to help people understand culture and religion and the impact they have on how we work and communicate.

Today, her company has grown, and gives seminars internationally. "Our market includes community leaders, educators, law enforcement officers, the military, government workers, corporate executives, and managers," its website says. "We have conducted training all over the United States and the world."

After the September 11 terrorist attacks, she feared her business would dry up from the backlash against Muslims. But the opposite happened: Americans became more curious than ever to hear about Islam and Muslims.

Indeed, Uncle Sam was one of her biggest clients. A month after 9/11, the Community Relations Services at the U.S. Justice Department hired Luby's company to begin training police officers and community leaders.

"After 9/11 and the wars in Afghanistan and Iraq, there has been a backlash against Arab and Muslim Americans. Our training provides key information about the Islamic faith and culture and how to effectively communicate and build relations with the community," Luby explains. It is also designed to help end the vandalism, desecration, physical attacks, and arson at mosques and other Muslim facilities.

At one of her recent sessions, held in Fort Lauderdale, she and a Sikh representative talked about their faiths to police officers, most of them from southern Florida. Luby emphasized that if police officers have to remove a suspect's turban or head scarf, this should be done in private, as these are religious symbols. She also wanted to sensitize the officers into understanding that a Muslim having a Quran in his car isn't a sign that he is an extremist.

"We want to explain the meaning of symbols such as clothing and religious practices to diminish fear and misperceptions."

The federal government has also hired Connecting Cultures to help officers in Iraq who are training Iraqis how to patrol and do other police work. She briefs them about the Iraqi culture and how Iraqis may, in turn, have stereotypes of Americans.

It may be painful but Luby recommends that the officers talk openly about these stereotypes—unfair characterizations of Americans being hard workers but also greedy, selfish, aggressive, promiscuous, and uninterested in their families. Luby feels strongly that cultural understanding is a two-way street. To her, a strength of the American people and their government is their eagerness to better understand Islam and Muslims.

Even Fortune 500 corporations are coming to her company to learn more about their Muslim employees, an interest that gives Luby what she calls her "greatest hope."

She believes that American Muslims can invigorate Islam world-wide with their emphasis on the heart and soul of Islam and interfaith exchange. American Muslims can also help bridge the gap between the United States and the Muslim nations.

She sees herself as something of an ambassador. She's also a work-ing mom, a PTA volunteer, and a soccer mom ready to carpool—all of this despite her MS. Diagnosed with the disease years ago, Luby has occasional flareups. She can't walk far and needs a wheelchair to man-age longer distances. But she's not one for regrets—or asking why she got the disease. She chooses to see MS as simply another of life's chal-lenges, one that has made her a better person. She's found she can per-severe despite her physical limitations, and she takes nothing she's accomplished for granted. Her personal trainer reports she has more upper-body strength than a lot of other people. And while she may not be able to ski she can go snow tubing with her family. Her next dream vacation might be kayaking in Crete.

She loves the spirit in America, that sense of where there's a will, there's a way. From her travels, she knows that it's not the same in some other parts of the world, especially for those with physical dis-abilities. In the more traditional Muslim societies, she says, organiza-tions or accommodations for the handicapped don't exist. In America, though, it is almost taken for granted that handicapped people should be out and about and living a full life. For what Luby calls "our just-do-it culture," Luby is grateful.

As strange as it may seem, MS has given Luby a deep sense of thankfulness for what she has: a loving husband, two sons, and now the surprise gift of an infant daughter, named Laila. "I really count my blessings. This fate of mine has made me more aware of what I have and all that I should be grateful for, thanks be to God."

❦ 13 ❧

FAY: A GOOD HEART IS MORE IMPORTANT THAN RELIGIOUS RULES

LIKE A TYPICAL TEENAGE GIRL of the 1960s, Farrukh "Fay" Peshimam loved the Beatles and miniskirts. Once she snuck into her home a pair of red-and-black stretch pants—all the rage at the time, but taboo in her Muslim community in Bombay, India. Relatives clucked at her wildness but she didn't care. She knew she was a good Muslim.

Now as a mother with grown children in Florida, she is still defying tradition, wearing makeup and fingernail polish as well as jeans and T-shirts in public. (She gives cosmetics as presents to her cousins in India, and they clamor for her latest stateside buys.) Her soft and wavy shoulder-length black hair frames her delicately featured face—no head coverings for her. She shrugs off the finger-wagging she gets from the more orthodox in the south Florida Muslim community.

"I don't need to wear the *hijab* because I know what I am," Fay declared recently as she sat in her café and catering business, Khana Kh'zana ("Food Treasures") in Coral Springs, a long cherished dream of hers. The *hijab*, she adds, is a relic of the past, and she still rebels at the thought of others telling her how to live her life. "They say, 'You can't do that,' but why?"

And what is worse, Fay asks: having a good heart but not always obeying the rules of the faith to prove to the world that you are a "good" Muslim? Or being a "good" Muslim in public who privately violates the Quran command to love one another? For her, the worst hypocrites are the religious who make a show of their piety but have hardened hearts and cheat and lie to others.

To her, it is a sign of progress that Muslim women are wearing clothes they want—as long as they are modest. She applauds that women in Afghanistan are regaining rights, and that in other Muslim countries women are enjoying new opportunities for work and education. "Women are waking up," she says, in spite of the Islamic zealots throughout the world who try to impose their values on others. "There are a lot of fanatics," she says. "It's sad to see."

Many years earlier, Fay's relatives were only trying to help her when they criticized her Western clothes. She would answer them by pointing to her heart. As she once told a criticizing "auntie" in India, "I have a clean heart. I love everyone."

And in fact, she prays every day, just like her family does in India.

Her customers at Khana Kh'zana appreciate not only her Indian cuisine (from her own recipes—Indian gourmet cooking has been a hobby of hers for years). They value Fay herself, the warm proprietress who will ask how her customers are doing. She runs the cash register and knows her customers by their first name. If she doesn't, she asks.

Recently a reserved Indian couple came in to sample one of her dishes. They didn't get out the door, though, before they told Fay where they were from: he from Bombay, she from New Delhi. Soon they were chatting about the ways of India and how they missed the cuisine. Fay regaled them with food stories—how she trains her cooks and prepares dishes from family-held recipes—and had the Indian couple laughing. By the time their food was served, they were promising to come back.

"Fay is wonderful; very sweet," says one regular customer, who has a taste for ethnic food but who doesn't always feel comfortable at some restaurants. Fay, on the other hand, has always been friendly and welcoming.

Fay says it comes naturally. Her mother and father were open to all people and cultures. "My parents were very broad-minded even though they were religious," she says. Her father liked nothing better than a good murder mystery; her mother subscribed to the American magazine *Good Housekeeping.* Like many other Indian parents, they emphasized education. Fay went to a convent school and later a French convent college. As the schools introduced her to Christian holidays,

Fay spread ashes across her forehead for Ash Wednesday, celebrated Easter, and sang Christmas carols. While home in Hindu-dominant India, she became accustomed to celebrating Hindu festivities as well. To this day, this multicultural mix of holidays has stayed with Fay, who still carts a Christmas tree into her Florida home each year. She knows that some local Muslims raise their eyebrows at that but Fay shrugs off the reproaches. "I love all holidays," she says. She is known, after all, for the rich banquets of food she prepares during Ramadan, when Muslims are able to eat only at sundown, after fasting all day. It is Fay, after all, to whom Muslim friends go to ask what her plans are for the Ramadan dinners.

As a teenager she fell in love with an Indian boy five years older than she, who was going to college in the United States. At the same time, her mother became seriously ill with cancer, and died. Now that her mother—her champion for a love match—was gone, relatives were fretting that "no one is in the house to monitor her," meaning Fay. Their solution: an arranged marriage. They had already been match-making, picking out a doctor for her. Fay would have nothing to do with it. "They were going to marry me off to some stupid guy who is a doctor," she wailed to her boyfriend's mother. But the older woman had a solution: marry her son first. Fay eloped: She was seventeen, he twenty-two. In 1969, the couple moved to America, first to the Washington, D.C., area and later to Florida.

Fay adapted to life in the United States quickly and positively. "I feel it's the only country in the world where immigrants don't feel like second-class citizens." Likewise, she'll have none of the talk of other immigrants who pine for their native country. All she has to do, she says, is remember India's trash-strewn streets, its polluted skies. "Here," she says, "it is so clean."

For Fay, the United States has been a place of opportunity. She was able to quickly find a job in Washington and, later, to work as an administrator for Motorola in Florida. She quickly worked her way up the corporate ladder to become the senior administrator for facilities. "My boss used to say I was the boss," she says with a laugh. "I loved every day at Motorola. I was treated very well."

Motorola had a policy of allowing its Islamic employees to meet in a room for prayer on Fridays, the traditional day of the week for

Muslims to attend mosque. Fay treasures those times. Today, as a business owner who works six days a week, "I don't have time" to go to services, she says.

Her bosses were also sympathetic when, while fasting during Ramadan, she would be dragging by mid-afternoon after not eating all day. "By two p.m. I would be exhausted," so her bosses allowed her to take afternoon naps—compensation for time saved by not going on morning and lunch breaks. She would wake up refreshed and able to finish her work without breaking the fast.

After 9/11, friends at work came up to her to offer comfort. She still remembers how sweet they were, assuring her that they knew she as a Muslim wasn't part of any terrorist plot. They knew that the terrorists were not like Fay and other hard-working, patriotic Muslims they had seen at Motorola.

She stayed with the company for twenty-five years until accepting a buyout to open her eatery and catering business. She is grateful for her time there but glad she has been able to achieve her dream of making a living from her hobby, Indian cuisine. She loves having her own business. At first, her husband didn't want her to run a restaurant, so she started a catering business. With its rich offerings of saffron-spiced goat, chicken or vegetable biryani, lemon-spiced chicken, fish masala fry, and beef grilled on skewers it took off quickly. When the state food inspector complimented Fay on her cuisine, he suggested that she should have a few tables in front, so he could sit down and enjoy all the good food! She took his advice, and within nine months, Khana Kh'zana became so popular that Fay had exhausted her supply of business cards and nearly all of her menus.

Since that time, one Muslim customer commented that he saw only Hindu art in her eatery. Not true, Fay was quick to retort. She pointed to a work of Muslim art on a wall near the kitchen. And she offered to put up any art that the man wanted to give her. If a Jewish customer brought in a Star of David she would put that up as well, she adds. "I love all cultures."

As Fay gets older, however, she feels she is the one who's a stickler for tradition. She has witnessed changes in her family in India. The women are now wearing Western-style dresses and pants. Fay can't bring herself to do that, at least when she is visiting her elderly relatives in Bombay, especially her grandmother. On such occasions she wears the traditional Indian clothing. But in the United States she dons comfortable jeans and khakis.

She also is distressed at seeing the way her native country has grown to favor what she considers cheap, tawdry entertainment that features nude women. Indians have become worse than Westerners, she claims. That, in her opinion, is definitely not progress.

Still, she has seen traditional Indian ways work for her family, even in the new millennium. Her shy son couldn't find a wife in Florida despite being six foot two and good-looking. At one point he urged his mother to look for a bride for him. "Who, me?" was Fay's response. Nevertheless, she decided to help. When the family next went to Bombay they made an appointment with a family who had a marriageable daughter. Fay's son was quite taken with her—and so was Fay. The young couple, after corresponding with each other by e-mail, fell in love in cyberspace. They are now happily married, also living and working in Florida.

Things have worked out for Fay. She is grateful that as a young girl she ended up in a country where her family could freely choose how to live, and where Fay could wear and do what she wanted, working and succeeding at a career she wanted.

❖ 14 ❖

CASSY'S CRISIS:
REMOVING HER SCARF TO
GET HER DAUGHTER BACK

A LOOK AT NINETEEN-YEAR-OLD CASSY DAVID would never hint that this polite, freshly scrubbed Midwestern teenager in jeans is anything other than a young woman taking her college entrance exams in the hope of studying nursing. Cassy has already experienced more than many do in a lifetime. She has been married to a professor, lived in his native Egypt, given birth to his daughter, endured emotional abuse in a strange land, and fled home to rural South Dakota. Even there, she was far from safe. Forced by her estranged husband to appear in court to defend custody of her now toddler daughter here in the United States—the judge ultimately deciding her husband was better educated to take care of their daughter, at least for now—Cassy last heard her daughter shrieking for her mother as she was taken away to board a plane to Cairo.

"It was heartbreaking, terrible," Cassy admits. "I remember it in a blur, yet it seems as if it just happened yesterday. To this day I can hear my daughter screaming."

As Cassy tries to get her life back in order, and regain custody of her child, she wants other young Muslim women to know that this, too, can happen to them, especially if they are American-born.

Cassy is still a Muslim but she has given up wearing the *hijab*. As soon as she got out of Egypt she took it off—and hasn't put it back on. Much of the reason for this is practical: She wants to get a job and earn enough money to go to college and pay for her daughter to visit her for

90

ten weeks in the summer, as the judge required in his final order when
he awarded the father primary custody.

"I realized that if I was wearing the *hijab* it would be harder for me
to get a job," she says matter of factly.

When she herself was an infant, her single mother, Anisah David
(see chapter 27), converted to Islam and Cassy was raised in a Muslim home. Growing up in rural South Dakota, Cassy was sometimes
painfully aware that she was "different."

When she was in middle school she tied a tiny scarf around her
head as a sort of hijab. She didn't want one too big. "I didn't want the
other kids to freak out." This was in a small rural school and everyone
knew each other. "They knew I was different. They knew I didn't eat
pork, that I had a special diet. They knew I got out early on Friday to
go to the mosque."

By the end of middle school she was ready to be home-schooled by
her college-educated mother like her brother had been. It had bothered her that some of her teachers didn't know the subjects they were
talking about, especially in history classes. Cassy says she had been to
historical re-enactments such as Civil War battles with her mother and
knew the facts behind them better than her instructors did.

"I had a friend who had problems with a counselor harassing her
about her head covering," she adds. "A couple of times some kids tried
to rip off her scarf. I didn't want to deal with that."

At the same time she wanted to get married right away. "I knew by
age twelve I wanted to be married young. I didn't see anything wrong
with that as long as I found the right person."

By the time she was fourteen or fifteen, she was trying to follow
the Islamic rules as she knew them, and she appealed to her mother to
be her gatekeeper and help her find a husband. The first candidate, a
college student, didn't work out: He decided he couldn't support her
while he was finishing his education. Then, a friend of the family, who
was studying for his doctorate at South Dakota State University said
he would look for a husband for Cassy. He even suggested his brother
but it turned out that he was secretly engaged.

The grad student profusely apologized, telling Cassy "how beautiful he thought I was and how he thought I was a nice young lady." Her

mother told him not to feel bad and then suggested with a teasing laugh, "Why don't *you* marry her?"

The next thing she knew, he called and asked to speak to her mother and stepfather. It turned out that he *did* want to marry Cassy.

Her mother told her it was up to her. For two weeks, Cassy pondered the thought and then agreed to the marriage proposal. At the time, he seemed like an ideal husband. She thought she knew him: He had been visiting her family's home for five years as it was one of the few Muslim households in South Dakota. As she later learned, she had never really gotten to know him—he was in her home for the adults, not her—but she had always been struck by his good manners.

"I thought he was a very nice gentleman," she says. "He seemed to be sweet-natured, very respectful. He seemed to know how to treat a lady."

With excitement she looked forward to her marriage, which took place just six days after her sixteenth birthday in February 2002. The groom was in his early thirties—twice her age. Cassy didn't believe the age difference would be a problem, as her grandparents had had a great marriage and there had been twenty years' difference between them.

Plus, she says, "I had always wanted to go to Egypt."

They did move to Egypt after they were married a few months and her husband had earned his doctorate. He'd had a little flat built—a condo with three bedrooms above his parents' home, with which they shared a courtyard.

Cassy grew acclimated to Egypt. She loved watching the water buffalo pass by her house, usually with a little boy in tow. She even adjusted to the climate. "The weather was humid—difficult at first to get used to."

But once she got used to Egypt's weather, she says, "I just loved it. You would see huge puffy clouds. It barely rained, though. I think while I was there it rained only about five times and I was there two years."

She is not sure when the marriage started going bad, perhaps when she became pregnant within months after arriving in Egypt. They had wanted to hold off from having children until she was older, but it was hard to obtain birth control in Egypt, Cassy says. "We kind of took chances," she says.

In the fall of 2002 and early 2003, her husband began expressing anger at the United States for its intention to invade Iraq. He would watch Arabic television and seethe at the images of Iraqis being killed. "He was starting to hate the American government," she says. "In a way I think he wanted me to hate the American government but I couldn't. Things started going downhill. I also think there was the pressure of the baby coming."

Even though Cassy's husband was a professor at an Egyptian university, he didn't make much money. Today, Cassy can earn more in a week as a factory or office worker in the United States than he does in a month in the Middle East.

Cassy tried to apologize profusely to keep peace in the home. "He had me apologizing for anything," she says.

Her mother had always taught her that it was best that couples didn't go to bed angry with each other and the only way to avoid that was for her to apologize so he wouldn't remain mad.

He also was angry at Cassy for not studying more. He wanted her to study math and science four hours a day. She had her GED and wanted to go to college in Egypt and study early childhood development. But in her husband's opinion she first needed a good background in the subjects he loved. The only problem: Cassy hated math and science.

In addition to this, he demanded that the house be immaculate. Cassy was supposed to spend hours a day cleaning the floors with an old vacuum cleaner. "He was concerned about bacteria and viruses," she says.

Then Cassy's mother came to visit. It had been agreed upon that she would come when Cassy was in her last months of pregnancy. She lived at their condo for about six months, to help with the birth and later with infant care, a situation that only added to the tensions.

By the time Cassy's mother returned to the States the marriage was in shambles. Cassy was miserable.

Incredibly, she had *lost* thirty pounds even while pregnant: At five foot four, she had dropped to 150 pounds and while it was good that she had lost the excess weight, she was worried she wasn't getting enough nutrition—especially milk and dairy products—for the baby. Her husband had put her on a diet in which she ate a cup of rice, a quarter pound of chicken, and salad.

He was also making her nervous by attempting to mold her into the person he thought she should become.

"He thought I didn't have a system. He would tell me you can't run a household without a good system. He would get upset if he thought I was falling behind."

He also worried aloud that she wasn't educated enough to raise their daughter, that perhaps others in the family would have to help out.

The blowup came in February 2004. Cassy had a baby shower at their condo for an American friend living in Egypt. Her father-in-law— whom she adored—became upset that Cassy was spending too much time with this friend and other expatriate Americans. "He seemed to have the idea I shouldn't trust these American women," Cassy says.

Her husband exploded at her, even though she insists he had given permission for her to have the little party.

"He said I was a burden to my family," Cassy remembers. "If it wasn't for him taking pity on me, I would be a high school dropout. I probably wouldn't go to college if it wasn't for him."

She cried as she had many times before. She even considered killing herself, but no more, and not now. She was ready to leave.

She telephoned and e-mailed her family back in South Dakota: She had had enough and wanted to come home.

Cassy's stepfather phoned her husband, and very casually cajoled him into letting her go home for seven weeks.

Cassy was eighteen.

She felt dispirited as she and her baby boarded the plane to the United States. But it only took a week home for Cassy to feel stronger, even confident.

"After the first week," she says, "I e-mailed him to say I'm not coming back. I want a divorce. I can't handle the pressure."

He then promptly called her to warn that her family was turning her against him and had even "imprisoned" her.

Cassy ignored that. Within three weeks she got a job on the night shift helping make electronics. She moved to her own apartment after a month and a half of her return to the United States. Later she took another job—with day hours—to please her Egyptian in-laws who criticized her for working nights. She tried to cooperate with her in-laws who by then had hired an attorney so they could see their grand-daughter in the United States. Soon after, her husband filed for custody of their daughter, and that case was heard first before her own divorce was decided.

The judge never met her estranged husband. Instead, his testimony was given as part of a telephone conference call. Ultimately the judge decided that the father could better care for his daughter because he was better educated and had family nearby.

Cassy's mother, in fact, found out about the judge's decision before her daughter did. Cassy's attorney had mailed the judge's written notice to her mother's home. She read it to her daughter over the phone.

"I just started crying," Cassy says. "I didn't want to hear it. . . . All of a sudden I heard my daughter coming down the stairs. I felt her hand and her saying, 'Mommy?' She had heard me crying. All I could do is grab her and hold her."

More action followed: Her husband's U.S. lawyer petitioned that Cassy not leave the state and that the judge order Cassy to turn over her daughter to the court within days.

"I admit I thought about running away with her—I was ready to do it," Cassy says. What stopped her was the idea of breaking the law. She didn't want her marital problems to turn her into a criminal fugitive. Instead she decided she wanted to fight within the system to get her daughter back permanently.

So she geared herself to turn over her crying child. It still hurt. She was determined though. As she told her mother, she had to simply place her trust in God.

Nearly a year later, however, she is not so sure about God or how she feels about Islam. She doesn't understand. She did everything she was supposed to, yet she still hasn't been reunited with her daughter. In the spring of 2005, her ex-husband asked the judge not to require him to fly the toddler back to the United States for the summer visit— at least not until she is six years old. Instead, the ex-husband proposed, in a motion, Cassy should come to Egypt for the visits. The judge agreed, despite Cassy's argument that she was afraid to return to Egypt.

The judge also ruled in favor of the ex-husband's request for child support. Cassy says she is now paying $150 a month. Her ex-husband does allow her to call their daughter every day but only in the morning. Cassy worries that they will have problems communicating in the months ahead. "She says, 'Hi, Mommy. I love you,' but otherwise she is barely speaking English."

The one bright spot, Cassy adds, is that she met a Muslim convert on the Internet, Eric Payne, a twenty-three-year-old petty officer in the United States Navy. They married and Cassy is now living in Virginia, where he is based. "He has been helping me through my depression," she says. "I realize that despite everything I have a lot to be grateful for."

❧ 15 ❧

RAHIMA: FAR FROM HER BURQA— AND HER FAMILY

RAHIMA MOHAMMADULLHA doesn't have to wear the dreaded burqa anymore. At one time, in her native Afghanistan, she was confined to the head-to-toe covering. But now she is in America, free to choose what she wants to wear.

Good-bye, burqa, good-bye, in fact, to any kind of covering. No more scarf, veil, chador, burqa, you name it.

Nowadays she goes out in public with her glossy black hair on full display, styled in a pageboy.

However, while she is tasting this essential freedom, something even more precious has been taken away from her in the United States, something not even the Taliban attempted to wrest from her: She is unable to see her two younger sisters and brother. The elder of the four children, she has been excluded from raising them. The older sister is now fifteen, her brother twelve, and the younger sister ten. They are growing up without Rahima. She hasn't seen them for more than a year.

"I cry a lot," she says.

Rahima, now twenty, and her family were once Afghan refugees who fled, like so many others, to Pakistan to avoid the wars, the Russians, and later the Taliban. They settled in a refugee camp just over the border. Conditions were not good but at least they were together, Rahima says.

When her mother died in the camps, and the children were orphaned, the United States intervened. Officials decided to fly the four kids to America where they would be able to start over, go to school, and have a better life. In 2002, when Rahima was still a teenager, she and her siblings arrived in, of all places, Michigan, where they were placed with a foster family. Soon a major problem developed: The foster family was Christian.

Nationwide, this has been a growing issue. Many Muslims have objected to non-Muslims taking in Muslim foster children and not raising them with Islamic principles. A group in New York has pleaded for Muslim families to come forward to become licensed foster families to help Muslim children within the state-run system. In Ohio, Muslim leaders have gone to court to plead that Muslims be given custody of Muslim children, in particular the small children of a Yemeni immigrant who was jailed for being an alleged terrorist. (After his arrest, his American-born wife had a nervous breakdown and was hospitalized; the children were placed in foster care.)

Rahima says she had no one to turn to when their new foster parents insisted on taking her and the other children to church. The children were given Bibles instead of the Quran. They were served pork, which Muslims, like Jews, aren't allowed to eat. The children were not fed anything remotely like a Quran-approved diet, but to be fair to the foster parents they probably didn't know there was one to follow.

Rahima says there were no other Muslims in the neighborhood who could intervene, or for the children to go to for advice.

She says their social workers never asked them where they wanted to go and they are not sure why they ended up in their overwhelming Christian city when the Detroit area has a large Muslim population.

All she knows is that her complaints fell on deaf ears. The foster family, in fact, became hostile and kicked her out. They accused her of being difficult and uncooperative—in short, a troublemaker. They kept her sisters and brother, though, and they forbade her from seeing them.

Rahima ended up with another foster family nearby, but she is still not allowed to visit her siblings. She is in the process of going to court to try to be reunited with them.

She recently married a fellow Afghan refugee and the couple is making their home in the Virginia suburbs of Washington. They enjoy the company of other Afghan refugees and frequently spend weekends with their friends. Rahima is already speaking reasonably good English and wants to learn more. Furthermore, she is already preparing for her own new family: She will be having a baby soon. She and her husband are both excited about the pregnancy. And if Rahima can convince the court to reunite her with her brother and sisters, she looks forward to eventually moving them to the Washington metro area so they can all be together again. This time they hope to create their own American dream as *they* see it.

❧ 16 ❧

SHAHIDA: SHE GOES TO
MED SCHOOL; HER HUSBAND
BECOMES MR. MOM

IT WAS SHAHIDA SHAKIR'S husband Mohammad who came up with the idea: Here she was in the United States, near Caribbean schools that would admit her to medical school. So why not go for it? Wasn't that her dream, to become a doctor?

It was, and she did.

While Mohammad became Mr. Mom—he and his relatives in Miami taking care of their two small daughters—Shahida set out for medical school at the American University of the Caribbean in Montserrat. It was the realization of a dream she had put on hold since moving from her native Pakistan to the United States. She is now an executive helping run two hospital labs in Miami Beach.

"Back in Pakistan, I always wanted to go to medical school," she reflected. "However, my grades weren't good enough to get me into medical school there." Nevertheless, they were good enough for her to study chemistry; eventually she earned a master's degree from the University of Karachi while still a teenager.

Mohammad felt he was to blame for his wife not going to med school. "She was destined to get the degree but she decided to forgo it for marriage," he says. "This was my way of making it up to her. I definitely wanted to get married but I didn't want to wait five to six years for her to go to medical school in Pakistan."

Mohammad, Shahida's first and only sweetheart, proposed marriage while she was still in her teens. No arranged marriages for them. Shahida thought that an outmoded custom, in which couples would meet each other only on the day they took their marriage vows. (They did, however, follow tradition insofar as Mohammad's family elders visited her family to ask permission for the two to marry.) Though young, Shahida knew Mohammad was the love of her life. He was fun, and eager to see the world, just like she was. He was also kind, responsible, and hard-working, the sort of man who would both work and study, who would save money so that all his brothers and sisters could come to the United States.

It was mutual attraction: Mohammad liked how close Shahida was to her own siblings. He also was attracted to her because "she has a very calming personality." He calls her a "great source of my strength—she complements me. She is a fulfilling element of my life."

Both Shahida and Mohammad believed in getting a good education and pursuing careers. Now it seems a matter of course, but more than thirty years ago they were ahead of their time, both in Pakistan and America. Mohammad was the rare man who encouraged his wife to have a career. Indeed, he saw nothing objectionable to working *and* raising children.

As kids, they both dreamed of going to the United States. This was at a time when Pakistanis held Americans in high regard, when schools, roads, and hospitals were named after American presidents. (One Pakistani highway, for example, was named after former president Eisenhower.)

So Shahida accepted Mohammad's marriage proposal. They married in Pakistan while he was on break from his studies in the United States. Then he whisked her to America.

Because during that era, the 1970s, young people in the U.S. were indulging a fashion for Eastern foods, faith, and clothes, Shahida fit right in, with her brightly colored silken tunics and pants. She wound her long, jet-black hair into a ponytail and it swung from side to side as she walked. She looked like any other young American woman. Having not worn a Muslim head covering in Pakistan, she didn't wear one here, either. She believed that as long as she was wearing long, loose-fitting clothes she was faithfully following the Quran's dictates for modesty. The Shakirs came of age at a time when many educated Muslims had grown away from the traditional ways. Like their Jewish and Christian counterparts, they thought they could follow their faith without necessarily following ancient ways. Not until years later did great numbers of Christians, Jews, and Muslims return to literal readings of their scriptures. Decades later, Shahida's daughter, born and raised in the United States, would be part of a new generation that chose to return to some kind of head covering.

Eventually, the Shakirs settled in Miami where Mohammad had been studying. As a recent immigrant with a green card, he was required to report to the draft board and was convinced by recruiters to join the armor division of the U.S. Army. The Vietnam War was winding down, and the Shakirs, who had come from halfway across the world, suddenly found themselves engulfed in a controversial conflict they had little understanding of. Nevertheless, a patriotic Mohammad felt duty-bound to serve in his new country's armed forces. "I take that stuff seriously," he says. He showed up for basic training and his new wife went to stay with relatives in Milwaukee. She still remembers a reunion in the Chicago train station when he got a furlough, running to each other on the platform. "It was," she said, "like the movies."

Mohammad might have been ordered to Vietnam after basic training, but fate intervened. During training, he fell from a height of eight to nine feet, landing on his back. Army doctors took a barrage of tests and discovered he had been born with a curved spine—he shouldn't have been serving in the military at all. He was honorably discharged.

The Shakirs returned to Miami where Mohammad could work full-time and go to what was then called Miami-Dade Community College. He signed his wife up for classes so she could practice the English she had learned in Pakistan. "I also learned how to drive," she adds, laughing. "I hated it but I learned."

When she grew more self-assured and her English was more polished, Shahida ventured out to look for jobs. Her English still wasn't proficient enough to understand complicated scientific exams, and she flunked her first test to become a lab technician. "I failed royally because I had no idea about multiple choice questions." But she managed to get hired as an assistant in a small mom-and-pop lab, became more comfortable with test-taking, and passed the licensing test the second time around. Soon she got a better-paying job at a bigger company.

By then she and Mohammad had had two daughters, Sofia and Sadia—about five and four—born only fourteen months apart.

This was when Mohammad encouraged her to apply to the American University of the Caribbean in Montserrat—and she was accepted. Mohammad's sister and brothers had since arrived in Miami and they readily agreed to watch the little girls while Shahida went to the Caribbean university during the fall and spring semesters.

After she graduated, Shahida was ready to apply for internships but the bad news hit like a sledgehammer: The U.S. government announced it was cracking down on accepting the degrees of med school graduates who had studied in the Caribbean. A scandal had broken out. Some schools were selling diplomas to those who hadn't earned them. Despite all her hard work, Shahida found her graduation didn't qualify her to be licensed as a medical doctor.

Bitterly disappointed, Shahida blamed herself. Now she thinks she shouldn't have been so timid and ought to have fought harder for her diploma to be recognized. Others from her university did, and are now practicing medicine in the United States. (Indeed, the policy was later reversed and most of her classmates became doctors.) She went back as a lab technician, eventually going to Mount Sinai Medical Center where she began to earn a steady stream of promotions.

But like every working mother she had to juggle, particularly since she and her husband worked to help their brothers and sisters emigrating to the United States. At one point, while she was working two lab jobs, Sofia, her elder daughter, asked hesitantly, with a woebegone expression, "Mom, do you have time for me?" That was it. Shahida quit one job and took a graveyard shift at the other so she could come home in time to take her daughters to school and then sleep before they returned home. On this schedule, she could spend hours with them before they went to bed and she to work. "I did that for years," she said.

Her medical training came in handy at Mount Sinai where she was put in charge of the lab of its recently acquired Miami Heart Institute and Medical Center. She was then given additional responsibilities to direct Mount Sinai's lab processing center. "It was a mess and they said if anyone could take care of it, it was me." She is now in charge of more than sixty lab technicians and other workers.

"I feel a real sense of accomplishment," she says.

Nowadays, Shahida's daughters are grown up and thriving. Sofia works for the Miami-Dade State Attorney's Office; Sadia just graduated from law school in Michigan, where her husband, a doctor, went to medical school. They have a daughter, Hanan, now a toddler and Shahida's first grandchild.

Sadia is causing her mother to rethink her ideas about the *hijab*. Sadia has taken to wearing a head covering, as do many women in Michigan's large Muslim population. She has also adopted the traditional Pakistani woman's long robe or long tunic and pants. Shahida notices how her daughter has become more spiritual, with more peace of mind, by going back to traditional dress. Someday, she says wistfully, she may do that, too.

For now, she admits, she has such a busy life that she cannot always pray the required five times a day. Especially at work, she finds it hard to accommodate Islam's requirements for prayer. Nor does she regularly go to mosque, because Islam has never required women to do that. All the same, she does believe in following her faith, in reading and quoting the Quran. She tries to lead a good life and be good to other people.

While she is grateful for her life in America, she does have a tough time explaining U.S. foreign policy to her family back in Pakistan. For the first time they see the United States as hostile to Islam. They don't understand why the United States invaded Iraq and they mourn the dead there, both American soldiers and Iraqi civilians. "That doesn't get on the news in the United States—the number of Iraqis killed," Shahida says. She and Mohammad try to explain to others that the United States' policy on Iraq doesn't reflect the kindness of the American people. Indeed, Shahida loves the United States because of the people. She loves how orderly things are, how people follow rules, and that Americans generally treat each other as equals and with respect. She has seen that civility erode over the years but to her mind America is still the best place for friendly, respectful people.

Over the years, she has seen her family take root here. Her daughters went to public school and absorbed the open culture. "My daughters are Americans," she says. So, she adds, are she and Mohammad. Like other good Americans, she tries to reach out and help others. She recently took in Maria (see chapter 11) who had been abused by her husband, making sure she ate well, took her medicine and regained her mental health.

Mohammad, currently the executive director of the Miami-Dade County Council of Asian-American Affairs, is helping set up a group of volunteers in Miami to help Middle Eastern and Asian women who have been abused or abandoned by their husbands since their arrival in the United States. It is more of a problem than he realized, he says. He is grateful that his wife helped Maria and tried to turn her life around. Not every woman would have been so generous, he says. Shahida could have easily excused herself because of her heavy workload.

Shahida says she is merely following both the Islamic and American way of helping others. "That's what we are called to do."

❧ 17 ❧

SABRINA: A MUSLIM MOM
ON THE RUN

SABRINA HOSSAIN WALKS BAREHEADED into her mosque in Virginia, hugging her friends. She's at ease, comfortable at her place of worship. Here there is not any sort of "cloth war." Many of her friends at the mosque do wear some sort of covering or veil over their hair, but many others don't. And that choice is acceptable at this mosque.

The *hijab*, Sabrina points out, is "not something that shows my faith as a practicing Muslim. I wear the *hijab* when I pray. That's mandatory. But at other times, I go without. Islam requires both men and women to dress modestly at all times—and I can comply with that without the *hijab*."

She has an ally in her husband, Mukit, who also does not see the need for his wife to cover her head all the time. He, like others, says it is not mandated by the Quran and that, more to the point, it is largely a cultural custom, practiced mainly in the Middle East. Many women in his native Bangladesh did not wear them, he adds.

Sabrina is twenty-five. Her family is also originally from Bangladesh and she did not grow up with the majority of women wearing the veil.

"No one covered, except my grandmothers," she says.

Not that she thinks every Muslim woman must go bareheaded like she does. Each woman should have the choice according to her own conviction. Islam allows it, and America thankfully does as well, she says.

"I admire women who don the *hijab*. They have to face a lot of prejudices. But they wear it based on their interpretation of our religious laws. I don't see the need for *hijab* for myself now. In the future, if I do, I'll wear it."

Sabrina was born in Iraq but with a father who is a petroleum engineer, Sabrina grew up in the countries where he worked, Kuwait, Canada, Bangladesh (mostly for long vacations), and the United States. She is used to seeing women wearing some sort of veil, particularly in Kuwait.

Her father was stuck in Kuwait for months when Iraq first invaded Kuwait during the first Gulf War—a scud missile burst into flames near where he was working. Sabrina and the rest of the family were vacationing in Bangladesh at the time the war broke out and spent an anxious month waiting for his safe exit out. Today he is retired in Canada, amid the mountains of Calgary.

Sabrina lives in Virginia where her husband works. She is thankful that she is now in the United States, which feels like home to her.

She is home schooling her oldest daughter, Maya, age five. Her mosque has a home schooling group where other parents can get together and share ideas. Sabrina says she has learned a lot from them. At home, she says, she can accelerate her daughter's learning. "Maya is a gifted student," she says.

Like other home-schooling moms, though, Sabrina can get tired from her hectic schedule. She also cares for her younger daughter, Hana, who is two and a half years old.

"It's a lot of work," she admits, "but anything good takes hard work. Mainly it is a test of my patience. If I do it the right way, it will benefit my children."

She wants her two daughters raised in a religious community and likes her mosque because it is family oriented with a wide range of children's programs. Her daughters thrive in the play groups and classes. Her older daughter has begun learning some Arabic and about the Muslim culture.

"I want her to be well-rounded," she asserts. "She is a Muslim in this country. She has to be proud of what she is."

The girls are also growing up with lots of sports. Her older daughter already has run the field as a soccer player, thrown balls as a softball player, and will soon start ice-skating and karate lessons.

All this emphasis on education and sports—from the mosque to the soccer fields—means Sabrina is driving a lot.

"I live in the car," she jokes.

That's okay with Sabrina. She wants her daughters to get off to a good start. Later, Sabrina will think of a career for herself.

PART III

✄

The Converts

Once Islam was for immigrants or black nationalists. Not any
longer. More whites, Hispanics, and Asians are visiting a
neighborhood mosque—and staying. Many are women. In
fact, some mosques are now reporting most of their "reverts" are white
women, according to University of Kentucky associate professor Ihsan Bagby.

The new *Muslimah* interviewed for the book say they became Muslims by choice, not because they married into the faith. Many were attracted to Islam because it promotes a strong family. Some say their
new faith strengthened them to endure difficult lives. Many were also
attracted to Islam because it promotes education. *Muslimah* Converts
tend to be educated, with at least some college.

Many of the converting women reflect Islam's diversity in America. Photographer Zulayka Y. "Zuly" Martinez says in chapter 26 that
there are an increasing number of Tex-Mex *Muslimah*. When she first
converted, she says she was one of the few Muslim Latinas in the
Houston area. She admits to being a bit lonely. She felt the immigrant-
born *Muslimah* were standoffish. That all changed with a rush of new
Hispanic converts. Zuly and other "veterans" provide classes and social activities to the newly arrived. Now Zuly feels her mosque is a lot
more welcoming.

Zuly and other Converts say in interviews that they had trouble
understanding their families' faiths, especially Christianity and its
Holy Trinity. Islam makes more sense to them. African American

converts to Islam say they had a problem with an American-flavored Christianity that was too linked with the country's past racism. Miami's Patricia Salahuddin, who grew up in the then-segregated Mississippi, says that she saw Christianity as part of the South's problem, with white ministers preaching in favor of Jim Crow laws. Like other African Americans, Patricia became part of the Black Muslim movement in the 1970s. Researcher Bagby says that conversions of African Americans to Islam "peaked in the 1970s, declined in the 1980s, and rebounded in the 1990s."

It was not only African Americans who had problems with what they viewed as a racist Christianity. Yuko Davis, a Japanese American now living in the suburban Phoenix area, says that she turned away from her Louisiana fundamentalist Christian upbringing when her church stopped picking up black children to bring to Sunday services. She says she wanted a faith that was more accepting of all.

Other Converts talked of how Islam is liberating to them as women. This is puzzling to many Americans. Haven't they seen on TV that Islam oppresses women around the world?

In fact, many *Muslimah* newcomers admit that the religion *has* been used to discriminate against their gender. But, they say, that is more a reflection of a predominantly Muslim country's cultural practices rather than Islamic law. They point out, for example, that Saudi Arabia dictates women's dress while Jordan doesn't.

Thus, the new *Muslimah* look to a time in the past when Islam was a leader in promoting women's rights. "The emancipation of women was a project dear to the Prophet's heart," religious scholar Karen Armstrong writes in her book *Islam: A Short History.* "The Quran gave women rights of inheritance and divorce centuries before Western women were accorded such status."

A few "reverts" have become disillusioned with the underground polygamy that they say goes on in the United States. Just weeks after her Islamic marriage, Juwayrich says that she discovered her new husband already had a wife. Juwayrich divorced him. She has since discovered she is not the only woman to be duped. Still, Juwayrich does not blame Islam but rather opportunistic men. She remains a devout Muslim.

Most Converts stay, too, because they have found Islam enriches their lives. "I had been searching for the right religion since I was very young," says one recent Convert. She found it in Islam. "There is," she adds, "something different and something special about Islam."

In the following chapters you'll read about ten women's spiritual journeys to Islam.

❖ 18 ❖

CATHY'S CONVERSION: A MINIVAN
MOM TURNS TO ISLAM

CATHY DRAKE COULD BE the ideal mother as envisioned by the Republican Party or an evangelical megachurch. She's a college-educated stay-at-home mom in one of America's fastest-growing exurbias, in northern Virginia—a solid red county in a solid red state. She home-schools all three of her kids and wants them to grow up with religion. And, yes, she drives a minivan.

Cathy is also one of Islam's newest converts, becoming a Muslim three years after 9/11. But even after the terrorist attacks—and in spite of the wars in Afghanistan and Iraq—Cathy was undeterred from exploring Islam. She decided it was best for her three children although her eldest, at age ten, is none too thrilled about becoming a Muslim.

"Kids don't like change," Cathy says. "Kids like to do the same things. And my son didn't know any Muslims."

But Cathy thinks he will come around just like she has.

"I had always been interested in Islam," she says. "I feel very comfortable with it."

It goes without saying that she finds Islam's emphasis on the family very reassuring. She also likes her suburban mosque, which like many churches has a plethora of programs for families. There's a home-schooling chapter that meets at the mosque, whose members help each other out. There's also a Daisy troop for her younger daughter. And, of course, there are classes in Islam for both adults and children.

"It's a very welcoming community. I can't enter without being greeted by half a dozen people."

Cathy grew up in a nonreligious Christian family that never went to church. She didn't want her children to grow up like she did. (Her husband is not keen about organized religion, but tolerates that Cathy and the children go to religious services.) At first, Cathy picked Catholicism because it had been the religion of some members of her extended family.

"It was the faith I was most familiar with."

She and her family began going to Mass. As families were expected to sit together while the priest gave his homily, it could be hard on Cathy: The church had no nursery for the children. Cathy found it hard to listen *and* manage her small children. She also felt a bit uncomfortable because the congregation didn't seem very friendly. She and her kids could go to church and not be greeted once by name. "I don't think people even knew my name," she says.

Then she hit a crisis. When her oldest son was taking first reconciliation and communion classes, Cathy discovered she didn't agree with a good deal of what was being taught in his classes. Take the idea that Catholics must go to confession to tell the priest their sins. "I was having difficulty with that," she admits. "I always thought you talked to God yourself."

She realized that she was becoming one of those "pick and choose" Catholics who ignored some of the Church's doctrines and followed others.

She also was dismayed by the Church's nationwide sexual abuse scandal. She was horrified that hundreds of priests had used their position to sexually abuse children. But she was more outraged over how the hierarchy had tried to first hide and then downplay the scandal. In her opinion, the Church should have responded openly and immediately.

Not that Islam doesn't have its problems, too, she is quick to add. It comes with its own "cultural baggage," some countries denying equality to women, some mosques still separating the sexes so husbands and wives and their children can't sit together. These things give Cathy pause. She says she can live with the segregation of the sexes because it is in the Quran, but she objects to the social inequality of women because that is *not* in the holy book. "People think this is Islam and it is not." Her mosque, she is happy to declare, treats men and women equally.

It was for that very reason that Cathy deliberately picked her mosque, which allows women to pray in the main room, not in a tiny basement room or balcony. The mosque also allows both sexes to enter through the main door, unlike others that relegate women to the back or side door. "I wouldn't feel comfortable with that," she says.

Certain traditional Muslim customs she has taken to quite easily. She now wears a scarf to cover her hair. "I want to identify myself as a Muslim to the non-Muslim world," she says.

She has noticed a change in how people treat her, especially strangers. "Sometimes I can sense someone staring," she says, "and sure enough, when I turn around, someone *is* staring at me." Some are hostile, she says. "But for the most part people are pretty friendly" — albeit curious. She also feels that people are more watchful, waiting to see her reaction before they enter a conversation or even sit next to her. Then, she says, invariably they relax when Cathy flashes them a smile. "They see that I am just like anyone else."

Cathy says she can handle that curiosity. It's worth it to be part of a faith-based community she believes in and her family can be part of, she adds. "I don't want my children growing up without a faith."

❖ 19 ❖

SAMIRAH: THE HIGH COSTS OF BECOMING A MUSLIM

SAMIRAH BINT JACKIE DEAN TODD has no way of knowing where her daughter is. Her ex-husband doesn't call her and their telephone number in Florida has been disconnected. Her voice almost breaks as she talks about how it has been fifteen months since she last spoke to one of her two daughters. She would be almost ten years old by now. Maybe she's still in Florida. Or maybe she is back in Maine.

Samirah tries to keep calm: She has been warned that she may have multiple sclerosis and needs to avoid stress in her life to help prevent an attack.

Ironically, it is her Islamic faith that keeps the thirty-something Samirah on an even keel—the very religion with whose marriage practices a judge disagreed, naming it one of the reasons he awarded custody of Samirah's younger daughter to her ex-husband. And it is the same faith that Samirah's older daughter, then thirteen, objected to, causing her to ask to live with her grandmother.

Samirah can't understand the objections to Islam: It has changed her, she says, for the better. "I have noticed how my belief in Islam has fortified me with patience and faith," she says. "I do not believe I could handle the trials I have gone through without my faith. Islam has changed me as a individual."

She lives in New Jersey where there is an active Islamic community in Newark and a smaller one in Camden. "I usually go to the community in nearby Philadelphia," she says. "It is more established there and closer to my home than the one in Newark."

116

Samirah started looking at Islam about four years ago. "I was at a low point in my life and started searching for ways to better myself. I always have had a hard time accepting Christianity. But when I started studying Islam I found answers to my questions and was amazed that Islam taught what I had always believed."

She became a Muslim on July 5, 2001, a mere two months and six days before 9/11. She was thirty-three and recovering from a broken back. While in the process of moving, she was carrying boxes and lost her balance on a flight of stairs, fell and broke her back. Doctors then became concerned that she might have MS, as loss of balance is one of its symptoms.

Samirah was grateful that she had her newfound Islamic faith to help her get through the ordeal.

"You can't go through things without faith," she says, and she has gone through a lot.

"I am Native American from the Cherokee nation. I come from a broken home with an absent father.

"When my parents were married we traveled. My father was in the Air Force," she says. "I spent time overseas as a child and have lived in various places."

The family ended up being in the military too, so to speak. Samirah remembers their life as being as regimented as if they too were serving a tour of duty. Everything was controlled. She has not seen her father since she was eleven.

As she puts it, "I had a troubled childhood and an even more troubled adult life." She was only twenty when she had her first daughter, though she says she was more mature when she had her second at age twenty-seven.

Samirah has had trouble disciplining her older daughter who would fight with other children. Samirah says she once whipped her daughter after she had gotten into some fights which left marks on her little body. Someone at her daughter's school noticed and asked about them; her daughter explained that her mother had hit her. That was true, except that Samirah says she hadn't caused the bruises. Nevertheless, a child abuse complaint was filed. Samirah says this was the only time this happened. "Otherwise, I have a clean record," she says.

She herself was the victim of domestic violence. Her jaw was broken during one attack, she says.

For five years, then, she was on her own raising her two girls by herself without any child support.

The father of her younger daughter, then age seven, suddenly reappeared, demanding custody. This occurred just after Samirah had become a Muslim and agreed to an arranged marriage that her "guardian"—an older man at the mosque—had set up for her. Samirah married her current husband after seeing only a picture of him, but, ironically, this marriage, of a kind that seems so outdated to many Americans, has worked out the best for her.

"I have a wonderful and caring husband. I have truly been blessed with that. He is also a revert. We don't say 'convert' as we believe everyone is born Muslim. My husband and I just happened to be raised in a Christian household."

However, the judge in her child custody case didn't agree. He made note of her arranged marriage when he gave custody of her younger daughter to her ex-husband. It was, Samirah says, "a nasty custody battle in which my religion played, it seemed, a major role. I have a seven-year-old stepdaughter. The same judge gave residential custody of her to my husband. The judge wasn't aware my husband was a Muslim when he appeared in court."

Through all this, Samirah says her faith stands strong. Like many other Converts, she enjoys wearing what she considers the full *Muslimah* apparel: She covers herself when in public from head to toe, even wearing gloves.

"I enjoy studying other religions plus learning my own," she adds. "I am also an owner of an e-group for Muslim women. I channel my trials into knowledge to keep me strong." She also makes hijab pins in her spare time.

She used to be a supervisor at a McDonald's, but she no longer works outside the home. She concentrates on taking care of her husband and stepdaughter. The life of her immediate family is warm, but many of those in her extended family have broken away because of her faith. Her mother, for one, told her not to call until she was a Christian again. "She thought I was brainwashed," Samirah says.

Sadly, that means she doesn't have contact with her older daughter because she elected to stay with her grandmother and be raised a Christian.

"Except for one sister, my family has disowned me for accepting Islam. They want nothing to do with the 'terrorist.' "

Yet, Samirah can't see how she can live without her faith. Islam has strengthened her too much to give it up, despite the sacrifices she's made to practice it. She tries to deal with these crises with patience and faith. Eventually, she feels, she will be rewarded.

"Allah tells us, 'Who are you to think you will not be tested when you say you believe?' I truly believe my reward will come in time for my patience. I love this thought and I love how Islam has changed me for the better."

❧ 20 ❧

EMMA: A NEW BABY AND
A NEW ISLAMIC LIFE

EMMA AL-AGHBHARY was sixteen when she began an online romance. It didn't start out that way—just two students chatting online. But as she e-mailed the young college student, she discovered they were a lot alike, both valuing family and education.

But they were also different. He was from Yemen and a Muslim. She was a sixth generation New Zealander who hadn't grown up with much of any religion. Her family was spiritual but not into organized religion.

They decided their love would overcome any differences and so they married. Now, at twenty, Emma is expecting their first child while her husband finishes his degree at a university near Chicago and works to support his young family. She is also a devout Muslim.

"I have worn the *hijab,* including modest clothing and abaya [the outer garment that is long and loose] since the beginning of 2002," she says. "People's reactions have not been bad in Chicago. In New Zealand many people don't quite know how to react—some make rude remarks or gestures. My family had and still has a bit of trouble understanding and accepting it but they are getting used to it as time goes by.

"Here in America," she adds, "people usually mind their own business. Some people stare at times but most don't. Muslims are more visible here. There is a big Muslim community in Chicago and you can't go for long without seeing other Muslims. People in this city treat us like anybody else."

Emma is grateful that she found Islam at an early age and that it keeps her on the right path. "Islam," she says, "gives you direction, meaning, and understanding of yourself, the world around you and the world you will go to after this life."

She likes to study Islam by reading books and browsing websites. She regularly reads the Quran and Hadith (a collection of the teachings of the Prophet Muhammad) so she can gain as much knowledge as she can. "I think it's important for every Muslim to read the Quran regularly. There are study groups here in Chicago but I don't attend because my husband and I prefer that I stay at home.

"However, I plan to go to some sort of study group once the baby arrives so that my child and I can have the support and company of other Muslims."

Emma grew up on the north island of New Zealand. She is the middle of three girls who remain close to each other and to their mother. The sisters are grateful to their mother for providing a strong family despite much hardship.

"We come from a broken home and never had a stable male figure in our lives," Emma says.

When she met her husband online, she realized that he was a different sort of young man. He was five years older than her and serious about his religion. Emma became curious: She too began studying Islam, and discovered it was what she had been searching for. In retrospect, she feels she was always religious—she just wasn't exposed to any faith growing up.

"I had been searching for the right religion since I was very young. Whether that had something to do with being from a broken home, I'm really not sure. But for me, really, it was the truth, clarity, and actual simplicity that made me stand up and say, 'There is something different and something special about Islam,' and that's what really attracted me to Islam."

Her soon-to-be husband had been living in the United States since he was nineteen. Emma moved to the United States to be with him when she was seventeen and right out of high school.

"Unfortunately, I had to return to New Zealand for a year while he got himself in a more stable position to be able to support a family." He has now been in the Chicago area for about six years and Emma for a year. She is a young housewife. Her husband prefers that she stay at home.

"But I do have my own goals, hobbies, and ideas. I am working on my poetry with the hope of publishing a book. I'm soon to be published in an anthology of writings by Muslim women and I have had a story published in a book in New Zealand. I also have my own website, which keeps me busy."

For now, her main focus and top priority is her family: "Being the best wife I can be and preparing to be a mum."

She and her husband had their daughter Henna after enduring a year of infertility. She is glad they are Muslim because she believes the faith will help her nurture her baby and it will help her teach her future children—she plans on having several—about why they are here on Earth, their purpose in life, and who created them.

"Our children will have a purpose and values and morals and they won't have to search and won't go through the questioning of who they are, where they belong, and why they are here," Emma says, before adding, "I am somewhat concerned about bringing my child up in America. I have many concerns about possible discrimination. I plan to home-school my children so that hopefully I can keep them from becoming confused or tempted by un-Islamic things."

She plans to stay at home with their future children, "as long as nothing happens that forces me to work to provide for my family. I like to say I'm a stay-at-home wife soon to be promoted! For me the greatest achievement I could ever have is raising good, strong, and pious children. My husband and I both believe in the traditional roles of men and women and that it is best for us and our family that I am at home."

Islam supports that idea of family coming first. The Quran decrees that men are to take care of the family financially, to provide food, clothing, and shelter, and are encouraged to help out around the house when and if they can. A woman's responsibilities are to take care of the family, to feed them and to take care of them and the house. Women are allowed to work, and if they do, that money is theirs. However, she places her duties to home and family first.

Because of the emphasis on women overseeing their home and family, Emma feels an obligation to protect them. That's one of the reasons she is thinking of home schooling. She is suspicious about American pop culture.

"There are many, many things that go against our Islamic beliefs and morals," she says, "to the point that I don't want to send my child out into schools where the influence of non-Muslim teachers and/or other children can be in many ways stronger than the Islamic influence at home. Home schooling will give us the chance to teach the children not only reading, writing, math, and other studies, but the morals we hold as important and as fundamental, and about Allah, prayer, and fasting."

She also likes the idea of time shared between mother and children. Home schooling, she believes, gives children an opportunity to nurture their talents and interests while they learn.

"School was never the best place for me," Emma adds "I was very intelligent but the school environment wasn't right for me. My mum tried to get the school to allow me to do correspondence studies, but because I wasn't a 'troubled child' I wasn't allowed."

Now Emma feels secure, happy, and content knowing that her husband "is a good, religious man who respects and values our Islamic rights and responsibilities. I feel absolutely thankful that Allah has given my future child two parents who love each other very much, especially a father who loves and respects the mother."

❧ 21 ❧

THE LESSONS OF
CANCER-FIGHTING LESLIE

IN HER OWN WORDS, Leslie Sinclair tells of her journey to Islam:

"I was raised in a secular household; my father was Lutheran in name only, my mother an unbaptized secular. I remember attending a Lutheran church in Fairbanks (I was born in Alaska) as a kindergartner and being frightened by the booming, angry tone of the preacher. Thankfully, we never returned.

"My father read the Bible and occasionally burst into song, usually spirituals, but he was a rather formidable figure, and I don't remember him teaching me how to live a Christian life.

"Although my mother's parents were Christian Scientists, I was not aware that they espoused any formal belief; they never spoke about religion or taught me anything religious. My mother was scornful of most religion.

"Curiously, she took my two brothers and me to the church closest to our house after we moved to Edmonds, Washington, in 1952. She wanted us to go to Sunday school; I'm not sure why. The best part about Sunday school was the cinnamon toast and tea we three shared afterwards, while playing canasta with an elderly Alaskan family friend.

"Occasionally, my mother and another woman friend would get dressed up and go to church. As a child that puzzled me. I regularly attended Sunday school, and later was part of the Methodist Youth Fellowship in high school, I never gained much appreciation or knowledge about the merits of being Methodist.

"As secular Americans, my family gladly celebrated Christian holidays, such as Christmas. I don't remember any prayer around those times, but I had a tender heart for Baby Jesus and a distant respect for religion.

"Years later, one of the attractions I felt toward my first husband was the fact that he was Catholic, something I assumed would prevent divorce. My parents' divorce after a sometimes treacherous marriage had been both welcomed and met with fear. Many of my friends' parents wouldn't permit them to pal around with me anymore, once my mother became a divorcée. The apparent solidity of the Catholic Church and my future husband's intact family was appealing. My mother had remarried and made it clear to her children that her new partner (whom I eventually loved as a parent) came first.

"When I married, I signed the contract to raise our future children as Catholics. After a year I took instruction classes to become a knowledgeable non-Catholic mother raising Catholic children. I believed in honoring my promises, even if I made them without much knowledge.

"My world knew only Christians and seculars; it never occurred to me to investigate any other religion.

"After my husband and I became parents we continued to worship at Mass and to observe the practices and restrictions of the church. We seldom read the Bible, but we took pleasure in our children's Catholic education. We celebrated all holidays in the church, belonged to and worked with our church organizations, and eventually led an engaged couples' class. We became Marriage Encounter Team Leaders and later we received the Baptism in the Holy Spirit.

"I was baptized into the Catholic Church when I was twenty-one. Religion brought stability to my life; it was a structure that I appreciated, and I believe that it benefited my family. We taught our values to our children. I believe this was a good thing and that it helped keep our children away from addiction and greed.

"My journey to Islam likely began with my journey away from Christianity. A Mother's Day church scene is burned into my memory, after which I was never the same Catholic. My daughter was part of a small chorus of sixth-graders who sang the beautiful song 'Simple Gifts' while facing a statue of the Blessed Virgin Mary. Try as I might, I watched them sing to a statue and I could not call it anything but idolatry. This was a watershed moment for me.

"My departure from Catholicism was not instantaneous, but was furthered along a couple of years later when I returned to college, despite tremendous emotional experiences at campus Masses. The end of my marriage compelled me to examine my commitment to Catholicism. Shortly afterward, my oldest son suffered a traumatic brain injury. Clearly, I thought, if I *am* still a Christian I will act like one through this crisis. The shock was so profound I was unable to pray; I let friends, community and family do this for me.

"Throughout this nightmarish time, I continued graduate school. (I am an artist. I was in the studio on weekends, and in the hospital room during week days.) I had no religion, but considered myself a person of faith. During grad school and after receiving my M.F.A., I was increasingly aware of a huge void in my life, although I felt a gentle pull on my heart. This I interpreted as the Holy Being.

"On the first evening of Desert Storm a fellow grad student who was not a Muslim strode into our cavernous studio. He loudly proclaimed: 'This is going to be a different war; they are not like us. They believe they are going to die for God; for them it's a holy war!' Astounding! I thought. This prompted the selection of my next book: *The Autobiography of Malcolm X.* I began reading it while on the plane to Texas to visit my son at a brain-injury rehabilitation facility, and could scarcely put it down. I was intrigued by the historical solidarity of religious people, and was startled by the intensity of this American man's conversion to what I thought of as a religion of desert dwellers. My ninth-grade social studies' textbook had introduced this strange group of believers as Mohammadans (that's how the book spelled it), adherents of Mohammadanism. Although I gained a significant measure of respect for practitioners of the religion, I have to say I never considered Islam as a potential spiritual home for me.

"Nevertheless, the spiritual pull continued throughout the many and repeated crises that occurred around my son's medical and rehabilitation needs.

"Then I met and married an immigrant Muslim. I qualified as a Christian still, according to his Imam. Once again, my new husband's religious affiliation was a strong attraction. Even so, I preferred observing him practice his faith rather than explore it myself.

"I visited a few Christian churches, affirming each time my aversion to praying through anyone, even a figure as holy as Jesus. Yet, when my second marriage was in danger, I did turn to a Pentecostal church and even accepted a new Bible when I became a member. But I didn't make a serious attempt to feed my spiritual hunger there.

"I did realize, though, that the foundation of the marriage was my husband's religious practice, as wacky as that sounds. But the close bonds he maintained with other Muslim men, so attractive to me before our marriage, eventually divided us. I had expected our marriage to take priority and that he would be at everything, from weekend breakfasts to extended family gatherings. I thought he would oversee our financial accounts. Instead he preferred spending his time with other immigrants, leaving the household responsibilities up to me. I ended up filing for divorce.

"He chose to handle the idea of divorce by telling the judge at the first hearing that he didn't want to separate.

"During this time, I came upon a copy of the Quran. I found it surprisingly simple and its truths easily comprehensible. My day job had ended when I sprained my ankle. Crutches and the bulky oversized splint caused me to trip in my own living room. That brought on a full foot-and-calf plaster cast, and as a result of limited mobility, I had lots of time for reading. I searched for books on Islam at the public library. I divided by reading time between the Bible, the Quran, and other religious books, as well as those about Muslims, prayer, and artwork.

"A blanket of certainty settled around me and I realized that one day soon I would make my declaration of faith as a Muslim. I shared that insight with a few family members and close friends. My grown daughter gave me her endorsement; she too had left the Catholic Church.

"But my men friends, both Christian and non-religious, were furious about my decision. I knew that I was soon to lose them, as Muslim women do not tend to retain individual friendships with men not their husbands. But I didn't waver in my desire to live an Islamic life, although, frankly, I wasn't sure what that was. When I made the decision to become Muslim, I thought of myself as refining my practice of submission to the one and only God, not to a God who is part of a Holy Trinity.

"My family is at best neutral about my conversion to Islam. Although my daughter supported my decision to become a Muslim, she has shown minimal interest in my faith. My married son indicated his lack of interest. He and his wife share an appreciation for his Catholic upbringing and are raising their children in the Church. Interestingly, it is the opinions of my oldest son—who was brain injured sixteen years ago and remains markedly impaired—that have had the most impact on me. He is opposed to my covering my hair. At times I wonder if he would have been as forthright with his comments had the injury not transformed his life. Still, he is empathic and compassionate about certain personal or political events, even as he refers to us as 'those Muslims.' Seldom does he initiate a topic of conversation. But the occasional reference to my style of dress—typically loose American clothes worn with a headscarf and sometimes a hat—can reveal his own feelings about being different from mainstream America since his injury cut short his senior year of college.

"My mother is most resistant to my adoption of Islam, although after a year or so, when it became obvious to her that the conversion was likely to stick, she remarked: 'Islam isn't a religion; it's a way of life!' I cheerfully acknowledged the correctness of her assumption.

"Within the span of a few months I experienced multiple upheavals in my life—breast cancer, divorce, conversion to Islam, loss of a job, death of my stepfather, move to a small apartment, and the departure from my life (and my mother's) of my closest brother. My art imagery changed, as I incorporated abstract shapes into even my written journals, where I replaced collages of photocopies and photographs with abstract images. They became surprisingly meaningful and eventually emerged as cohesive watercolor drawings. I named them 'Chemo Journal Drawings' and did one daily for sixty-five days of chemotherapy. They melded my religious experience with the first cancer trip.

"Later, when I was diagnosed with thyroid cancer, I turned those same images into 3D clay wall pieces. Treatment for thyroid cancer

seldom requires chemotherapy of the traditional sort but rather inges-
tion of a radioactive iodine tablet in the hospital. This treatment required a week-long period of starving the thyroid hormone, during
which all my faculties slowed down. I drew images inspired by my experiences on small sheets of handmade paper.

"The post-thyroidectomy journey was long. After nearly one year
I began to move and speak as before. New pounds were finally shed.
I continued my ceramic series and made tile pieces that incorporate
Arabic Quranic verses along with their English translations.

"Seattle Eid celebrations are often held at the Washington State
Convention Center. After Eid al-Adha in 2004, in full holiday mode I
parked my car outside the hospital where a Muslim sister lay bedrid-
den. Because I was in a holiday frame of mind, I mistakenly thought it
was Sunday, and I was grateful that I didn't need to find quarters for
the meter. I returned to find two tickets flapping on my windshield.
But I have learned from Islam that nothing is lost: From those tickets
I created some art pieces that I used as examples for classes I taught
to cancer patients.

"Islam places a strong weight on the value of the married state, for
men as well as for women. It is considered, in effect, half the religion.
I've come to see that to live with another requires constant adjustment
of one's attitudes, thoughts, feelings, and actions, something often
lacking when one is single. Personally, I have refrained from seeking
another husband until I spot the broken link in my chain of illnesses
and accidents.

"Ancient cultural (as distinguished from religious) practices
among Muslims demand total separation of genders in all venues outside the home, and often promote female seclusion within the home.
Many contemporary American Muslims, both men and women, are attempting to remove those cultural biases in practices here in the
United States. Barriers, nevertheless, do remain, such as those which
prevent women from seeing (as opposed to hearing through a speaker
or watching over television) the Imam.

"As a result, Seattle Sisters' Caucus was conceived by me and similarly concerned local Muslim women for education and action. We acknowledge the wisdom of the Islamic admonition to speak truth to

power. We recognize that our energies must be used wisely so we don't
burn out or spin our wheels.

"As we educate ourselves, with the goal of realizing a holy and refreshing mosque experience, we will, with God's blessing, move on the
Path, with both men and women sharing a voice."

❖ 22 ❖

FATIMA REBORN: FROM PARTYGOER TO MUSLIM MATRON

IN INDIANAPOLIS, there was a twenty-something party girl who hit the bars in miniskirts. She loved going to clubs, dancing and flaunting her looks. She was the blond, blue-eyed beauty who relentlessly kept up her appearance, working out to tone her tummy, never missing her weekly appointment at the nail salon, and always searching for the latest mascara or lipstick. She had her bikinis, too.

Now, in Chicago, she wears long, flowing—and shapeless—gowns, her blond tresses completely hidden under a scarf. (She once even considered covering her face with a veil, but her husband told her she was going too far.)

She's now Fatima Az Zahra, a young Muslim matron still wanting to be attractive to her husband. But that's all. Sexy is fine—at home with her husband. After all, sex is a gift from God. But she's not interested in looking good for other men. She now believes in the Muslim woman's code of modesty.

Fatima legally took her new name (she got the legal forms from the Internet and filed a civil action in Indiana courts. Total cost: $300) because she was so impressed by Fatima, daughter of the Prophet Muhammad and the perfect wife and mother. Her new last name also reflects her love of Fatima: Az Zahra is Arabic for "very brightly shining."

"Fatima was resplendent," she says, "a wonderful human being. I don't think there will ever be as unselfish and kind a person as she was.

131

She was such a good daughter, a good mother—she is my role model. It makes me feel great that I carry her name."

The new Fatima was born in Ohio but later her family moved to Indianapolis, which she still considers her hometown. Her mom was a teenager whose boyfriend felt he couldn't be part of the new family. Fatima never really knew her real father, but after a while her mother met and married a kindly man who adopted the girl. Today she is close to both. She is proud of her mother who went back to school and became a registered nurse who now works with cancer patients in Tennessee. Her mom is also special in another way: She had her youngest children when she was in her forties. Fatima's little brothers are twenty-five and twenty-seven years younger than she.

As a child, Fatima didn't understand Christianity even though her grandmother dutifully took her to church. Fatima dreaded the long services, which included the minister's long-winded sermons. Fatima found them incomprehensible and boring. She colored pictures in the pew instead of praying. And she knew that this wasn't the faith for her.

"I don't think you should have any mistrust or doubt about your religion and I had those my whole life with Christianity," she says. "It's just a label. I mean, what is Christianity, anyway? How can God have a son who is also the Lord? Isn't God our Lord? So that means His son and He are one? These are some of the things I was confused about. When I was young, I would ask my grandma about it. She would actually tell me, 'You just have to believe it, that's all. There isn't an explanation, you just have to believe it.' So I never accepted it."

Still, she knew something was missing in her life. In her twenties, though, she seemed to have it all, including an active social life. But she was spiritually adrift.

At age twenty-four she discovered Islam. Her first time inside a mosque was almost comical: An older colleague from work, an Arab American, invited her. She went trustingly. "I was very naive," she now says. She pinned on a *hijab* to enter the mosque. He brought her to the Imam who asked her to repeat Arabic words. No big deal, she thought. But it turned out she was repeating the vows to conversion. Her co-worker wanted her for his wife. "He should have explained things to me." But he didn't, and subsequently, Fatima ignored him at work. Then he turned on her, and treated her meanly. She feels bad that his feelings evidently were hurt, but she maintains he never explained his intentions.

However, that first trip to the mosque did whet her interest in Islam. She began researching the religion.

"As I was reading the book *What Islam Is All About,* by Yahya Emerick, questions that I had all of my life were suddenly answered—just like that. This one book about Islam contained all the answers. After this, I knew Islam was the truth and I should follow it."

Since then, she adds, "I am so much more spiritual, it's unbelievable. I am definitely kinder and much, much better inside and out. I have morals and values that I never possessed when I wasn't a Muslim. Now, as a Muslim, I will not miss one of my five daily prayers. Never."

As a convert, she knew she wanted to wear the traditional Muslim women's apparel. (She has noticed that converts like her can be more excited about obeying Islamic traditions than those born to it.) But it took courage to do so. None of the hundreds of employees at the Indianapolis HMO where she worked wore the veil. She forced herself to, and found that donning a *hijab* was not as hard as she thought. She was especially touched that her boss, a devout Jewish man, never said a word to her about her new attire and let her say her daily prayers privately in the conference room.

"You'd think we would have clashed," she says. "I think he respected me. I was very lucky. I certainly respected him for his beliefs."

She was not as lucky with her mother, at least at first. Her mother couldn't understand why she had to become a Muslim. There were, Fatima says, "screaming matches."

"After two years she saw that I wasn't changing my mind and she got a little hot under the collar. She told me that I was going to Hell because I didn't believe that Jesus was the son of God."

Then 9/11 happened. It was life-changing for her mother. She told friends and co-workers that those terrorists couldn't really be Muslims because her daughter was Muslim and they did not have her daughter's giving heart. They did not study the Quran like her.

Fatima is now proud that her mom supports her and brags about her. She also considers herself blessed that she fell in love with a

Muslim man—Islam forbids Muslim women from marrying out of their faith.

Her husband was born a Muslim in Lebanon. He came to the United States as a fifteen year old after civil war broke out in Lebanon during the 1980s. It was a time of anarchy and violence. His brother was spirited away like so many other young Lebanese men and tortured, but his father managed to find him and have him released. He then sent his sons to the United States to ensure their safety.

When first in America, her husband had to go back to high school even though he had gotten his diploma in Lebanon. But he was eager to conform with American rules and so he did, finishing high school in a year. Then he went to work while attending college at night.

Fatima is glad that her husband is devout and as interested in Islam as she is. It makes it easier that they pray together and keep Islamic traditions, she says. "It's true what they say: The family that prays together, stays together."

Her husband helps her learn the Quran from his years of studying it in school in Lebanon. "In the Middle East they are forced to learn the Quran," she says. "They know a lot about it when they come to America." But many Muslim immigrants lose touch with their religion as they don't live near a mosque. In Fatima's opinion, "America doesn't cater to Muslim people."

But, then, that is to be expected in what is a predominantly Christian nation, Fatima says, and Muslims must make their own communities—and she is proud to say one is thriving in Chicago, where they now live.

Her friends in Chicago are an even mix of those born to the faith and converts like herself. "Chicago is absolutely the best place for Muslim people," she says. "I love Chicago for its diversity and beauty. I wouldn't want to be anywhere else. I love the Muslim community here and all it has to offer us here."

But as a new Muslim, Fatima reports that she has had moments when she realized she had to tone down her enthusiasm for Islam. One such time was when she was considering wearing a veil over most of her face—everything but her eyes. Other friends had been discussing the pros and cons of such a veil. Her husband's reaction: "Getting a little extreme?" her husband gently chided her. Fatima saw his point.

The "extreme" veil stayed off.

Then, she says, "I went through the stage I wanted to get rid of TV and radio," thinking this would make them better Muslims. Her husband convinced her otherwise.

"You can't do that," he told her. "There are no extremes in our religion. We are commanded to be moderate—no extremism. You are not being good by doing this. The Quran says you are not to make the religion hard. Islam should be easy to follow. Don't make it a hardship."

The television and radio stayed.

And Fatima says she learned to take a path of moderation.

Islam, she adds, is a faith that keeps her spiritually grounded in her everyday life. She seeks God in prayer five times a day, no matter if she's in a car or her living room.

"I have come to love all the prayers. They are not cumbersome and shouldn't be looked at that way. Praying keeps you out of trouble—if you are thinking of God five times a day you won't go wrong."

❧ 23 ❧

Juwayriah's Journey

Juwayriah, who doesn't want to state her full name because she wants to speak frankly, offers the following advice: Love Islam—but beware of some of the brothers. She wants to make it clear from the start that what she says doesn't apply to *all* Muslim men in the United States.

"Indeed," Juwayriah says, "there are many who fear Allah and the Last Day, thereby doing right by their wives and families. However, there are some brothers who may try to take advantage of trusting and innocent women coming into the faith who may not fully know Islam.

"Islam gives many rights to women, especially wives," she adds, "but new 'reverts' [converts to Islam] may not be aware of them. And some brothers may take advantage of this lack of knowledge, especially when the sister is American and the brother is not."

For example, she knows of numerous cases of immigrant men in the United States who marry American women to obtain green cards, then leaving or divorcing their wives once a green card is acquired. These men might already have a wife and children back in their homeland, she says, and are only waiting to get a green card in order to bring them to the States. A couple of her friends have married immigrants, and discovered that the men were using them.

Such immigrant Muslims may also be tempted by opportunities for romantic involvement—even casual sex—in the United States that is unavailable in their native country. Dating is not permitted in Islam but some may try to do that anyway with American-born women, even those who have converted to Islam.

"A brother cannot come at a sister from his own country like they do us American sisters," Juwayriah says. "In the Middle East, women have fathers and brothers to protect them. Here in the United States, unless a sister is close to the *masjid*, other sisters, and her Imam, she can be caught unaware. Many American sisters do not have Muslim families and as such they are vulnerable. And it is not only the foreign brothers."

Juwayriah has been a Muslim since 1998 and has been married three times—all to African American brothers. "It just seems like a lot of Muslims bring their cultural baggage into Islam," she says. "And that is the biggest part of the problem. Islam is supposed to be for all people and for all time. Cultural bias and racism have no place in Islam."

Juwayriah was practicing Judaism when she married a Muslim. She is grateful that he introduced her to Islam. She "reverted" to Islam during this marriage. She read a lot of the Islamic books in her husband's extensive collection and began to learn about the rights of women in Islam. What she learned was not exactly what he had told her. Differences surfaced, and friction escalated into domestic violence. When she tried to get the Imam to help them, her husband divorced her. She was devastated. She knew his violence was not right, but she had thought that they could work out their differences and have a good, peaceful marriage. She hoped for a reconciliation because Islam, like other religions, promotes marriage.

"We are taught in Islam that of all permissible things, Allah hates divorce the most. It shakes His throne," she says.

Juwayriah found herself in deep financial difficulty that eventually forced her into bankruptcy. She also became physically ill. She had been off her menstrual periods for close to a year when she started bleeding. Doctors feared she might have uterine cancer and conducted exploratory surgery, but it turned out that her emotions were causing internal havoc. "There was no cancer, *Alhamdulillah* [a Quranic phrase that means "All praise to Allah"]," she says.

Juwayriah and her first husband were eventually able to talk and forgive each other. This helped them both to move on.

"We did this because in Islam we cannot hurt each other," she says. "Not only do we need Allah's forgiveness for our sins, but we also need the forgiveness of the person we hurt."

Soon after, she was approached for marriage by another Muslim brother. Juwayriah was attracted to him for what seemed to be his deep faith, his commitment to Islam.

"At first, he was asking me to be a second wife. Well, actually, it was his wife who approached me for marriage to him," Juwayriah says.

Although Islam permits Muslim men to have up to four wives, Juwayriah knew that this man's finances could not support two families, and she declined their offer. However, he called her almost a year later and told her that his wife had left him, and that he was alone with his two children. Juwayriah then agreed to marry him. After three weeks of marriage, he let his first wife move back. Juwayriah found out from her co-wife that she had not left, but was thrown out by their husband!

"It seemed to me that he had been engineering a way to have two wives when he could not afford to do so," Juwayriah says drily.

She left him.

Juwayriah, now fifty-five years old, married again, and she says, "Even though there may be problems from time to time, both my husband and I fear Allah and let that be a guide for our marriage."

She met her new husband on the Internet in one of the Islamic marital websites. Less naive now, she checked his references. They were able to vouch for him and his character. She married him. She says she has high hopes and prays to Allah to guide her and her husband.

Despite her two bad experiences with marriage, Juwayriah is glad she came to Islam. Looking back, she sees her experiences in marriage as a result of bad choices (as she says, "I own them!") and naiveté.

"However, the most important part of it is that it is all part of Allah's plan for me," she says. "I was to learn something from each experience that would help me be a better *Muslimah.*

"I was not born into Islam in the conventional sense," she adds. "As Muslims, we believe that everyone is born a Muslim and that their parents make them some other religion. To that end, my mother was Catholic and my father was Jewish. My father was the first to intermarry in his family, as my mother was in hers. Being politically correct, or in an attempt to blend together, we celebrated the holy days of both religions. We had Hanukkah and we had Christmas. We had Easter and we had Passover. I went to church and occasionally to synagogue.

"When I was around eleven years old, my parents divorced. My mother returned to her hometown and she put us into a Catholic school. We were baptized, were confirmed, made confession and accepted Holy Communion all in the first year there. It was an adjustment, but the Catholic Church gave me some comfort. I liked the beautiful church and its rituals. I was a child in a great deal of emotional pain."

But after her teenage years, when she could make her own decisions, she returned to Judaism.

"Despite my love for the Catholic Church, I never could understand the concept that Jesus was 'God' or the 'Son' of God," she says. "Returning to Judaism also emotionally reconnected me with my Jewish family."

Judaism, like Islam, can be culture-bound; both are more total ways of life, she points out. Both sides of her family were from Eastern Europe, but her Jewish family was more tied to Eastern Europe and its values, customs, and history. "Maybe World War II and the Holocaust also had something to do with it—that Judaism is intertwined with one's identity as a person," she says.

For her, becoming a Muslim unifies her background: Islam draws from the richness of both Judaism and Christianity, she says.

"Actually, Jews and Arabs are the same people. We are both from the Prophet Ibrahim—the Arabs from the line of his son, Ismael; the Jews from the line of his son, Isaac. The role of Jesus clearly connects the three faiths as well. He was a Prophet of Allah, sent to the Jewish people to guide them back to the straight path."

While Islam has also given Juwayriah peace and firm grounding, it has allowed her to see, for example, how she can live simply but fully. "In America," she says, "we have so many wants and so few real needs."

Islam has also helped her cope with her past. She comes from a tough childhood that might have overwhelmed most people. Her mother died an alcoholic; her father was a criminal and drug user who married several times. Amid such turmoil, Juwayriah was vulnerable. She claims to have been repeatedly molested by an uncle and four cousins. Scared and trusting no one, she told no one. Her mother "didn't catch on," she says. But then, Juwayriah adds, "no one wanted to know."

She began to abuse drugs around age nineteen. Her drug of choice: heroin. She ended up on the streets, but she didn't care. She supported herself and her addiction through prostitution. She says she had numerous negative experiences in the streets, including being raped. She finally got clean and at age thirty-three started a new life.

"What made me get clean? I was sick of going to jail," she says. "And after numerous overdoses, I was afraid I was going to die. I hit bottom, by the grace of God."

A twelve-step program and faith in a higher power helped her recover. "I've been clean for twenty-two years," she says proudly. She came to Islam when she was about fourteen years clean, re-establishing her life working full-time while attending college part-time to earn her bachelor's degree in psychology. She is now a substance-abuse counselor.

Juwayriah remains a contented woman proud of her faith and continually learning more about it—and from it.

"Everything is a test and a lesson from Allah," she concludes. "There are no mistakes in Islam. Allah is the best of planners."

❧ 24 ❧

PATRICIA: AN EXTRAORDINARY TEACHER CHANGED BY ISLAM

PATRICIA SALAHUDDIN LIFTS A FINGER to her lips. *Shhh.* Her high schoolers, loud and boisterous in the hallway, become silent as she leads them into her darkened Miami classroom. Two small lanterns are the only light. Soft rhythmic music plays in the background. The kids grope their way to their desks and sit down, snickering nervously. This is not their usual English class. They tend to be chatty but the strangeness has left most of them quiet. They stare up expectantly at Patricia.

She smiles. She is about to give them a breathing lesson: Breathe in slowly, breathe out slowly. Now the class becomes pin-drop quiet as they follow her instructions.

"Welcome to meditation," she announces.

Now calmer, more tranquil, they're ready to write in their journals and still later to give reports.

They're used to such creative approaches: Patricia is a National Board–certified teacher who is on her way to earning a doctorate in Curriculum and Instruction at Florida International University. Now teaching at one of Miami's well-regarded magnet high schools, the Design and Architecture High School in the heart of the city's design district, Patricia is trying to pass on her expertise to the growing number of teachers in Muslim schools throughout South Florida. As a leader in the Muslim Teachers Association, she has helped assemble a conference called "Educating the Muslim Child: Ingredients for Success."

Volunteering to help improve private Muslim schools justifies the grueling schedule of teaching Patricia has assumed while working on her doctorate.

"During the first semester I was asking myself: What am I doing here? Why am I doing this? The reason is, I have always wanted to help Muslim teachers. This was God's way for me to spread knowledge."

Then she laughs. "I think I am crazy sometimes. I'm suffering with doing all this course work. But I think God wanted me to do this. And God is Number One in my life. I attribute everything in my life to Him—in all aspects of life. I know I have choices and I pray that I have His guidance to make those choices."

And, she says, she obeys the command: Make the Quran the light of your path.

This degree of religious conviction might make many nervous but Patricia is sincere as she speaks it. She is from the Bible Belt South and is used to piety as a part of everyday life. Her father, after all, is a Baptist preacher, now age seventy-nine and retired. She didn't grow up with him; she lived with her mother and stepfather on a farm they owned in Mississippi. They were active church-goers, and so Patricia went, too.

She grew up at the tail-end of the South's segregation and Jim Crow laws. She knows she was lucky. Her family was relatively prosperous. In addition to the farm, her mother had her own business. "I worked in our fields—I worked hard—but we owned the land. That was a big difference."

Because of her family's relative financial comfort she says she was largely sheltered from the worst of segregation, and did not encounter many white people at all while she was growing up. A white man did own land next to their farm, and they would see him in his pickup, but they did not wave to each other or even acknowledge each other's existence. This was the South: Black and white people went their separate ways.

Patricia went to all segregated schools. Today she is glad: Some of her friends volunteered to help integrate the whites-only high school, and as a result they endured much abuse, from slurs to fights.

"When I think of the difficulties of my classmates who went to the integrated high school, I don't know if I could have stuck it out. I might have quit school."

After she graduated from high school, she went to Mississippi State University, which had already been integrated for a few years. There, she began searching for spiritual answers. She was eighteen.

"Maybe I was in my rebellious years. I prefer to see it as the age of awareness."

The truth was that Patricia was not comfortable with Christianity. Segregation in the pious South was the worst on Sunday mornings. There were white churches and there were black churches, and no one dared cross from one to the other, even though they prayed to the same God. There was no need to put up a sign, "Whites only" or "For the Colored." People *knew*.

To Patricia, this made no sense. Christianity seemed to be part of the South's problem.

"I saw religion *participating* in segregation. To me, that is not religion. I did not want to practice that."

Her friends were searching, too, for a new faith, and in 1969 they encouraged her to attend a Nation of Islam meeting. The speaker: a young Louis Farrakhan.

"He talked of a positive self-identity for the black person. I was very impressed with his message of self-help—that God has given us everything we need, that the black man did not have to go pleading for help to the white people. I was so impressed with the language, the self-reliant attitude, I started attending the meetings."

Patricia had to tell her Christian parents, and she was surprised how receptive they were, even her preacher father. (Patricia's mother warned him in advance.) Today he still goes to his Baptist church and she goes to her mosque.

While still in college at Mississippi State, Patricia met another student who also was interested in the Nation of Islam. They met, of all places, in a Chicago factory, where they both had taken summer jobs to pay for college. Patricia was staying with relatives in Chicago. The son of Panamanian immigrants, he was from Chicago, the home base of the Nation of Islam, and was studying at Southern Illinois University in Carbondale. He would share his books with her, heavy-duty stuff like Frantz Fanon's *The Wretched of the Earth*. They fell in love and married in 1971, the same year Patricia graduated from Mississippi. They decided to change their last name to Salahuddin, which in Arabic means "one who protects the faith," or "one who looks out for the good and right." (Patricia decided to keep her first name but chose Zahirah as a new middle name.) She moved up to Carbondale to be with her new husband while he finished school. At one point he worked in the nearby coal mines because, as Patricia explains, "That's where the money was."

When he graduated, they opted to settle in Mississippi. Things had changed for the better. By then Mississippi had improved its race relations and was more hospitable to African Americans. "I wanted to go back to Mississippi because my family was there. I had been in Chicago and couldn't stand the cold."

Soon after relocating, they had two young babies. (They would go on to have five children in six years.) Patricia went to work in a child-care center, while her husband started his own business and eventually earned a master's degree from Mississippi State.

In 1983 they moved again. This time, it was his idea. He was losing the Spanish he had grown up with, and as few people spoke Spanish in Mississippi, he wanted to go to Miami, where many people were Hispanic. He landed a good job with the county government. Today, he is deputy director of the Miami Port Authority.

They go to a mosque in inner-city Miami that is predominantly African American but not affiliated with the Nation of Islam. Like many other African Americans today they have moved away from the Nation of Islam toward the practice of a more orthodox Islam. They welcome anyone to their mosque, and it attracts some immigrants for the customary Friday prayer services, but it is primarily African Americans who gather on Sunday for classes and other mosque activities. The Sunday habit of going to church is entrenched in African-American culture, Patricia observes with a chuckle.

She faithfully goes both days. Islam has been a comfort to her.

She's made lifelong friends at the mosque; she has learned from the Quran; and her five daily prayers replenish her. Even the *hijab*, which she feels she is required to wear, is not a problem. She is a stylish woman who wears beautifully patterned scarves that cover her hair

Zainab Elberry, an extraordinary Muslim activist, Democratic Party volunteer, insurance executive, and early feminist, lives in Nashville. (Photo: M. Nour Naciri)

Deedra Abboud *(left)* and Yuko Davis became best friends after meeting at a Phoenix-area mosque. Both are from the Bible Belt South and converted to Islam. (Photo: Ali Asim Abboud Al-Janabi)

Artist Leslie Sinclair grew up in Alaska and now lives in the Seattle area. She became a Muslim as an adult. (Photo by Leslie Sinclair)

Growing up in the Deep South, Patricia Salahuddin didn't like that some Christian ministers promoted segregation, so she became a Muslim when she was in college. (Photo courtesy of Patricia Salahuddin)

Lobna "Luby" Ismail, her husband, Alexander, and their two sons and infant daughter at their suburban Maryland home. Luby is an entrepreneur who teaches Americans about Middle Eastern and Muslim culture. (Photo by Lobna Ismail)

Michaela Corning *(seated)* designs flattering fashions for *Muslimah* around the nation. American Muslim women want their own distinct "look," she says. *Inset:* A model shows off one of Michaela's creations at a *Muslimah* fashion show. (Photos: Usman Khan)

Okolo Rashid helped start the first Muslim Museum in the nation in Jackson, Mississippi. (Photo: H. Abdul Rasheed)

At the Arizona Refugee Community Center: standing *(from left)* are two students of English, Sheima Siffati and Deman Zubar, and teacher Batool Shamil, herself an Iraqi refugee; another two students, Hawa Khamis and Sakina Ghulam, are seated with the head of the nonprofit center, Rosalind Rivera. (Photo: Arizona Refugee Community Center)

Edina Lekovic began wearing a *hijab* after learning more about Islam—her immigrant parents' faith—at college in California. (Photo: Muslim Public Affairs Council)

Sireen Sawaf is another southern Californian who began wearing a *hijab* as a young woman—after her uncle was murdered. (Photo: Muslim Public Affairs Council)

Ingrid Mattson, a college professor in Connecticut, is, as a vice president of the Islamic Society of North America, an important female Muslim leader in the United States. (Photo: Hartford Seminary)

Riffat Hassan, at the University of Louisville in Kentucky, has led research on Islamic feminist theology and started an international group to end honor killings. (Photo: Riffat Hassan)

Sarwat Husain of San Antonio started a Muslim newspaper and is a tireless
Muslim advocate. (Photo: Mohammed Zakir Husain)

Farida Azizi grew up in a refugee camp and helped educate women in Afghanistan as a young woman, despite the Taliban. She later made a daring escape to the United States with her two young sons. (Photo: Alyse Nelson Bloom)

In New York, Dalia Hashad works to help Muslims at the American Civil Liberties Union. (Photo by Dalia Hashad)

Anisah David has found other Muslims in rural South Dakota. (Photo: Eric Wenger)

Zulayka "Zuly" Martinez was about the only Latina in her Houston-area mosque when she joined five years ago. Now she says there are many more Latinas. (Photo: Zuly Martinez)

and match her clothes. As seen on one winter day, she is particularly striking, dressed in a smartly tailored brown pantsuit with matching heels and a lighter brown patterned scarf.

Faith is not a burden, she adds, but a reward.

"I know it helps," she says. "Through God's help I have been able to do a lot."

She ticks off her accomplishments: She was able to raise five children close together and still work. She was able to take in her mother after she developed Alzheimer's disease and care for her until she passed away. She was able to focus on her passion—teaching—while working on her doctorate and keeping up volunteer work.

"God helped me do all of it," she says. "He put people in my life. It's been hard, but I would have done a lot less if I hadn't had God in my life."

⋖ 25 ⋗

YUKO YEARNS FOR
FAMILY AND FAITH

THIS WAS THE WAY Japanese American Yuko Davis went to school in
rural Louisiana, just outside of New Orleans: Every morning she entered the classroom to sit on the girls' side of the room. The boys sat
on the other. The playground—and playtime—also was segregated, as
was lunch. She didn't have significant conversations with the boys;
that was discouraged.

She wore her skirts long, her blouses buttoned up to the neck.
Card playing and dancing were considered sinful. She grew up not
collecting rock 'n' roll records. ("I did like the Beatles," she confesses
years later.) She didn't go to movies either, not even G-rated ones. (In
Yuko's graduating class, a classmate was stripped of being named vale-
dictorian after she was caught her senior year leaving a G-rated movie
at the local cinema.)

Such were the rules of the fundamentalist church school Yuko
grew up in, and they shaped her childhood. Yuko felt comforted by
such structure. To this day she tells of how she automatically accepted
the rules in exchange for the order in her life. No rebellion for her.

"I was a goody two-shoes," she says candidly. "I only sat in the
front of the class. I loved the environment. It was protective."

She never missed church on Sunday, contentedly enduring the
long hours required for both Sunday school and services. She even accepted the congregation's pride in being strict. Said one leader to
Yuko: "We're narrow-minded and we're proud of it."

And she agreed with the church's philosophy that a woman's first priority was marriage and family. Foreign to her was the notion that a career was a young woman's goal. Although she did want a professional career, Yuko wanted first to rear happy and successful children, then go to work. Mothers were her role models. Ultimately, she believed success was found in following God.

She might still be in rural Louisiana today, except that everything changed when the bus rules did.

"The last straw," she recalls, "was the bus ministry."

Yuko was one of the teen volunteers on the bus that picked up children for Sunday-morning services. One day, she says she was told they would "no longer be picking up any more black children."

Yuko couldn't believe the new rule, but she was assured this was the best for everyone, including the black children who were no longer welcome at the church. "That didn't feel right. When they said that, it really disturbed me."

Although church members told her that segregation was good this didn't seem like the teachings of Christ. And when she asked questions, she was told, "We have to obey church leadership." Being the polite girl she was, she fell silent.

But in her mind began whirling a lot of thoughts—rebellious ones. Why, she asked herself, was it the church's dogma that it was a sin for the races to mix? This meant that one of her mother's Asian-born friends was going to hell because she had married a black. And the friend's biracial child was, too, as a product of a so-called sinful union. That made no sense to Yuko.

"This wasn't coming from God. These sounded like man-made rules." She thought so because, as she points out, she and her mother were accepted—although her Japanese-born mother had married a Caucasian. It didn't seem to bother the church that Yuko was biracial. "That's different," church members reassured her. "You're one of us." Yet Yuko was aware of her darker skin, her "otherness."

Her father, a Louisiana farm boy, had been a GI stationed in Japan where he met Yuko's mother and married her, and where Yuko was born. When Yuko was about a year old, her father finished up his Japanese tour and, discharged from the military, he brought his young family back home to Louisiana. Yuko and her mother quickly absorbed the American ways they encountered. Yuko's Buddhist mother went to her husband's Baptist church. They were a close family and Yuko might still be a Baptist today, were it not that her father died young and Yuko's mother, seeking refuge, started going to the stricter fundamentalist church whose members seemed so open and welcoming. She enrolled Yuko in its school.

Yuko and her mother were always told how welcome they were in their church, despite their obvious Asian looks. Yuko was always told not to worry about her heritage: The church didn't consider her Asian ancestry a "minority." But Yuko began feeling like an outsider after the black children were excluded. She still marvels how church members never could understand why she was upset at the exclusion.

Yuko's rebellion extended to church doctrine. She began having second thoughts about the idea that only Jesus was the answer to salvation and that non-Christians automatically didn't go to heaven. "That meant everyone on Mother's side was going to hell," Yuko says, a thought she found disturbing.

Again, Yuko went to church leaders to answer her questions. What if her mother's family hadn't been told of Christianity? How could they be doomed if they never knew Jesus? She asked her mother whether there had been missionaries in Japan and her mother vaguely remembered some when she was in her twenties. Bolstered with this evidence that her mother's family might have never had the opportunity to know about Christ, Yuko asked her youth leader how could they be doomed to hell. "Basically, he couldn't answer me," she remembers. He just reiterated that people had to accept Jesus Christ into their lives in order to go to heaven, and warned her: "Don't ask all these questions. It's the devil at work."

Yuko accepted it, at least outwardly. But, she says, "In my heart I didn't agree with him. I kept thinking, God gave me this mind and I can't use it?"

After graduating from high school, she decided to leave the church. She felt terrible—she missed her faith. She began searching for a new religion.

Yuko found it in a doctor's office.

In a magazine left in the waiting room, she saw an article about Islam. She became fascinated by the religion. "This, of course, was no accident: I believe this was an answer to my many prayers for guidance," Yuko claims. She became attracted to its diversity, its welcoming all races and anyone interested.

"I loved it," she says. "Islam is a lot more tolerant. It's amazing how much diversity you see."

She started wearing a scarf over her hair, and soon got used to her new Muslim ways.

She met her future husband, Ahmad, a Lebanese student studying engineering. He had a diverse background too: His mother's side was Turkish; his father's family was from Syria. Some of the family members looked European, others more Middle Eastern.

Yuko didn't know it at the time but Ahmad was looking for a wife. In the Middle Eastern way, he felt he couldn't come right out and ask Yuko for a date. He needed an intermediary. So Ahmad hooked up with a friend from the mosque, who also knew Yuko. "Do you think he's cute?" the matchmaking friend asked Yuko.

"He's got Coke-bottle glasses," she replied. (This was the 1980s; now, thanks to technology, he has thin lenses.) They didn't talk to each other for a month. But when they did, Yuko became interested in him—Ahmad was a serious young man who wanted to take care of a wife and children. They began a formal courtship, chaperoned when they saw each other. "We talked mostly by telephone," Yuko says. "This was pre-Internet."

Her mother approved of the formal courtship, which resembled how it was done in Japan. Both she and her daughter were impressed with Ahmad's gentle ways, and his regular attendance at mosque. They were married three months later.

They've now been married for seventeen years, and have five children: Safiya at sixteen is the oldest; Malika the youngest at three. They gave their oldest son a name that had both Arabic and Japanese roots. Unfortunately, Osama—which means "king," in Japanese—is now indelibly linked to terrorism. The boy now goes by his "safer," more neutral middle name, John (the name of Yuko's father).

Yuko is grateful for her close family. They read together, play together, go to mosque together. Yuko's mother lives with them. "Thank goodness my husband is Middle Eastern and is used to in-laws living in the same house," Yuko jokes.

She keeps an immaculate house. There's no clutter; the family lines their shoes up against the wall. For now, Yuko home-schools Safiya, their eldest. But Safiya is looking forward to going to high school next year—she will be a junior. Their other children are going to public schools. When her youngest starts kindergarten, Yuko will go back to school, too. "My husband says it's my turn." Probably she will major in psychology or religious studies at college. Like many other American women, she plans to have a career after all her children are in school.

They now live in suburban Phoenix and Yuko is grateful for its Sunbelt openness. No one says much when she wears her *hijab* in public. Arizona has been much more accepting of her Islamic dress than Louisiana, she reports.

The Muslim community is growing in Phoenix, and Yuko and Ahmad have become volunteers at their mosque, helping new arrivals adapt. Ahmad has been a leader, teaching about Islam to the non-Muslim public as well as doing administrative work for the mosque. Meanwhile, Yuko teaches Islam to children in classes held at the mosque. Eager to help Americans understand Islam, she recommends that visitors read the Quran, and gives them a prayer rug—along with her homemade cookies and other delicacies. She is eager to talk about the religion that has brought so much peace and spiritual renewal to her. It is a faith open to anyone, she says. She likes that her mosque has both immigrants and non-immigrants, converts and those born into Islam. She and her husband regularly read the Quran and pray the required five times a day. In particular, Yuko appreciates what she calls the "physical aspect" of *Salat*, the prescribed prayers, "the physical mechanics of worship." It puts her closer to God.

Their Islam, she adds, is a far cry from the extremism that has Imams calling for holy wars. To her, this is a misguided minority—although it gets most of America's attention.

"We are mainstream Muslims," Yuko says.

And they are comfortable with American ways. Ahmad, for example, shakes the hands of women; more traditional Muslim men do not. At home they wear jeans and T-shirts just like anyone else.

For Yuko, Islam became not only a religion but a way of life. It has helped make her family strong and widened her circle of friends. Her life, she says, can't get any better.

❖ 26 ❖

ZULY: A LATINA FINDS ISLAM

A LATINA TEXAN, Zulayka Y. Martinez (nicknamed Zuly), has discovered cultural differences at her mosque and a backlash after 9/11. In her own words, "Zuly" tells her story:

"In 2000, I converted to Islam during December, the month of Ramadan. You can say I am a typical Latina. As the child of a strictly religious family in Houston, I went to Catholic youth groups. I even dreamed of one day becoming a missionary nun.

"But as a young woman I converged on another fate and faith: Islam. My story begins with a group of friends that I went to middle and high school with. Back in those days, you never spoke about religion, and I had no idea that some of my close friends were Muslims.

"After high school, I kept in touch with a few of them, and one day I found out that a cousin of one of my best friends had arrived from Lebanon. I went to welcome him and to tell him that he would find in me a good friend—just as his cousin and I were friends.

"He simply smiled and said, 'Thank you for your kindness but I don't believe in friendship between a man and a woman.'

"That confused me. When I asked my friend (who was a guy, by the way) why his cousin said that he told me not to worry about it.

"Months passed by, and as I used to hang out with that group of friends, I bumped into the cousin again and asked him why he felt that men and women couldn't be friends. That's when he brought up Islam. To be honest, it was a religion that I had never thought or heard about.

"To make a long story short, I decided that he — and his religion — were wrong. I could not get it through my mind that there was a religion that didn't believe in Jesus as the Son of God. I decided to prove to him that he was wrong.

"I began to research this religion and to find any fault with it that I could. One day, while at a Catholic retreat, I brought a Quran (which had been given to me). I read it during the times of silence and reflection. It spoke to my heart, which made me very confused about my faith and whether I was a Christian.

"Of course, as a good Catholic girl I went and confessed to my priest that night at the retreat. The memory is still vivid of how he responded. I remember him promptly telling me, 'I've read the Quran. I'm not saying Muslims are bad people, but I assure you that our faith is correct and theirs is not.'

"When I tried to ask other questions, he looked at me and said, 'Never doubt your faith nor question it.'

"His response only made me more curious. I began to ask my Muslim friends for more information. Meanwhile, I read any material I could find about Islam.

"After a few more years of studying, I took the plunge and followed in the footsteps of thousands of Latinas. I became a *Muslimah* in a ceremony at the mosque.

"Now, four years later, I see how my way of thinking has changed. Islam has made me a better person in understanding myself and getting closer to my family. It's allowed me to have a one-to-one connection with God. And it has taught me to love everyone. Whether you are Muslim, Christian, or Jewish, we are all loved by the Almighty. I feel that I'm very open-minded. I'm friends with Christians, Jews, and Muslims.

"Before the 9/11 terrorist attacks, people were very courteous when they learned I am a Muslim or when they noticed my Islamic head covering for women. Here in Houston, they smile at me, hold the door, and greet me. I have encountered some ignorant people, but in general Texans have been wonderful.

"At first it was hard to let my family know. I come from a family of thirteen children, of whom I am the baby. I'll never forget something one of my brothers-in-law said at a family gathering (which as typical Mexicans we have almost every weekend). He told a friend of the family, 'I'm proud of Zuly and I'll back her up in her choice of becoming Muslim. I've seen her change and now she's made the right choice. May God guide her and all of us.'

"I'm a wedding photographer. I also take pictures of families and beautiful scenery. When I am working, people are stunned to find out that I am a Muslim, since they think that as a Muslim woman you are supposed to be locked in the house all the time. Some of my co-workers, you could say, make jokes about me being a Muslim or tease me. I just hold it in, because I know how a few people can be pretty closed-minded. But the majority respect me and don't bug me.

"There was a big difference in how I was treated after 9/11. Before then, I used to wear a *hijab* — and it was easy. They didn't know who you were and they didn't care. They figured you were like a nun. But, of course, it got hard after 9/11. People started thinking all Muslims were terrorists. The sudden difference in how I was treated was a big shock. I'm a very sociable person, not the type to stay at home. So I started not wearing the hijab just so I could go on with my life without being stared at. Another reason is that when I was doing my photography while wearing my head covering, people would look at me like they were wondering, Why is she taking pictures? Is she going to blow something up? I felt more at risk.

"I do not wear long gowns like some Arab or Pakistani women do. I dress in a westernized way, because that's who I am. After all, I'm a Mexican American. Not that I wear a miniskirt — I never was into that, it never has been my style. I dress comfortably but conservatively. I dress like Turkish women. I love the very Western and very modern way they dress.

"Unfortunately, I have encountered discrimination as a Muslim woman in America, even among my own race. I would be wearing the hijab and they didn't know I was Hispanic and I could hear them say things in Spanish like, 'Look at one of the wives of Saddam Hussein,' or 'Look at that Taliban woman.' I would then start speaking Spanish loudly on purpose so they could understand I was a Latina. And they would just freak out.

"I thank God for the type of woman I am. I feel and *am* independent.

"Everyone assumes I am married to a Muslim from the Middle East. That must be, they figure, why I became attracted to Islam. But I tell them, no, I didn't convert for a man but for God. They are invariably shocked.

In fact, I myself was shocked and dismayed at the marriage process. I would be introduced to a man at the mosque or at a Muslim function and after a two-hour conversation, he would say, 'You seem like a good prospect. Do you want to get married?' That blew me away. As they were trying to get me to marry them, they would say, 'Marriage is your *deen* [way of life].' I do want my own family one day. But I believe in my rights as a woman. I do not want to be pressured.

"I am not worried. I am very happy the way I am. And I know I will find my future soul mate, *Inshallah*.

"As a Latina, I didn't feel well received when I converted to Islam. The Arab and Pakistani-born women at the mosque were not that welcoming — or maybe they are not sociable like I am. It was hurtful. I felt more like an intruder than a sister.

"Now it's different, and I helped make it that way. In Houston there's a growing community of Hispanic Muslims and now we throw a party for the new girls. We have a class about Islam for them in Spanish. We tell them we were the pioneers and that we are happy we are here for them as they discover Islam. We tell them we are their friend, their sister.

"I am grateful to Islam. It has changed my heart. I believe in one God and that is what brought me to Islam. It was always very hard for me to kneel down to the Virgin Mary and the other saints in the Catholic faith. Other girls could — and would start crying, too. I couldn't do that. I believe in worshipping one God and nothing else.

"And so I am content in the Islamic faith. It has brought me peace and harmony.

My recommendation to new Muslims is this: You have to open your mind and listen to your heart."

❦ 27 ❧

ANISAH: LIVING VEILED IN RURAL SOUTH DAKOTA

ON SOME MAPS, Bushnell, South Dakota, doesn't even exist. But nestled off Highway 14, less than seventeen miles west of the Minnesota state line sits the hamlet: all four paved streets, two stop signs, and twenty-seven homes.

"I think we have about as many animals—dogs, cats and horses—as we do people," speculates Anisah David.

She's not joking. The town is so small, its roads so little traveled, that it has become known for such eccentricities as a horned white goat named Schnee (German for snow). Schnee liked to rest in the middle of one of the town's roads. Bushnell residents had to carefully select when they were going to travel: They didn't want to butt horns with Schnee. If disturbed, Anisah remembers, "He would stand up and lower his head, threatening to ram his horns into your radiator."

But the town tolerated the goat—until he passed away of old age—just as it does the human residents who admittedly march to a different drummer. This is a town, after all, where a six foot eight resident—"just a big walking wall of a man," Anisah says—dons fairy wings, leotards, an aviator cap and goggles on Halloween to launch pumpkins from a medieval catapult. Then there's the woman who liked to walk her mule on a leash. Most residents are artisans: They paint, sculpt, and weave. There are also songwriters, dancers, and potters.

Anisah, forty-two, fits right in. She's a webmaster, Muslim matchmaker, community activist, lecturer, writer, and textile artist as well as

an Islamic convert who since 1988 has worn some sort of head covering as well as long dresses. No one notices what elsewhere might seem
unusual clothing. Anisah still marvels at the level of tolerance not only
in Bushnell but throughout South Dakota and, indeed, her stretch of
the Midwest. She says she only receives an occasional stare when she
ventures out to do business in larger Brookings (population 18,604).
Or she may get a few long looks if she travels to the even bigger Sioux
Falls—with just over 100,000 folks—south of Brookings. "I would be
wearing an extremely big cape and a long gown, and some not used to
diversity would point at me and stare. Sometimes they would only be
a foot away from me. I would usually wave at them."

South Dakotans, she says, have made peace with the state's unusual religious groups, which include Native American and conservative Anabaptist Christian sects. "They're extremely tolerant. I have
been so amazed. I'm just as welcome here as anyone else."

Or at least she used to think that.

Anisah has had to reconsider that after a South Dakota judge recently ruled against her daughter, Cassy David, in a custody case (see
chapter 14). The judge decided Cassy's estranged Egyptian husband,
who has a Ph.D. and a large extended family, is better equipped, at
least for now, to care for their baby daughter, saying Cassy's extended
family was "questionable at best." The judge singled out Anisah as a
poor influence, citing her online Muslim matchmaking service, her
pro-polygamy views (Anisah, who is monogamous, says she accepts it
in theory, as the Quran tolerates polygamy under strict guidelines),
her Muslim garb, and her past criticism of the Israeli occupation of
Palestine.

"He used every derogatory, inflammatory claim against me to
make me look like a raving fundamentalist. I was attacked for encouraging Muslim women to wear the veil and I was even attacked for having done matchmaking. The judge claims that I may have the right to
free speech, but he can use that against my daughter in making his
decision."

Only a couple of other incidents have made Anisah feel unwelcome in the Heartland, and they all occurred after 9/11. On one occasion, a man made a menacing gesture when he saw her at a grocery

store. Luckily Anisah's six-foot-five husband, Eric, who is also a Muslim convert, was nearby to intervene.

Throughout the years, neighbors have shown their support for Anisah and her family. Anisah got numerous supportive calls when a high school teacher told Anisah's son that he shouldn't use his study hall to go to mosque on Fridays. She told him he needed to go to "Sunday services like normal people."

Anisah was incensed, but local folks were even more so. The controversy made the regional newspaper and people approached Anisah to tell her how wrong they thought the teacher was.

She's also found that, as a Muslim advocate and founder of the not-for-profit organization Human Interactions for Religious Understandings, people will listen—including other judges. Anisah once helped a young woman who had converted to Islam and was trying to go to Egypt to be with her new husband. The only problem: Her father sued for custody of the woman's five-year-old son, saying his grandson would be safer with him. According to an Associated Press report, the grandfather claimed his daughter "had been engaged in some bizarre behavior, including wearing Muslim garb and declaring herself a Muslim." Anisah says the man submitted to the court pictures of his daughter wearing a veil at her ceremony in which she formally became a Muslim.

An attorney for the grandfather later told an Associated Press reporter that he and his wife were not biased against Muslims but, rather, "concerned" about the child being taken to Egypt because his mother "had been somewhat inconsistent in her behavior."

At first, the court agreed with the grandfather and gave temporary custody to him and his wife, leaving the young Muslim mother without her son.

"She was devastated," Anisah remembers. "It destroyed her sense of justice in America, that we have freedom of religion. Nobody would ever think to remove children for what their parents wore for their religion."

But the judge ultimately sided with the young mother, ordering the little boy returned to her thirty days later. The woman was able to rejoin her husband in Egypt with her son, where they now live.

As director of Human Interactions for Religious Understandings, Anisah helped that woman free of charge, just as she does other people needing her help. She's also on the board of a Minneapolis-based nonprofit group, Sisters Need a Place, that helps Muslim women and their families throughout the Midwest who face domestic abuse or problems with housing, employment, transportation, child custody, and divorce.

She also lectures about Islam, including at colleges. Because of her conversion to Islam, many think she has conservative views and are surprised when she turns out to be progressive. On the subject of gay rights, she asks college students, "Why is that an issue?" When some say it is a sin, Anisah then asks the students to raise their hands if they are living with a boyfriend or girlfriend, or know a friend who is. Invariably, most raise their hands, and Anisah points out they are sinning, too. "I have to say I have a strong sense of justice," Anisah admits. "I also have a big mouth. I can't keep quiet when I see injustice. I get myself in trouble sometimes. But that's just the way I am. I think God put me on earth to be a squeaking wheel."

Then, she is used to fighting what most take for granted.

"I learned early in life to struggle for what I wanted, being born with a severe speech impediment and respiratory infection that, at the time, was expected to end my life in infancy," she writes on one of her many websites. She survived, but "throughout my childhood I battled yearly bouts of respiratory infections and chronic illnesses, which interfered with my schooling." Anisah says she also had to overcome child abuse and the horror of seeing her mother beaten.

By her mid-twenties she was on her own, struggling after she ended her first marriage. Her first husband, who had served in Vietnam, had violent flashbacks that could be dangerous to others. Then, just as her divorce was to be finalized, she discovered she was pregnant.

As she remembers: "Everyone was trying to pressure me to have an abortion, since I was a soon-to-be divorced mother with a three-year-old to raise all by myself. I went against the social pressure and gave birth to [Cassy]."

She was now alone in northern Wyoming with two small children to support. Refusing to feel sorry for herself, she went on welfare while attending the local college.

"I dealt with the social marginalization of being on welfare while attending school. We lived in the ultimate state of poverty so as to comply with all the federal regulations that are imposed on welfare families. I tried hard to give my kids a 'normal' childhood, by getting involved in hobbies that would allow all of us to be together and have fun. We camped, hiked, participated in historical re-enactments."

It was while she was attending college in Wyoming that she became interested in Islam.

"I met a foreign-exchange student there—I love talking to people about cultures—who happened to be a Saudi. You can't separate their religion from their culture. As I was trying to understand his religion, I asked him, 'Do you have some sort of Bible you follow?' He took it kindly. He said yes, they have the Quran." He helped Anisah find a copy in the library and she soon became immersed in it.

The Quran changed her life. She felt she had found her religion.

"Islam is an amazing religion to me. It gives answers about diversity and human rights. It talks about the rights of the homeless versus the rights of the wealthy, the rights of the imprisoned versus those who imprison them. Everyone has rights—and responsibilities. I like that Islam acknowledges that."

She also was struck that the Quran "is so straightforward and did not seem to have gender bias." In it, she could find out more information about Mary, the mother of Jesus, than what is in the Bible. "I found that refreshing."

So Anisah decided to become a Muslim in 1988.

Soon afterward she moved from Wyoming to Portland, Oregon. While driving there with her two small children in their loaded-down car, they passed through a large fire on a mountainside, with flames on both sides of the road, that had erupted in Yellowstone National Park. To her, going through the fire was deeply symbolic.

"I went from being a Christian to coming out at the other side a Muslim. I went through this parched, charred land—what I was leaving behind."

That included friends who didn't like that she had converted.

But Anisah persevered, despite her family's efforts to dissuade her from becoming Muslim. But she ended up starting a family trend: One of her brothers also converted and married a Muslim woman from Singapore.

A year after Anisah became a Muslim, she moved cross-country from Oregon to New York where she thought there would be more Muslims. She settled in Brooklyn near a mosque. It was at a time when Afghan rebels were fighting to overthrow their Soviet invaders. She can remember federal agents trying to recruit young Muslim Americans at the mosque to fight against the Soviet Union in Afghanistan. She now finds it bitterly ironic that the same government is accusing some of the same men for being possible terrorists. "They were asked to go," she stresses. "I witnessed it with my own eyes. To me, it's hypocritical."

She eventually moved back West, where she had always felt most at home, and settled in Bushnell in 1990. She's been there ever since.

Bushnell, after all, has been good for her. There, she met her new husband, Eric, a red-headed former Lutheran who sculpts and welds. They met because of her son, who discovered that Eric's house had the perfect rooftop on which to slide down on a toboggan during one winter when the snowdrifts were as much as twenty feet high. In remarkably tolerant Bushnell, Anisah's future husband had no problems with the kids using his roof as a sledding hill. Eric soon met Anisah and became interested in Islam . . . and her. Bushnell's population now included one more Muslim. They married in an Islamic ceremony. "In Islam, I don't lose my birthright when marrying. I kept my own name," Anisah says. "That is my right."

To help others, Anisah started a matchmaking service, at the request of many of her friends and family. Even total strangers asked for her help, including Christians who were finding it hard to find mates.

They, says Anisah, "were fed up with the lack of decent places to meet decent life partners."

Most of those whom Anisah helped were Muslims trying to find spouses in a nation overwhelmingly Christian. Many felt isolated — they didn't even know there were other Muslims in their Midwestern communities, let alone which ones were looking to marry. "I started the matchmaking service because we are so spread out. Because Muslim men and women don't socialize together the single men didn't know if a single woman was available." Thus began her Internet service, www.angelfire.com/nd/MuslimMatrimonials.com.

Her matchmaking became international when Muslims throughout the world wrote in, asking to be considered. "We do it for free. It's not a paid service. Bringing couples together to start a family is not something I would want to be charging for."

She says she has helped ten couples marry, including a cardiologist from Jordan who was living on the East Coast. Anisah was able to match him up with an American-born woman, a convert who was, in fact, living in Jordan. Nowadays, with more matchmaking services available nationwide and online, Anisah is not as involved. Still, she is proud that she helped some couples get together.

Today, Anisah prays that her daughter Cassy will find peace with a good Muslim husband and that her toddler will be returned to her. Bushnell is a good place for a grandchild to visit, she says.

"It is a quiet and peaceful place where time itself slows. The people here are neighborly and speak to strangers and friends alike, but don't meddle. Privacy is respected and so is neighborliness."

This is, Anisah says, a place to take root.

And so she has.

PART IV

The Persecuted

Many of America's newly arrived *Muslimah* endured years of squalor in overcrowded refugee camps. What even the poorest Americans take for granted—from running water to electricity—many of these refugees are enjoying for the first time in the United States. They are the faces behind the headlines of violence erupting in Somalia, Sudan, Ethiopia, Bosnia, Afghanistan, and Iraq. Since the 1990s, more than 229,000 Muslim refugees have settled in the United States, a dramatic influx unseen in previous years.

In 1999, a record 44 percent of all refugees arriving in the United States were Muslims, according to the Washington-based Cultural Orientation Resource Center that receives federal funding to help refugees. By 2004, that percentage was down to 33 percent but still significantly more than in the late 1980s when the Department of State was reporting that not a single Muslim refugee had entered the United States. Since the 1990s, however, the Muslim refugees have come from 77 countries, virtually every corner of the globe, according to a report published by the resource center to help educate the refugees' social workers and other service providers. Indeed, these Muslims newest to America are changing cities around the country. For example, with thousands of Afghans, Iraqis, and Sudanese now calling Phoenix home, the city has assigned a police officer to act as a liaison with its rapidly growing Muslim community.

Less in the news are those Muslims fleeing persecution as a religious minority. In India, for example, riots and racial fighting periodically erupt between Muslims and the Hindu majority. The Muslims invariably lose out. Salma, now living in Florida, still remembers when violence broke out in the Indian city she had grown up in. Shootings and beatings occurred in broad daylight. Homes went up in flames. "It was like destruction from Biblical times," Salma says.

The *Muslimah* applying for political asylum include victims of domestic violence. Tania tells how she is now applying for political asylum after fleeing an abusive fiancé who hit her repeatedly even before they were married. Her father had agreed to the arranged match in their tribal society before anyone realized he was violent. Tania managed to win a scholarship to study in the United States and, once here, refused to go back.

Many Muslim refugees flourish in the United States. They climb into the middle class, especially those who were already educated. Senada Alihodzic describes how she and her husband arrived in Erie, Pennsylvania, with only the clothes on their back after he was released from a concentration camp in Bosnia. Once white-collar, Senada's husband found himself taking any menial job he could find while Senada looked after their two small sons in a cramped apartment. Now he is a high-tech worker and Senada a social worker. They own their home and two cars. They are saving for their three children to go to college.

Muslim refugees from poorer Third World countries also fare well. Women especially benefit. Unable to go to school in their native countries, they are finally learning how to read and write here.

Still, the refugee *Muslimah* cope with overcoming fear. They may have left the violence of their homelands, but their anxieties follow them. Many Shiites from the persecuted Iraq city of Basra, for example, are afraid to talk openly. "In Iraq, they always felt like someone was watching them," says Rosalind Rivera of the Arizona Refugee Community Center. "They were afraid to even talk in front of their kids because of what their kids might say in school [one of the places where Saddam's spies lurked]." A slip of the tongue might have landed them in jail. Even now in the United States many Shiites from Basra remain guarded.

After growing up in cultures that emphasized female submissiveness, many of the refugee women in America learn for the first time how to be assertive, Rosalind Rivera says. This can bring discord in families, although most remain close-knit. "I think of my wife as my partner, my equal," says Detective Harry Sexton of the Phoenix police department, who is assigned to work with Muslim refugees. "That is not the case with men" from such countries as Afghanistan. In fact, American social workers were advised in the providers' guide published by the Cultural Orientation Resource Center that some of their male clients would balk at working for a woman and would need help adapting.

Still, despite the considerable obstacles, the refugee *Muslimah* are forging ahead. ⚓

❧ 28 ❧

When Voting Is a Joy

BATOOL SHAMIL was but one of the many Iraqis proudly displaying their inked thumbs to show they had voted in a historic ballot, taking place some 8,000 miles from her hometown in southern Iraq.

Batool now lives in the United States but she still wanted to cast her vote on behalf of Iraq's fledgling democracy. She had already taken the grueling trip once before to register for the historic January 2005 election. So she again left her Phoenix, Arizona, home at midnight to ride with a group of other Iraqi refugees more than seven hours to vote in the Los Angeles area, one of the designated polling cities in the United States. The task completed, they got back in the car to drive straight back home, returning that evening to their families and jobs.

"We didn't get any sleep," she says, but that was not important. "I was so happy. There are no words to describe how happy I was."

Batool, who teaches English to other refugees, can't believe that some Iraqis she knows in Phoenix are still afraid of Saddam Hussein and wouldn't vote, regardless of how far away they were from any possible retaliation.

"I was so upset. I don't know why they didn't vote, except they were really afraid."

But they were ashamed and embarrassed, too, she points out, when the election went smoothly, and a majority of Iraqis went to the polls despite threats from insurgents.

Not that Batool doesn't understand fear—it was a part of her life in Iraq. Batool is a Shiite Muslim who grew up in the south of Iraq in a large family of nine brothers and four sisters. The Shiites were, she says, a majority turned into a minority. Saddam Hussein had a huge network of spies that watched over the Shiites to keep them under control. "There was no house that wasn't visited" by Saddam's henchmen, she says.

Her then husband had it particularly hard. He refused to fight with the Iraqi forces during the first Gulf War and fled the country. He ended up in a camp in Saudi Arabia. After the war ended disastrously for Iraq, he returned home, only to face intense scrutiny.

"They didn't leave us alone," she says. "The situation was so hard we decided to leave. Life was too difficult there."

When they came to the United States in March 1996, Batool was only in her mid-twenties. She had been married at age sixteen to her first cousin and had their daughter a year later. Four years later, she had a son.

Life was difficult in America and her marriage did not survive. They divorced five years ago and Batool found herself a single mom, sometimes holding down two jobs.

Still, she clings to her dreams and she managed to buy a three-bedroom, two-bath home for herself and her kids. To Batool, it is a castle. She is proud she is able to provide her son and daughter with their own bedrooms. And she realizes she made a savvy investment: She estimates her home has increased about $110,000 in value.

Nevertheless, it is difficult being a single mom. In the summer of 2005, she faced a layoff from her job teaching refugees at the Arizona Refugee Community Center, because of budget cuts from a local school board. But now the center is trying to raise money so she and the other teachers can come back for a new school term.

It is also a challenge for her to cajole her children into learning about two cultures. They may live in America now, but she wants them to have an awareness of their Iraqi heritage.

But her number-one goal for her children is to see they go to college. She expects them to earn A's on their report cards. (Batool's daughter gets some B's but so far her son is meeting the straight-A quota.) Batool figures they can live at home while they go to nearby

Arizona State University in Tempe. She is already collecting information about scholarships and financial aid for her children.

"My dream is for my kids to go to college." In Iraq, she says, "there's no way the children could go to the university. I am working so hard." At the same time, she is also sending money home to her family in Iraq, and that places great demands on her.

Still, she knows she made the right decision to come to America: She and her children are already better off in their new home. Meanwhile, her family in Iraq has less of a struggle thanks to Batool's regular contributions.

Most importantly, she says, her children have a chance of achieving, with a solid shot at college.

❧ 29 ❧

SENADA: THE REFUGEE WHO
NOW HELPS OTHERS

SENADA ALIHODZIC WANTS TO HELP the traumatized, newly arrived
refugees fleeing war and persecution. These days they're coming to
her Pennsylvania town from the far corners of the globe: Somalia,
Liberia, Sudan, Russia, Ukraine, and Uzbekistan.

She knows their fears can be overwhelming: flying into the United
States, thousands of miles away from their homes. Many don't speak
English or have any understanding of American culture. Their wealth
is often limited to the clothes on their back. They're coming to one of
the colder parts of the United States: Erie, Pennsylvania, where win-
tertime high temperatures are below freezing even in mid-March. It's
a shock for most refugees used to the desert or subtropical weather.

But Senada (whose name is pronounced "sonata") is there to say:
You can do it. I did.

About a dozen years ago, she and her young family were uprooted
from their Bosnian city. She was in her mid-twenties, with a four-year-
old and a toddler, when the war started in 1992 in that part of disinte-
grating Yugoslavia. She had watched on television the old socialist
republic crumble as Croatia erupted into war the year earlier. But she
never thought it would spread and have an impact on her family.

"We were living in peace," she remembers. "It was a normal life.
My husband, Nedim, managed a warehouse distribution center and I
stayed at home to take care of our children. We owned our house free
and clear. My parents-in-law built a house for each of their kids. It was
a very good life. Then suddenly one day your whole life changes.

"At that time I didn't understand—I still can't comprehend. But you don't appreciate peace until something happens. Peace is standard—it comes as everyday life. But when you have war, you start thinking how lucky you have been. With peace, you didn't need to run from all the bombs."

Senada decided to go back to her mother's home in neighboring Slovenia, an area that had escaped the civil war. She didn't want to leave her husband, but her year-old baby was sick, and there was no medicine for him in Bosnia.

Her husband stayed behind to protect their home and his family. But the Serbian forces started rooting out Muslim men in Bosnia. "They just picked up all the males from sixteen to seventy," Senada says.

At the time it was a shock. For decades, Christians and Muslims had lived peacefully side by side. Under Tito, Communist Yugoslavia had banned religion but leaders looked the other way when people attended religious services. (Senada was considered a good student and offered a spot in a youth camp that trained young Communists. When she said she couldn't, since she went to mosque regularly, the school administrators said she could still be a Communist. Nevertheless, she declined.)

In the former Yugoslavia, Senada says that Christians and Muslims respected each other. Senada can remember learning about Catholicism from a parish priest in the Bosnian city Sanski Most, where her grandmother still lived and where Senada met Nedim. Indeed, her Muslim grandmother urged her to go to church: She wanted her granddaughter to learn about Christianity as a way of honoring their Christian friends and neighbors.

"My grandmother was religious. She would stress love and respect and health—and not to lie and steal."

Not only did Christians and Muslims intermingle, they intermarried. "Even after the war my brother married a Catholic. My other brother married a Serbian girl, an Orthodox Christian."

Yugoslavian Muslims were more secular from their years of Communist rule. Muslims and Christians even looked alike in that part of Europe: Muslim women did not cover their heads or wear clothing that separated them from other women.

To this day, Senada does not pray the required five times a day.

Nor does she believe she has to. She remembers her grandmother advising her to concentrate on the crux of Islam—being loving and respectful to others—rather than to follow rules about praying.

So it came as a shock to her and other Yugoslavian Muslims when the Serbs began their assault, supposedly to avenge the rule of the Muslim Ottoman Empire hundreds of years earlier. Those whom they had thought of as fellow countrymen were now their attackers, even their killers. The tanks, bombs, and other military equipment the Bosnians had once paid for as part of the country's defense system were now being used against them.

Her husband found himself facing soldiers and loaded guns. He was among those rounded up in May 1992. Destination: a barbed wire concentration camp. His head was shaved. He lost fifty-eight pounds.

By the time the International Red Cross found his camp six months later and demanded its liberation, he was emaciated and sick. He and the other liberated prisoners were taken to Croatia. Senada was shocked to see his shrunken frame. She barely recognized him.

While he and the others were recovering, the Red Cross gave him the option of leaving Bosnia and starting over in another country. As he felt he had nothing to return to in Bosnia, he asked what countries would accept him and his family. Only the United States, he was told.

They arrived in Erie in September 1993. As Senada explains, "They just assign you here—you don't choose where you are going."

It would be their luck that during that winter of 1993–94 Erie would endure one of the coldest ever. Senada, who had grown up in Slovenia where it never snowed, was stunned at Erie's frigid cold and icy winds.

"I thought, oh my God, this is Siberia."

On top of this they had the stresses of starting a new life. As a twenty-something she was embarrassed at not speaking English, but she was determined to change this. She began reading aloud newspaper ads. She stumbled over pronouncing the foreign words, but she kept at it. "My husband used to laugh at me," she says. Today she has her reward: She speaks fluent English.

Meanwhile, he was coping with a new job—the former manager

found himself doing menial work at a plastics factory and a bakery. He worked long hours for a small paycheck. Every penny counted. The family had to furnish an apartment, buy food, clothes, and toiletries. "You come and you don't have anything," Senada says. She and her husband also had to set aside precious dollars to buy a car so her husband could get to work. For a while, he had been forced to wait for buses, or for other refugees to give him a ride if they were working in the same factory. But a car would give him greater flexibility in finding a better-paying job. They scrimped for a year to buy—on credit— a small used car. He would eventually retrain for a job that helped elevate them to the middle-class: He is now a technical worker who helps prepare electrical motors for a small company that has a contract with General Electric.

At the same time, Senada's husband was trying to recover from the trauma of being in a concentration camp.

Then, in 1994, Senada discovered she was going to have their third child.

"I was very depressed. There were so many things to worry about, and then I get pregnant."

Her husband reassured her that everything would work out and that in the years to come they would be grateful for their new child. He was right. They treasure their youngest, a daughter, now ten.

Her husband, a hard worker, did find better work, and Senada found a career, too.

It was her kindness that led her to her present work. After plodding away at learning English, she was able to help other Bosnian refugees by translating at doctors' offices, government agencies, and schools. Staff members at the nonprofit International Institute of Erie noticed her volunteer work and asked if she would like a paying job. The agency helps refugees adapt to the United States by helping them find housing, counseling, jobs, and even food. "We are a resettlement agency," Senada explains. "We help the refugees with everything they need to start a new life." Senada started at the institute twenty hours a week, perfect for a mother. Now she is working full-time.

She is grateful for this work. Now, with two incomes, the family is assured of a comfortable life.

She finds her work meaningful, and crucial to those she's helping. She knows what it is like to be a refugee and she wants to help America's newest arrivals. She feels particularly motherly to a group she calls the "lost boys of Sudan"—orphaned boys who survived bombings, shootings, and even alligators waiting on river banks as they fled their country's violence. The boys ended up in refugee camps before the United States flew them to Erie for a new life.

"They are doing very well. Because they were very young, they learned English quickly."

Some are in college; others have started working, she reports. By helping the lost boys and other refugees, Senada feels she is giving back to a country that helped her family.

Not that her life here hasn't been bittersweet. She was never able to see her father again. He passed away in 1997. "It was heart attack. He was a young man, only fifty-six, when we lost him."

And she worries that her children are missing out on their faith. Erie is too small to have a mosque that practices the European style of Islam, and the family doesn't go to Friday prayers. Senada teaches her children at home about Islam.

The family also socializes with other Bosnians. Senada doesn't want her children growing up without knowledge of their heritage. So they go, for example, to the yearly Bosnian soccer camp held in Erie. "They play soccer, and after that we have a party."

Like most refugees she is willing to struggle in America for her family. Her older son is seventeen and will be ready for college in another year. Her younger son is an eighth grader and doing well at school, as is her daughter in fifth grade.

"I can provide for my kids. They can have a better life here, especially when your own country is destroyed by war."

Senada is happy that her children are thoroughly American and *think* American—they have that can-do attitude.

This summer, Senada is splurging and taking her children to Bosnia and to visit her mother in Slovenia. Finally, she will be able to see her family again. It will be the first time that she has been back to the Balkans since war changed her life. She's longing to see the towns she grew up in, and she wants her children to get a taste of the life she knew.

Not that she wants to dwell on her golden years in Bosnia, when she could stay at home with the children, when life seemed so much easier. "I will never have that kind of life again," she says.

And she is determined to stay in America. "It is good to sacrifice. I know my kids will have a better life."

❖ 30 ❖

FARIDA'S JOURNEY BACK
TO FREEDOM

FARIDA AZIZI was supposed to be living in the new Afghanistan, the one liberated from the repressive Taliban by the United States. But she found herself resorting to wearing the burqa in Kabul and trying to escape from an angry husband who demanded she submit to him and stay in Afghanistan. He had already taken their two small sons before. Ultimately, he would obtain an Afghan court order to keep her and the boys with him. And Farida, who had appeared in Washington, D.C., with President and Mrs. Bush as well as Senator Hillary Rodham Clinton, was trapped. The United States government could not help her, because she was still an Afghan citizen and not yet a permanent U.S. resident. So she did what she has had to do for almost a quarter of a century, since the Russians invaded Afghanistan in 1979. She lived by her wits.

The thirty-three-year-old managed to find a ride to the Pakistani border and smuggle herself and her two small sons to freedom. The head-to-toe burqa came in handy after all. Concealing her boys inside the bulky gown, the border guards couldn't recognize them as the runaway wife and sons.

Today, they are safe in Arlington, Virginia. The boys are back in elementary school and Farida is once again a special adviser for Afghanistan and the Middle East for the Washington, D.C.–based nonprofit group, Vital Voices Global Partnership. She also returned as a founding member of the Policy Group on Afghan Women that lobbies the United States Congress for direct support to Afghan women.

And she sits on the board of the Tahirih Justice Center, the same pro bono legal agency that helped Farida win political asylum in the United States.

There is, however, so much work to be done. As Farida recently said in a Voice of America broadcast, the best way to promote peace and economic advancement in the Third World is to empower the women there by educating them and giving them work.

"If you invest in women you invest in the whole family," she asserts.

She sees the need in her native country. The Taliban may have been toppled but Afghanistan still is repressive to women.

"It's not just the Taliban. It's the way of life, the culture, the daily life. For one hundred years it has been this way. In Afghanistan, change comes so slowly."

Still, that doesn't mean Farida is going to give up. Not by a long shot. She is used to struggle.

She was born into a prominent family in Afghanistan. During her early years she enjoyed wealth and comfort. Her father was a doctor in the Afghan army. She once described to a *Washington Post* reporter how she grew up on army bases amid the fragrance of orange blossoms and narcissus. Her family went on picnics and attended concerts and movies. That all ended in 1979 when the Soviet Union invaded Afghanistan. The Soviets bombed the country. Soviet tanks and troops rumbled in. Terrified, her family fled to the refugee camps in Pakistan and ended up living in tents.

"I was nine years old," she remembers. "We missed the whole school year. At first it was very strange. We couldn't go out; we couldn't speak the language. Even the food was strange. And we had little water and no electricity."

Nevertheless, the family had to adjust to those bleak conditions as their stay stretched into years. Her father treated fellow refugees for free while her mother emphasized the need for the children to become educated. One of her brothers got a good job and was able to move the family to a one-room house with a concrete floor.

"At least we had a roof over our head," Farida says.

It even had a pump that gave the family running water twice a day, when the water was flowing. Even better, Farida got to go to school and attend a makeshift university of women. She wanted to study medicine, like her father.

"I wanted to be a doctor. It is a highly honored profession. As a doctor or teacher people will protect you because you are helping them as a professional."

But at her so-called university, she and the other students had to make do with little. "We had no facilities—no labs, no library, no books, no photocopies." Instead the students had to rely on their professors' lectures. "We just took notes," Farida says.

But even that was not to be. Conservative religious leaders (the Mujahideen) in the refugee camp decided her university shouldn't remain open. They decreed that girls shouldn't go to school and that to educate women was not Islam. Farida's father tried to protest. He knew the Quran didn't prohibit women from learning, and wanted his daughter to go to school.

Her mother, who was not educated but could quote the Quran, also protested.

"But society was not on their side," Farida says sadly. In the refugee camps, she points out, "you can't control what you want to do," especially after the Mujahideen raided the school, its windows and doors shot up. Even the school's guards were shot at. The university was soon closed down.

She later married a former Afghan army officer that her parents had picked for her. It was an arranged marriage. He was a good man but he had been disabled from a bombing and had few skills beyond the military. All the men in the refugee camps were jobless, but Farida didn't think to refuse the marriage—it was so ingrained in her culture for the woman to agree. "We don't want to disrespect the family, so women sacrifice themselves."

By this time, the early 1990s, the Russians had left and her new husband decided they would go back to the capital, Kabul. Both returned to Afghanistan with high hopes, but they were soon dashed. War had broken out between the various tribes and factions trying to take over from the fleeing Soviets. "There was heavy rocket fire," Farida recalls. "I was scared." Some seventy rockets, she counted, ended up near their Kabul home. A hole was left in their living room, and the ground shook whenever a rocket landed nearby.

Like many others, they survived by living underground, amid open sewage. People became ill from the cold, dank, smelly conditions. Farida heard of women being raped. After a week of this, Farida and her husband decided they had no choice but to return to Pakistan. They crept out at one A.M. during a lull in the rocket fire and walked for hours. "It was winter, and we were freezing," she remembers.

For more than eight hours, they walked until they reached an area just outside of Kabul where there wasn't rocket fire. After a week there was a ceasefire and they scrambled to find a bus to Pakistan. Finally they came upon one—which had one empty seat. They shared it.

"My brother was looking for us. When we got there, he was amazed we were alive. He was so happy and shocked to see us."

Farida worked for a while as an English teacher. But times were difficult: Her husband couldn't find work and they struggled just to eat. Then Farida discovered she was pregnant. As they had no money for her hospital stay, she sold her jewels. Giving birth to their first son, Farida had no anesthesia. "You have to suffer with the pain until the baby comes," she says simply.

A mere two weeks later, it was back to looking for work. Her husband did manage to do construction work for three days, earning the equivalent of $6. But they ran out of food. "We had no food for three days. We had tea with sugar. At least I had breast milk for the baby so he would not die."

The Norwegian Church Aid offered her a job to help Afghan women, and once again Farida was willing to venture back to the war-torn country. The salary was generous, enough to keep her and her husband and their new baby comfortable. They would never go hungry again, and she would be helping her countrywomen learn how to read and get jobs.

But once again, fate intervened. Just as she was re-entering Kabul in 1996, so was the Taliban. There were more rockets and land mines, and once again her young family was on the run.

After three days and nights, she and her family made it back to Pakistan and her Norwegian Church Aid boss was relieved. He was confident that Farida would find her way back.

The agency came up with a new strategy: Farida would venture secretly back to Afghanistan. With the Taliban banning schools for girls, she helped set up secret schools at private homes, the Norwegian Church Aid paying teachers' salaries. "In the provinces it was not so strict," she says, and she could do more. She also was able to help the rural women with health care and suggest ways for them to earn money to support their families. She received death threats, but she kept on going, even after a short maternity leave to give birth to her second son.

Then she was sent to Eastern Mennonite University in Virginia for a three-month training program on peace-building.

"What a big difference when I came to the United States," she says. "I had thought no one is helping us. But I realized we are not alone in our suffering."

Re-energized, she returned first to Pakistan and then to Afghanistan, where she was promptly visited by the Taliban, who demanded to know why she had come back. She told them, "This is my country and I belong here."

She felt driven to help. "I saw how the women needed us. Even a very small amount of support means a big difference to women there."

One event that sustained Farida's convictions was seeing a woman give birth by herself, because there were no doctors or clinics. The woman had high blood pressure and couldn't push the baby out. "She died in front of my eyes. She could have been saved. I could not stay calm. I have to be able to help her and other women like her."

But the Taliban wouldn't let her alone, even venturing into Pakistan to threaten her. One official told her: "You know it is very easy to kill you and your children."

Fortunately, she returned with her two young sons to Eastern Mennonite University for more training, and this time she applied for political asylum. The Tahirih Justice Center, which advocates for women and children fleeing human rights abuses and violence, filed legal briefs in her behalf. In 2001, she won her asylum. It was a heady victory but soon Farida had to concern herself with finding work to support herself and her sons. "I just applied everywhere"—stores, restaurants, and offices—"I was not hearing from anybody." She managed to work a few days at a nursing home and was content to mop the facility and clean bathrooms. But, as a Muslim woman who is required to be modest, she felt she could not undress and bathe the home's elderly men, so ultimately she had to quit.

But fate intervened—in her favor. The Vital Voices Global Partnership hired her to help Afghan and Middle Eastern women.

Thanks to Farida's steady paycheck, she sent money home to her family and her husband, who were still in the refugee camps. She had applied for her husband to come to the United States, but after 9/11, the government froze the number of refugees allowed into the United States, especially Middle Eastern men.

Meanwhile, her career was taking off. Farida helped advise First Lady Laura Bush about the conditions of Afghan women and Mrs. Bush used information she provided for a radio address. Farida appeared with the President and Mrs. Bush when he signed a bill to give aid to help Afghan women. Farida would also work with Senator Hillary Rodham Clinton and other congressional leaders.

Meanwhile, her husband was becoming depressed and Farida promised to visit him. With their sons, they spent a month in Pakistan after the children were out of school. But when Farida said she felt she had to return to America for a better life for her sons, her husband balked. He wanted them to stay with him. Claiming that his life was useless, he couldn't see living without them. Farida urged patience— his U.S. asylum papers had to come through one day—but he only grew more upset, telling his wife that people were saying bad things about her.

Although accused of forgetting her culture, and not living her life in the Islamic way, she tried to reason with him. "I have a stable job. It is dignified and respectful. I'm helping people. This is a future for our children."

He would have none of it. He decided to flee with their sons. "He felt he had to take control," she says. And so Farida came back to America alone.

She was beside herself with worry for her children. But at least her husband allowed her to talk to them on the telephone, and after three months, her husband was complaining that their sons were faring poorly. They were crying for cereal and milk—nourishment they had taken for granted in America. Only then did her husband agree she could take them back to America.

To do so, Farida had to wait until she had accrued enough vacation time at work. However, by summer, when she was finally able to return to Pakistan, her husband had changed his mind. They would start over, he declared, in the newly liberated Afghanistan. Farida protested, but he took away her and their sons' American passports. Trapped, she went with them to Kabul.

Her brother tried to intervene but the husband was implacable. This was the end: She felt she had no choice but to escape.

When she could, she and the children crept from the house and hurried over to her brother's. She had assumed her husband would eventually come after her, which he did. But she had a plan. When he and friends began pounding on her brother's front door, she and her sons raced out the back and jumped over the side wall next to her brother's home. They landed in the yard of the family next door, who took them in overnight. The next day, Farida and her sons made it to the home of a former co-worker from her Norwegian Church Aid days and they at last had a safe place to stay.

While there, she became sick and, with a high fever, began to hallucinate. She thought she was going to die. She dreamed she saw a container filled with small bits of paper, each of which read, "All our prayers are with you."

"When I woke up there was no pain," she says. "I prayed and thanked Allah."

It was also Thanksgiving week and, of all people, Senator Clinton was in Kabul to help American troops celebrate the holiday. She tried to help Farida, but Farida was forced to sneak out of Afghanistan because her husband had obtained a court order to keep her and the children there.

The United Nations' Rina Amiri and friends in the United States pleaded with the U.S. State Department to speed up Farida's paperwork. She had so much support that Farida says a State Department official later told her that everyone was encouraging them to act, and it became their top priority to bring back Farida and her children.

She and her sons are now back in Virginia. The boys lost a year's schooling. Farida lost all their belongings because the landlord threw away her stuff when he evicted her for not paying rent while she was held in Afghanistan. But she was able to get her job back with the

Vital Voices Global Partnership. She now has a new, neatly kept apartment in suburban Virginia, and feels blessed that her sons will have a better life. She, too, has fulfilling work, which includes taking in other struggling Muslim women to her apartment.

And, of course, she continues to work to help bring peace to Afghanistan.

"There have been twenty-five years of war," she observes. "How can you have any stability with all that war?"

Many in Afghanistan, she adds, no longer know how to resolve disputes peacefully. "They are used to speaking with a weapon."

❖ 31 ❖

Tania, the Runaway

For years, Tania's family had eked out an existence in a refugee camp in a strange country, trying to wait out the violence in their homeland. It has been a familiar plight for millions of Africans and Asians fleeing wars and violence. Finally, there was word that Tania's family could go home: The oligarchy had been overthrown. There was the promise of peace.

To get home, Tania's family trudged hundreds of miles across mountains and arid lands. They were reunited with members of their extended family whom they hadn't seen in years. The welcome home was sweet, indeed.

But the reunions were soon to become a nightmare for Tania, now twenty-three. One of her father's brothers, who had remained in their country, rapidly made up for lost time with his long-absent brother. Both now had grown sons and daughters and within a month after the homecoming, the brother suggested to Tania's father that their two families cement their ties with marriage: Tania would marry his son and one of her brothers would marry his daughter.

Although in most of the United States marriage to a first cousin is illegal, in Tania's third-world country—one of the poorest on the planet—the tribal ways are very much in force. Families have inter-married for centuries, and the tradition still goes on today. As such, the proposal was considered not strange, but entirely proper. To this day, fathers like Tania's are arranging the marriages of their children, especially their daughters, for it is considered wise for the fathers to choose their daughters' husbands and it is a dishonor to the family if the daughter does not comply. Tania's father thought about the offer and agreed to it, thinking that his brother's children would be good for his. He had met his nephew and niece and was impressed with them.

Tania had also met her husband-to-be and thought he seemed acceptable, even pleasant. Well, he was family, wasn't he? "He seemed nice," she remarked, "but you know how some people change?"

That's what happened to her: The man she thought she was marrying turned out to be entirely different after the agreement was reached. The polite older man—he was about a half dozen years her senior—suddenly became arrogant, abusive, and controlling as soon as their engagement became public. As far as he was concerned, even before their marriage, she became his property to manage as he saw fit, an attitude that included meting out corporeal punishment.

"He hit me so many times," she admits.

The first time stunned her—he just smacked her for some minor thing she can't even remember. It escalated to beatings and threats that he would kill her family if she did not do as he said. Traditionally, opinion in her country was on *his* side: There have been honor killings before if family members thought they had been dishonored.

Tania was taken aback at this man whom she had trusted. "We never thought the family was like this, that they were so violent," she says. They were, after all, blood kin—and Tania's family was not violent.

He also ordered Tania about. "He would tell me, 'You are my property. You have to do what I tell you to do.' "

At about the time Tania was decided that she couldn't possibly go through with this marriage, her brother, who was betrothed to her fiancé's sister, began having second thoughts, too. She was not what he had thought he was getting, either. His and Tania's unease about their future spouses only worsened as weeks went by, but they suddenly found their situation impossible to get out of. It is a sign of disgrace if an engagement is broken and the other family was making threats if the marriages did not go through.

Tania did not see how she could marry this man. She had finished her high school education—a rarity for women in her country where many today remain illiterate—and was looking forward to college. She had a rare opportunity to study agriculture in the United States, and would be able to learn about farming techniques in a three-week seminar. The program was designed so that she could, in turn, then pass on to other people in her country what she learned. It was a great opportunity for her—the beginning of a fine education and a virtual assurance of work for her once she returned home. But there was one major problem—her fiancé refused to let her out of his sight, and refused to let her go to America.

By this time, Tania says, "I hated him."

She decided she could no longer endure being beaten and ordered about. She decided to tell him that she could not marry him. It was over. And, indeed, she went through with her plan.

Then she had second thoughts—and fears. What if he did come after her family? There had to be a better way to get rid of him without her family suffering retribution.

That's when she came up with the idea of apologizing to him and saying she had been confused. She told him it might be better for her to go to America, to have time by herself, to think things over. "That way I would pretend to miss him." Both of them, she added, would have time and distance to think over their future marriage. And it was, after all, only three weeks and then she would be back.

She was relieved when he agreed to the plan.

When she went to her family to tell them what she was going to do, her brother agreed with her. He, too, had decided likewise, and, indeed, would abruptly "disappear" so he would not have to marry.

At last, Tania boarded a plane to the United States for her course. It was at one of her classes that she met human rights activist Farida Azizi (see preceding chapter), who had endured some harrowing times herself in Afghanistan. Farida gave Tania hope.

After Tania had told Farida her story, Farida made a suggestion that changed Tania's life: Why not stay in the United States and file for political asylum? Tania would be free from any abuse. Farida was now on the board of Tahirih Center, a Virginia-based legal rights group that represented poor refugee women. She would ask if the center would take Tania's case. The center agreed.

Tania is eager to start making her way in the United States and is looking for a job. "I will do anything," she says. Her English is good and so are her prospects. Tania is confident she will eventually find work.

It is her family that she worries about. For that reason, she did not want to use her real name for this chapter, in case the publication of her story would further enrage her angry fiancé and his family. The fear was not misplaced.

After both she and her brother had escaped, her uncle's infuriated family arrived, with friends in tow, to her father's home. They demanded to know where Tania and her brother were. Tania's fiancé and the other men ransacked the house and threatened more violence if the two did not return.

"When I called my family, my mom was crying," Tania says. "It was a very bad situation."

Her ex-fiancé continues to demand her return. Tania is sometimes tempted, just to help out her family, but, she says, "I can't. I think I would be killed." Besides, she adds, "I have suffered enough. I don't want any more suffering."

❦ 32 ❧

DEMAN: SAFE FROM BOMBINGS
AND SADDAM

DEMAN ZUBAR, A KURD from northern Iraq, was only eleven years old when the bombs came. The planes flew near her Kurdish village and dropped the bombs on a nearby town, where members of her mother's side of the family lived. She never saw them again. "They died," she says, as did many others—men, women, and children—in the streets, in shops, in their homes. They were killed because they were Kurds, a minority making up about 20 percent of the Iraqi population, whom Saddam Hussein persecuted ruthlessly.

The village might have been one of those targeted for chemical warfare. Documents from the Iraqi secret police and military, captured in the 1990s, disclosed how Iraq gassed Kurdish villages as retaliation for the Kurds' support of the Iranians during the Iran-Iraq War and for starting their own rebellion. Human rights groups documented how the Iraqi military used low-flying planes to drop bombs containing nerve or mustard gas on Kurdish villages. "Saddam treated us different," Deman says. That is an understatement. In 1988 alone, the Iraq military killed 200,000 Kurds in an ethnic cleansing campaign.

Deman grew up in fear of Saddam Hussein and his military as the violence continued. In 1991, Saddam again sent troops to brutally suppress another Kurdish rebellion. Kurdish leaders thought the United States would support them after American troops chased Iraqi forces out of Kuwait during the first Gulf War in 1991. But President Bush did not send any troops or launch any bombing missions to help the unlucky Kurds. Once again, Saddam destroyed entire villages in the course of putting down the rebellion. Tens of thousands of Kurds died, while others fled to nearby Turkey.

Amid the years of bombings and military invasions, Deman's family tried to live a normal life. Deman went to school, eventually earning a nursing degree in her community near the Turkish border. She married, became pregnant, and had a daughter in 1996. But days after she had given birth, Saddam Hussein started another military campaign against the Kurds. This time, Deman and her husband decided they had had enough. With a newborn in tow, they fled to Turkey, where they asked for political asylum in the United States. Their baby was forty days old when they were flown to, of all places, a refugee camp in Guam, a U.S. territory in the western Pacific. They lived in the refugee camp for two and a half months before they could relocate to their new home in the Phoenix area.

Her husband found employment and they had a son. But the stresses of adjusting to America were too much. Deman and her husband divorced in 1999. Deman has been on her own since then.

Though others are too afraid, Deman, adamant in her dislike for Saddam, is willing to talk openly about Iraq and her new life here. A friend of hers, a Shiite from Basra near the Persian Gulf, says she fears to talk openly. "He was a dictator. Not good—horrible," she says. "He hurt my family. He forced my brother and cousins to go to wars." Three to be exact: the war against Iran, the first Gulf War, and the American invasion in 2003.

Deman's family was just as hurt by Saddam. But Deman is one of the most confident of Muslim refugee women, says Rosalind Rivera, director of the Arizona Refugee Community Center. Indeed, Deman is becoming acclimated to the United States, including its politics. "I like George Bush. Most of us like George Bush for one reason. No more Saddam Hussein."

True, she says, a violent insurgency is at work against the American troops and Iraqi people as Iraq tries to establish a new government. But she credits President Bush with transforming the country, giving it a chance to become a democracy.

She is grateful to be in America. She and her family are much safer. Her two children, now seven and nine years old, go to school.

She volunteers in their classes and helps out at the refugee center every week where she has lots of friends. She is hoping to start advanced English classes soon so that she can be a nurse here.

It has not been easy. She has struggled to take care of her children by herself. Her husband remarried and has a little boy with his new wife. Deman herself almost married again before her friends urged her to slow down the relationship and heal emotionally.

Now all her concentration is on establishing roots in America.

ᚖ 33 ᚖ

SAKINA'S MIRACLE: FROM REFUGEE
CAMP TO AMERICAN SUBURB

SAKINA GHULAM USUALLY KEPT to her home in an isolated mountain village in Afghanistan. It was too dangerous to venture outside: She feared her burqa might accidentally slip and expose her face for a few seconds—even if it was just her nose or a strand of hair.

Terrible punishment was in store for her or any other woman caught not obeying the Taliban's draconian orders for women to cover themselves in public from head to toe. Since the Taliban had taken control of Afghanistan, women's lives had been targeted by a fundamentalist government that kept women virtual prisoners in their own homes. Despite worldwide criticism, the Taliban imposed a harsh interpretation of the Quran's edict for women to be modest, even forbidding male doctors to see women and girls as patients. Sakina says women weren't allowed to give birth with a male doctor present, and some resorted to delivering their babies in backyards.

The women and small girls in her village were all illiterate. Above all, they lived in fear. The Taliban had its spies who helped maintain rigid control over the sparsely populated country. "Their followers were everywhere," Sakina says. And the Taliban had been known to impose swift justice on "bad" women. A "light" punishment was the public cutting of a woman's hair to humiliate her for a slipped burqa. An alleged adulteress risked being shot to death. By the time the United States had invaded Afghanistan, many women were terrified to venture outside their home.

Sakina's family was able to eke out a living until the Taliban rounded up her husband and oldest son. They were taken without explanation, and Sakima was beside herself. Even in a best-case scenario—that they remained alive—they would no doubt be tortured. And there was no way of knowing when they would get out of jail.

At home, she and her remaining three sons faced desperate circumstances. She had no way to support them. Food and water were already scarce.

Desperate people do desperate things and one night Sakina summoned the courage to abandon their home and escape with her three sons. In the dark of the night they crept out of their house. For five days and nights, they climbed through the mountains, trudging on treacherous unmarked terrain, not daring to use any roads.

And then their first miracle came.

Somehow, an Afghan man driving a farm tractor spotted them. Rather than turn them in, he took pity on them. He motioned for them to get on the tractor and he gave them a ride to the nearby border. They made it safely to an area just inside Pakistan, where the United Nations and charities from around the world were caring for refugees.

Sakina still talks about their second miracle in awed whispers. The family came upon what they thought were United Nations workers. Sakina was eager to feed her sons, and she had been told she had to sign papers with an *X* to obtain rations. Sure enough, the workers asked her questions; she patiently answered them and they held out papers to sign. She carefully wrote her *X*.

Only this wasn't an application for food. It was for U.S. refugee relief—and by sheer luck Sakina was signing to start the paperwork for her and her sons to come to America under a federal emergency program to help refugees. This, despite the hundreds of thousands languishing in refugee camps in Asia and Africa for years. A worldwide waiting list of refugees hoping to come to the United States grows longer by the day, applications being held up by extra screening of newcomers after 9/11.

Yet Sakina's extraordinary luck held. Two years ago, she and her sons were whisked from their sorrowful past to a new life in suburban Phoenix, where they moved into one smallish apartment. Later Sakina found a better one in middle-class Glendale, where they are close to the Arizona Refugee Community Center that provides them with

English classes and other social programs. They felt at home in Glendale: It turned out to be a Muslim refugee enclave. In some Glendale neighborhoods it is common to see women wearing *hijabs* as they walk or drive cars.

Life was not easy at first. Sakina's health in Arizona started out weak. She could not walk for great lengths or even climb stairs. She also had to come to terms with the trauma of her past life. She signed up for Catholic Charities' counseling for victims or relatives of those who have been tortured or experienced war.

The only problem was logistical. The therapy sessions were held on the second floor of a building without an elevator. That didn't deter Sakina. If she couldn't walk up the stairs, she crawled.

Sakina and her sons started adjusting and soon were thriving in their new life in America. For the first time they had something most Americans take for granted: running water. There was a dazzling array of groceries at supermarkets, and the United States government had provided food stamps. The family's health improved simply from eating regularly. Other amenities they enjoyed for the first time included electric lights, heating, air conditioning, and indoor toilets.

Best of all, Sakina says, there is peace in her new home, and opportunity. She and her children, she says, live in a quiet area and no longer fear being picked up by the Taliban. Americans are kind, she adds. Through a translator, she reports, "They have been helping people. They help us go to school—this is important for my children." And Sakina considers education crucial.

Consider her persistence: Despite being forty-something, she began assiduously attending classes at the Arizona Refugee Community Center, not missing a session. She labored over learning the Roman alphabet and writing in cursive.

Today, Sakina is proud to have graduated from her first reading class and has moved on to studying more advanced English. She is no longer illiterate and now signs her name with a flourish.

Sakina herself is amazed at her resilience: For a middle-aged woman, learning how to read and write as well as navigate a new and complicated country, with a different language and culture, cannot help but be daunting.

Sakina is equally proud of her sons' educational accomplishments.

They are all doing well in school. They also help Sakina by explaining American rules and customs.

Today, Sakina especially cherishes her family's new freedom. The burqa is now a thing of her past.

"We couldn't walk," she says of the bulky garment that hobbled her movement. "We couldn't see. We couldn't talk." Now she can go into stores at ease, or even take an evening stroll.

Not that she has abandoned Islamic dictates for modesty. She wears long-sleeved blouses and long skirts or pants to cover her legs, as well as a filmy chiffon scarf that she drapes around her head and neck—what she calls a chador.

According to Sakina, she likes the chador, wants to keep her Islamic faith. During Ramadan she is eager to get home to prepare the evening meal that breaks the daylong fast.

She has recently gotten good news. Her Taliban-jailed husband and son are alive; they both escaped to Iran. She spoke to her father, who assured her that the two are safe. When Sakina had fled to Pakistan, her husband headed toward the Iranian border and managed to slip across. Now they are trying to make it back to Afghanistan so they too can get help from American agencies to reunite them with their family.

Sakina hopes that eventually they will be together again. When that happens, her husband and son can start over in the United States, as she and the three other boys have. They deserve, she feels, what she and the other children now enjoy.

"We have freedom," she says simply.

❧ 34 ❧

SHAIMA: RECOVERING FROM HER
HUSBAND'S MURDER

SHAIMA SHIFFATI WAS EAGER to go to work in the United States after escaping Afghanistan where her husband was murdered. She and her four children had languished in a refugee camp where there seemed no hope.

As soon as they were flown into Phoenix, she signed up for whatever available job there was. It turned out to be in a candy factory, which was fine with her.

But it was not to be. When she arrived in the U.S., she was suffering from a host of physical problems, including headaches and body aches. These are symptoms of post-traumatic stress disorder, made worse when Shaima probably took on more than she could endure at a time when she was starting over in a new country. She was still grieving for her late husband while trying to care for her four children and adapt to a foreign land, language, and culture.

She became so sick she had to quit the factory and it is only now, about two years later, that she is feeling better. Shaima says she had a nervous breakdown. But what came to a head in the United States began when she became ill in Afghanistan. She remembers she was neatening up her house near Kabul when, in disbelief, she watched as men from the village carried her husband's body into the house. He had been shot to death at their small store in town. She collapsed at the shock.

It was too much to bear, she now says, almost five years later. She struggled during the months ahead to rise above the grief and

195

depression that engulfed her, realizing that she had to regain her equilibrium: She had four children to raise. And yet she was exhausted by the never-ending violence and the grief it brings.

"It was thirty years of war," she says through an interpreter. "They destroyed everything." And she never found out why her husband was murdered.

After her husband died, she suffered from relentless fear. She felt virtually confined to her home under the Taliban's edict that required women to be covered while in public. She had trouble collecting her thoughts, even thinking in a rational way, and she endured nightmares and physical tremors. "I was afraid to live in Afghanistan without my husband," she says. And it wasn't just the fear of a bullet. How was she going to support her family? As a woman she could not operate their former shop: The Taliban forbade women touching men not their husbands or relatives. So how could she be a shopkeeper? How could she even see in the store wearing a head-to-toe burqa that had only slits for her eyes?

Plus, she says, "I had heart problems after my husband died."

In desperation, she decided to abandon the family's house. She would join other Afghanis going to Pakistan. One of her husband's friends gave her money and helped her cross the border with her two sons and two daughters. Her children found work making Persian-style carpets, doing the tedious hand-threading of intricate patterns that such rugs are known for. It was very hard work, but for two years, like thousands of other Afghan refugees, they eked out an existence in Pakistan.

Then President Clinton entered her life. "He wanted to save widows in Afghanistan," she says. Shaima went to the refugee resettlement program and signed up.

Today, she loves the Arizona weather, especially in the winter. She likes that she can see mountains in her new home, much like the mountains she grew up near in Afghanistan.

She is within walking distance of the refugee center where she goes to school to learn how to read and write. Her son has saved enough money to buy a car. He takes her grocery shopping. Otherwise, she likes to walk in the neighborhood. It is so safe.

Shaima and her children are filled with hope. Her children go to school and study hard. They know how important it is to learn.

"Education for the kids," Shaima declares. "That's the most important thing to me. They have opportunity here. In Afghanistan, they had no future."

❧ 35 ❧

SALMA'S JOURNEY

MOST AMERICANS PRIDE THEMSELVES on their tolerance. They remain insulated from the religious strife that has engulfed other parts of the world. Indeed, they are unaware of ongoing clashes between religious groups that have sometimes endured for centuries. Muslim minorities have been particularly persecuted. In India, Hindu mobs have routinely attacked and killed Muslims, especially after the predominantly Muslim country of Pakistan was carved out of India in the 1940s. Human rights organizations have detailed this anti-Muslim violence for decades. But few Americans know of the ongoing tension. Except for an occasional story in *The New York Times* or on National Public Radio, the violence remains unreported in the United States.

As a teenager, Salma lived through the terror of some Hindus attacking her Muslim neighborhood in India in December 1992. Her family's Imam and his assistant were hacked to pieces a few blocks from their home. The horrified congregation discovered the strewn body parts as they arrived for Friday prayers. Around India, Hindu mobs went into a violent frenzy after militant Hindus rioted and destroyed the sixteenth-century Babri mosque. Hindu extremists had bitterly hated the historic mosque, believing centuries-old allegations that a Hindu temple had been destroyed to make room for the mosque.

Even Salma's father, a prosperous and well-regarded business owner, was terrified amid the sudden violence. The Muslims had lived in peace for decades in their Hindu-dominant city. Salma's family had felt comfortable with their Hindu neighbors. They have even invited them for holiday banquets and family dinners. Their Hindu neighbors liked to partake of chicken and lamb dishes at Muslim festivals. Salma remembers how her early friends were Hindus—and how no one thought anything of that.

But the sudden rampage ended those harmonious times, violence indiscriminately targeting Muslims while police did nothing. For the first time, Salma says, her family felt isolated, like outsiders in their own homeland.

Salma still remembers that bitter taste of betrayal. After the rioting, she could go nowhere. Her father forbade her even to visit her next-door neighbors. It was too dangerous, he decided. As a young Muslim woman, she was especially vulnerable wearing her Islamic *hijab* on the streets. So, day after day, she had to stay at home. Then came the murders—all over town. "In the name of religion, they were killing people," she said.

It was a heartbreaking time: One of the killers of Salma's Imam had been a close friend of Salma's brother. "He literally was brought up in my house," she says. "He was like a brother to us." His involvement was incomprehensible to the family. "How could he?" Salma still asks in wonder. Although the murderers' identities were known, the police arrested no one.

Today she is grateful for her new life: in a peaceful palm-shaded Florida suburb where neighbors are friendly. Her children play with others down the street; she exchanges cakes with neighbors. She is welcomed into her sons' elementary school to do volunteer work. She marvels how open-minded and friendly Americans are.

Salma counts her blessings: She married an Indian telecommunications executive, and they were able to emigrate first to London, then to the United States. She is relieved that their two sons will grow up in peace.

However, Salma's memories remain painful and vivid. A year ago, when Salma returned to India with her two small sons to see her family, she encountered hostilities at the Bombay airport. She was held up at immigration because the checker couldn't believe that, as a Muslim woman wearing a *hijab* and long gown, she carried an Indian passport. Salma was asked if she was "sure" that she was born in India. To prove that she was, she told the authorities, "I can speak seventeen Indian languages." Later, as she and her sons were in line, an Indian official sneered at her, muttering "We should kick all of you out of the country." When, after their return flight, they landed in London and Salma retrieved her luggage, she discovered that their cloth bags had been slashed open, her clothing hanging out and her jewelry gone. Salma was in tears. She claims that the airline promised her reimbursement for the lost items but none was ever made.

Since she relocated to the United States, she is still amazed at how well Americans get along. It delights her that she and her family can live in a community where neighbors welcome them. Nor is there the degree of illiteracy or ignorance that spawns wholesale violence, she adds. However, she was once accosted by a man in a pickup truck while visiting Atlanta. He apparently did not like her wearing her *hijab*. When he yelled and gave her the finger, she simply laughed him off. Salma cites this as an example of how safe she feels in America. She could not have guaranteed the same would have happened in India.

After 9/11, however, Salma went into a depression.

"I was literally in tears. I hoped Muslims were not involved." She was scared that there would be outbreaks of anti-Muslim violence, as there had been in India. But except for scattered reports of individuals attacking people they thought were Muslims, people were safe. It comforted Salma that President Bush attended mosque to show his solidarity with Muslims, as did other U.S. leaders. Salma marvels at the maturity of the American people during those times when everyone was stunned—and enraged—over 9/11.

When Salma and her husband moved to a new Florida neighborhood, where the schools are among the best in the area, Salma was at first apprehensive about wearing her *hijab* in public. But she was rewarded with indifference; she still marvels how most people don't single her out. If they do, it's because they are curious, she says, about her faith.

To celebrate her new neighborhood, Salma baked cakes for her neighbors. "This was my way of saying hello." She was touched to receive thank-you notes, and one neighbor returned the gesture and made Salma and her family a peach cobbler. "Now we all know each other—Christians, Jews, and Muslims."

She also wanted to educate her neighbors about Ramadan—but in a fun way. So she made cakes and her sons wrote notes about their faith. Then they delivered them. Salma has been gratified by how touched people have been by her culinary gifts.

Just like any other American mother, she volunteers at her sons' school. She was a weekly tutor at her younger son's kindergarten class. The children loved her for her sense of fun and mimicry. They felt they could ask her what was that thing she was wearing on her head. Salma playfully told them, "It makes me look prettier and it's for my religion." The children then asked if they could wear it, and Salma plopped her silken scarf on each child who giggled.

At the school's open house, Salma was stunned at how the children came running to her to introduce her to their families. "They hugged and kissed me," she says. The parents were surprised too, but only one woman refused to shake Salma's hand. Salma shrugs it off. The woman was probably a snob, she thinks. Salma is not interested in blame. The people where she lives are too nice and she's too busy to fret over slights. Still, she has noticed that some parents hold their children close to them when she passes by in her hijab. She stays serene, though. And she still keeps busy volunteering at the school. Teachers love her. They wish other parents were as diligent and caring.

All the same, these are disquieting times. Some Muslim families from Salma's mosque have moved to other countries, no longer feeling, she says, welcome in the United States. After 9/11, a Palestinian immigrant she knew at her mosque was abruptly arrested, and no one in the congregation has seen him again. He later was mentioned in the newspaper as a terrorist suspect who allegedly used Muslim charity money to support terrorism around the world. All of this mystifies Salma. True, he was a loudmouth, especially about the Palestinian cause, she thought, but he never seemed dangerous. After his arrest, the mosque helped support his family—he had a wife and three small children. But as his detention turned from days into weeks, and finally months, his wife gave up and went back to the Middle East, Salma says.

What Salma would like to see is an America before 9/11: full of serenity. She has dreams of America returning to what she considers a better era—say, the 1950s and 1960s, when family values were stronger, when piety was welcomed.

But even today, the United States, with its looser values, has a big advantage over other countries: its tradition of tolerance. Grateful to live in such a climate, Salma is repaying America for its generosity to her with loyalty to her new country. After all, she says, the Quran requires that. "You're supposed to be loyal and follow the rules," Salma says. "Otherwise your Islam is not complete, and you are not a good Muslim."

❦ 36 ❧

Hawa: The Queen Takes a Walk

Hawa Khamis wears a flowing white robe and scarf with bright blue trim as she adroitly maneuvers a stroller that seats her baby. Her two preschool boys are walking alongside her, clinging to her robe.

She is tall, perhaps more than six feet. Indeed, Hawa, thirty-one, is a striking woman with a wide smile that flashes brilliant white teeth. Her posture would be the envy of any queen, as she walks regally to the refugee center in Glendale, Arizona. Here is where she is learning English, and how to read for the first time. Here, also, she finds Arabic-speaking people who can provide a link to what now seems like a distant past.

She was only in her mid-twenties with two toddlers (she now has five children) when she arrived in the United States with her husband to escape the violence in their native Sudan. Today there's awareness among Americans of the genocide that is occurring there, particularly against Christians in the south. But Hawa, a devout Muslim, reports that people of her faith have been targeted for violence too. Humanitarian groups have documented how the predominantly Arab Muslim regime routinely attacks native tribes, whether or not the tribes are Muslims. They report of Arab militias raiding villages at night, burning every house and shooting those who try to escape. Sudan has also suffered serious food shortages and drought, driving many from their homes simply to survive. The war—and there has been war since 1983—has displaced millions. More than 10 percent of the world's uprooted population are Sudanese.

"It was very difficult—there were too many problems," Hawa says before adding quietly, "One of my brothers got killed there."

A sister remains in the Sudan but Hawa and her husband decided they had to get out. They took their two children and fled east, crossing into Ethiopia, where they stayed in a refugee camp. Hawa is not one to talk about the conditions there. Suffice it to say, they eked out a living until they could come to the United States. They were lucky: Many still languish in the makeshift camps.

Like many other third-world refugee women, Hawa was illiterate when she arrived in Arizona. The United States government estimates that about half of women in the Sudan can't read or write. Overall, the literacy rate is just over 60 percent, with more men than women educated. But Hawa now has opportunities to learn that she never had before, even though the demands of being a young mother restrict her, at least for now. With her husband working and studying, she needs to be at home taking care of the children. (Her husband once teased her that she had already had enough education in America, remarking in front of her, "I sent her to school six months and now she needs more?") Hawa may be too busy with a new baby to go to formal classes, but she *is* learning.

Hawa is glad that her family can have a normal life again and settle into a routine. She is grateful she can walk wherever she wants to, without fearing for her or the children's safety. It wasn't like that in Sudan.

However, because Hawa now lives in the United States, where few women wear traditional Muslim dress, doesn't mean that she is going to quit wearing her flowing robe, the long turban-like scarf that frames her face while discreetly covering her hair. She dresses as a proper Muslim woman would in her native Sudan. In that sense, America hasn't changed her, and it won't.

"My religion is very important," Hawa says. She's not one to go to the mosque, though. In her opinion, that's for the men. "Only my husband goes."

Meanwhile, she is busy tending her children, the oldest of whom is ten. By now, even he finds Sudan and its violence a distant memory. Hawa's youngest three were born here and are American citizens.

Hawa and her husband like the Southwest, where the weather

reminds them of their homeland. But the similarities end there: Arizona is peaceful, and they feel safe here. "We like it here because we are free."

Education, she feels, is the best benefit of life in America. Her school-age children are learning how to read and write. She herself must sacrifice her own English classes to take care of her youngest preschoolers. But soon they will be going to school and Hawa lights up at the thought that all her children will be educated. She's got a handful but she is the queen: All she has to do is gesture, or softly say a few words, and the children obey.

PART V

The Changers

I f they see something wrong, they want to change it. They are the Changers: Muslim women in America out in the forefront of politics, religion, law, academia, and human rights organizations.

One is following an unorthodox path: W. L. Cati is a former Muslim who became an evangelical Christian minister trying to help abused Muslim women. She knows their pain firsthand: She says she herself was abused, often in the name of Islam.

But the great majority of Changers remain in the faith as they sort out problems. Clareen Menzies describes how she also was a battered wife. But she stayed with Islam and became a Muslim leader in the Minneapolis-St. Paul area.

Many of the Changers have made inroads in more than one profession or cause. Zakia Mahasa, profiled in chapter 45, is believed to be the first Muslim woman appointed to a judicial position in the United States. She is a Master in Chancery in the Family Division of the Baltimore City Circuit Court. Master Mahasa also leads the Michigan-based Muslim charity Mercy USA as volunteer chairperson. "You have to have balance," Master Mahasa says. "You can't be all about your career." Indeed, Sarah Eltantawi took time out from her future academic career—she is working on a doctorate at Harvard— to help start the Progressive Muslim Union of North America. She says there's a need for another "voice" in the Muslim community as an alternative to the conservative imams in the United States.

Reforms are inevitable, declares Ingrid Mattson. As vice president of the Islamic Society of North America, she is one of the nation's top female Muslim leaders. Fighting for equal treatment of women, she says she does not want anyone to feel left out of a faith that has enriched her life.

Other women have helped reinterpret the Quran, such as Azizih al-Hibri, a law professor at Virginia's University of Richmond. She has analyzed the status of women in the Islamic family laws and found women benefited from its requirement that men support their wives and children. Through studying the Quran, she discovered how the Prophet Muhammad promoted the treatment of women. However, she says Islam has been misinterpreted by male religious leaders to shore up their power and keep women subservient. In Washington, D.C., she started a human rights group to help women globally. She named her group Karamah, after an Arabic reference to a Quranic verse that reads, "We have given dignity to the children of Adam." Her group has attracted the notice of President Bush and Secretary of State Condoleeza Rice (who was the country's National Security Advisor when she spoke at a Karamah gathering).

Many Changers say America's Muslims face pressing matters, including defending their civil rights. Muslims are under attack with the USA Patriot Act and other new laws, says Dalia Hashad, a leader in the American Civil Liberties Union. She describes how she is helping lead a national effort to protect Muslims' civil liberties.

Other *Muslimah* Changers feel the heightened tensions from the war on terrorism and are trying to educate non-Muslims about how Islam promotes peace. Sarwat Husain, herself the victim of a hate crime, started a newspaper to help educate about Islam, for both Muslims and non-Muslims. She is also a volunteer in San Antonio, Texas, for the Council of American-Islamic Relations and frequently holds press conferences to denounce terrorism and other acts of violence. Her loyalties and responsibilities are to both the United States and Islam, she says. "America is my home," Sarwat says, "and whatever I can do to serve this 'land of the free and the home of the brave,' I will do."

She is among the dynamic leaders profiled in the following chapters as changing America and Islam. ⌁

❧ 37 ❧

Sarah: Progressive and Proud of It

IT'S IN THE DEAD OF WINTER—frankly, drearily, January cold—and former Californian Sarah Eltantawi is flying to one of the coldest spots in the United States: Chicago. But it's important. The twenty-eight-year-old wants to speak to a group of Muslims to correct what she calls the "great misunderstanding." She wants to say that the newly started Progressive Muslim Union of North America—PMU as she affectionately shortens it—is not the bugaboo that so many conservative Muslims seem to fear. Just go to the website, for example, she says, and see how the PMU advocates reading the Quran.

But also make no mistake: The progressives want structural change, what Sarah calls "new institutions to reflect the values and lives of Muslims."

These changes include accepting gays as equals, women as clergy, and allowing men and women to pray side by side instead of the now segregated services that are conducted at nearly all the mosques in America. They want the faithful to read and interpret the Quran themselves instead of relying on Islamic scholars, many of whom over the centuries have interpreted passages of the Quran to treat women as second-class citizens.

"I'm traveling everywhere answering questions," she says before adding cheerfully, "It was a rough beginning but the PMU is going to survive."

She's still a bit surprised at how she came to where she is now: in the center of a hailstorm of controversy.

209

But then she knows what it is like to take on controversial issues. She has defended Palestinians on national television shows, walked through the front doors of a mosque that were for men only, and defended women's right to choose whether they wear a veil or not.

Such positions have earned her enmity from all sides, from conservative Muslims to those bashing her for being anti-Jewish.

"I need an 'enemy' and I found her. Her name is Sarah Eltantawi and this smug American of Egyptian background is a walking and talking 24/7 rationalizer for terrorism," wrote a man on the Internet who called himself Andrew. He was fuming after Sarah had appeared on Fox's *Hannity & Colmes* in 2002 and criticized Israel for "occupying three million people, humiliating them, setting up checkpoints, and turning their life into a hell."

But Sarah holds strong feelings—she was in the Palestinian West Bank just before the Intifada broke out. She says she saw the daily humiliations and violence the Palestinians were forced to endure. She remains concerned about what she calls the ongoing psychological and physical abuse of Palestinians. To her, it is as much a kind of apartheid as what blacks had to endure in South Africa.

"These people (like Andrew) who call me a terrorist sympathizer are like children throwing a temper tantrum on a playground, covering their ears, sticking out their tongue and screaming at the top of their lungs to avoid getting down to the nuts and bolts of this situation," she says. "I am confident that one day their racism will be exposed, and then we'll travel down the road of healing and peace."

Sarah feels just as strongly that reforms must come from within the mosque. That is why she joined other young Muslims in forming the Progressive Muslim Union.

At first, Associated Press reporter Carol Eisenberg marveled in the fall of 2004 when Sarah and others were forming the group: "They looked like any group of hip, young New Yorkers hanging at the Starlight Diner on West 34th Street. But this was no ordinary social hour. Crowded elbow to elbow around a long table strewn with coffee cups were eighteen men and women, mostly in jeans and T-shirts. They were thoroughly Muslim and thoroughly Western. And they were brainstorming ideas to transform Islam in America."

But then the criticism came. The Union didn't include enough voices, such as Republican Muslims. PMU had too many liberal positions. Sarah was even called a "radical."

The *New York Times'* Clyde Haberman wondered about the "conspicuous absence" of any discussion about terrorism. "Nowhere," he noted, "in the group's mission statement or in the members' remarks was terrorism mentioned. Why is that?"

Sarah tried to explain to Haberman: "We're not going to equate Islam with terrorism." Instead, she says, the PMU is trying to set a positive path for changing Islam within.

Then there is the criticism she has to fend off that the Progressive Muslim Union is too American and out of touch with other Muslims around the globe. Sarah grows exasperated when other American-born Muslims tell her that fighting for reforms within the mosque is bad and that it reflects "your American neocolonialist attitude."

"Cultural relativism is not an excuse. Abuse is abuse," she tells them bluntly.

Other Muslims in the Third World "are way more critical" and are, to her mind, clamoring just as hard for reforms.

Take the French ban on *hijabs* in schools and other religious markings. An Egyptian activist decried the controversy over the ban, worrying that women opposed to the new law were unwittingly helping promote patriarchy and the conservative faction within Islam that forces women to wear some sort of veil.

Like the activist she is, Sarah wants women to be able to choose without being pressured. She doesn't wear a *hijab*. She doesn't see a connection between covering her hair and being religious. It has wrongly become, she says, "almost a fetish piece of cloth for Muslims around the world." Sarah feels there is "weak theological evidence" for women feeling they have to cover their hair while in public. "It's not in the Quran," she adds. The actual Quranic verse that supposedly required women to cover refers to women throwing a cloth over their chest. In the seventh century, when the Quran was first being written, many Arabic women were openly walking about bare-breasted. But there is no actual demand for covering the hair, she says.

Most Muslim women today in the United States and even some predominantly Muslim Third-World countries do not wear the *hijab*, Sarah points out.

Sarah is convinced PMU members and other Muslims want change in the mosque to reflect how Muslims live in today's world. That's why many Muslims don't go to prayer services—they feel out of touch with their local mosque.

"People want to see change," Sarah emphasizes. "They want openness, critical changes."

As one such would-be reformer, she knows this firsthand. How can she be otherwise, she says, as an educated woman?

In March 2005, Sarah joined other men and women in New York, praying side by side—which is considered taboo—and listened to Amina Wadud, an Islamic expert at Virginia Commonwealth University, lead men and women in prayer, another controversial move. The participants had to brave death threats and people yelling at them as they went to the Friday service.

"It was amazing," she remembers.

Just the summer before at a West Virginia conference, she joined a movement to protest mosques' unequal, segregated treatment of women. She and four other Muslim women broke another taboo by walking into the men-only front door of a mosque and praying in the main hall. (A man joined them in solidarity.)

Normally, women are supposed to enter through the back and pray in the women-only segregated balcony. But Sarah and the activists felt enough was enough. While many Muslim women in America say they don't mind entering through rear doors, Sarah and others say they are tired of being treated as second-class citizens.

"As I was walking through the mosque," Sarah recalls, "I was not scared, but I can't say that my feelings were unambiguous. Our action drew a lot of media coverage, and it was clear that the mosque and its members were under a large amount of stress that day. Usually—given my work for the past few years—I've been on the other side of the camera, so to speak, helping the mosque fend off various accusations or threats. This time, actions I was participating in were bringing trouble and wrath to the mosque, and it was hard for me to watch older men, who reminded me of my father and uncles, looking worried, fretting, and perhaps fearing for their families and for the mosque. I'm too intimate and familiar with the fear Muslims are broadly experiencing in this country today to have not had this emotional response."

But, she adds, the women had to do it to jumpstart reforms.

"I know firsthand that no amount of politeness has been enough to get the powers that be to prioritize our rights," she says. "At best, Imams will tell you that the issue is 'too explosive' and now is 'not the time' or they don't want to offend their patrons in the Gulf; at worst, we women will continue to be called temptresses, and the 'spiritual health' of men will continue to be the uncritical priority. So I'm glad I did what I did, and I continue to admire, respect, and befriend the women I met that day, as well as the one Muslim man who marched with us."

Sarah is the daughter of Egyptian immigrants. Her father came to the United States in 1973 and her mother in 1975. They settled in southern California, where Sarah grew up. She remembers growing up in an upper-middle-class suburb of Los Angeles.

In some ways it was idyllic. She grew up in a multicultural area where Hindus, Christians, Jews and she, a Muslim, all went to school together. "I identified with everyone," she says. "I didn't identify with being a quote-Muslim-unquote."

When she asked her father about her identity, he told her she was ethnically Egyptian, her nationality was American, and her religion Islam. "That sounded fine with me," she says.

In retrospect she says she grew up in a remarkably tolerant, civil time. She and her friends socialized without thinking about religious differences. "I remember going to church all the time with friends because it was social, it was fun." She reciprocated by taking her friends to Muslim functions.

Like many other Americans, her family went to religious services off and on. Sometimes they would have spells of going every weekend to their mosque; at other times, years would go by with the family attending only on religious holidays.

Still, she remembers her father excusing himself for his daily prayers; both of her parents encouraged her to read and memorize the Quran. She is grateful for that early religious education.

What sometimes made her uncomfortable as a child of immigrants was the strict enforcement of cultural traditions that her parents brought from Egypt. Sometimes she chafed at the restrictions.

"I was never allowed to spend the night at someone's house," she says. "While I wore shorts and short skirts, it was never without a fight."

Dating? Sarah didn't even think about it.

But now she appreciates how her parents' conservatism helped her, and how savvy they were in protecting her. And they *did* allow some leeway. She could have both girls and boys as friends, for example. She could go to many social functions with her friends.

"I know there is this stereotype about Arab men but my father always raised me to be an outspoken woman. I was encouraged to have opinions, to read. I felt like I could speak to any man in the family about important issues and that was fine."

While she was growing up, her parents stressed education. They did not want her worrying about boys—finding a mate would come later, they assured her. That gave her a buffer. While other girls seemed to be excessively worrying over boys and sex, Sarah didn't have to face any pressure to be sexually active.

"Some of my female friends really obsessed about boys and sex—it took away from their intellectual development. You can spend too much time on that stuff. I was shielded from that, and I do feel lucky."

She feels she really came into her own when she went to UC Berkeley, where there were thousands of other liberals like herself. "It was utopia," she says. "I was a very driven, idealistic undergraduate."

She majored in rhetoric and English literature. After she graduated she worked for a year as a childcare coordinator at the San Quentin prison, helping provide activities for inmates' children while the inmates visited with their wives. It is there, she says, she learned how to pool other nonprofit resources to provide even more services. The local Humane Society brought in guinea pigs for the children to enjoy; other volunteers provided other activities.

Then she went to Harvard to study for a master's degree in Middle Eastern Studies. In Massachusetts, the California girl not only had to endure snow and freezing temperatures—which took a lot of getting used to—but Sarah also had to contend with what she considered an emotionally colder, more conservative, campus. Still, she appreciates what Harvard gave her. She learned how to be objective as a scholar, to not let her opinions seep into her research. "It gave me better skills," she concludes. "Your work has to be objective."

Her Harvard studies also gave her a life-changing experience: She went to the West Bank to study Arabic at a Palestinian school, just before the Intifada erupted. "I loved the West Bank," she says. "It was beautiful." But now she mourns that it has been "destroyed," with the Israelis setting up settlements everywhere. Even before she left she saw, to her chagrin and growing outrage, the increasing number of gun-toting Israeli soldiers patrolling and causing more havoc for the average Palestinian. "Even Israeli settlers carried Uzis," she says. It was apartheid, she feels. Few Americans realize how Palestinians are humiliated on a daily basis. She saw young Israeli soldiers pushing around unarmed older men—the ultimate indignity for Palestinians, who honor the elderly. "It's horrible to watch a grandfather getting beaten up," she adds. Americans don't realize that the Palestinians are being treated unjustly because the media doesn't show a true picture. "It filled me with anger of a kind I have never had," she says.

She carried that anger home, "ranting twenty-four hours a day—to my parents, family, and friends." Finally, they suggested that if she felt that way why not volunteer at the Los Angeles office of the Muslim Public Affairs Council?

At first she declined, saying, "They're going to make me wear the veil. I don't want to deal with that stuff. It's the politics I am interested in."

But she had respect for the executive director, Salam Al-Marayati, and so she went. She soon became immersed monitoring the media's reporting on the Infitada and preparing a report. This was in August 2001.

Then she was offered the job as communications director for the group in Washington. So, once again, she was back on the East Coast, arriving only a month after the terrorist attacks.

The media flooded her with calls on all subjects, from the plight of the Palestinians to how Muslim Americans feel about terrorists. Sarah tried to talk as frankly and honestly as she could. That got her into trouble—with hate e-mail such as Andrew's, that she says is "mired in fear, ignorance, and stereotypes." That can be scary, Sarah says. But she is not backing down.

"I do feel threatened and I do feel afraid," she says. But she relies on "help from friends and colleagues who go through the same abuse or worse. These people's selflessness is inspirational to me."

She also doesn't want to be lulled into thinking that giving CNN an interview is the final solution to helping solve Muslims' problems in the United States. Rather, she feels Muslims need other voices. So she is helping promote the Progressive Muslim Union, flying around the country to encourage others to stand up against conservative Imams she is convinced are holding back the faith.

She is also getting on with her own life, going back to Harvard to pursue her dream, a doctorate. She wants to study the progressive Muslim counterparts—the liberal Christians and those in the Reform Judaism movement.

She herself has felt a spiritual awakening in, of all places, crowded New York where she sees all races and ethnic groups.

"God created an amazing diversity of people, and when you put them together and leave them alone just a little," she wrote in a lyrical essay, "the result is an overwhelming sensation of peace and tranquility."

❧ 38 ❧

INGRID: THE LEADER OF
THE MOSQUES

INGRID MATTSON DOESN'T WANT women to feel unwelcome at a
house of faith that has brought her so much spiritual enrichment. As
the first woman to become vice president of the Islamic Society of
North America she feels she has a clear mandate to push for reforms.
It might seem a trivial issue, but if some women are offended that
many mosques require them to enter through a back or side door—
while the men use the front—she believes that must change. If some
women feel victimized that they are relegated to an overcrowded balcony or a basement while the men have the mosque's entire main floor
to themselves, that, too, must change. In her opinion, the recent resistance to making changes is a sign that substantial reform is in the
offing.

"We are in a struggle," she says. "I believe the struggle is now out
in the open and that it will get better soon.

"Look at it historically: Conflict increases just before a major
breakthrough. We will see a major breakthrough soon. There will always be very conservative mosques, but over the years they will come
to be marginalized."

Her own mosque in Hartford, Connecticut, is being renovated and
the new building will have a front entrance open to everyone.

In other cultures, reforms at the mosque might not be so important. Indeed, in some predominantly Muslim countries, women do not
go to mosques. "They pray at home; they have women's groups," Ingrid says. "They don't see this as a big deal."

In America, it *is*. The mosque has become a community center, much in the way synagogues and churches are used by their members. Mosques now host all sorts of programs, from marriage counseling to youth groups. It is also a gathering place for the Muslims who might not otherwise see each other.

"The mosque is such an important place," Ingrid insists, "that women need to be represented in any decisions."

She herself knows the pain of exclusion. When she was on the road, volunteering to help Afghan refugee women in Pakistan, there would come the time of day to pray. But, as a woman, she would not be able to go into certain mosques. She remembers seeing a man sweeping at the front of one—a gatekeeper to keep her and other women out. "I felt, Who are you to keep me from praying?" she remembers. "It was very frustrating."

Once, as newlyweds, Ingrid and her husband were traveling in Pakistan and the time came for prayer. They found a mosque, but it was for men only.

"My husband and I just decided I would come in," Ingrid says. "I was not going to pray on a dirty sidewalk. They weren't very happy, the doormen." Nevertheless, she and her husband were allowed to pray peacefully.

If you had told Ingrid as a teenager that she would be so concerned about prayer that she would flout rules (normally, Ingrid is quiet and soft-spoken), she would have looked at you in polite disbelief. She was born into a Catholic family in Ontario. Her father was an attorney, her mother a homemaker who cared for their seven children. Ingrid stopped going to church at age sixteen. "I just didn't have any conviction," she says. "I had no faith. By the time I was a teenager I had put religion behind me. I wasn't interested. It wasn't that I was angry—religion just had no hold on me, no grip."

While at the University of Waterloo in Canada, she began studying engineering but became taken with philosophy and made it her major. Studying philosophy helped her to think more clearly.

"I was always a thoughtful person," she says, "always thinking and reading. I wanted to live a life of integrity. But I guess I was kind of a dissatisfied person. There are things missing . . . the way people behave, the life around you. I felt there should be more meaning to life than just having fun and enjoying yourself."

She found it one summer when she went to Paris to study the history of film. There, she met some West African students who changed her life.

"They were the most incredibly generous, kind, and balanced people I had ever met." They were also Muslim. "Not overtly religious," Ingrid adds, but quiet, practicing Muslims.

She became intrigued and began asking them questions and reading about Islam. She continued her reading when she returned to Canada. Over the next year, in fact, she read and read and thought and thought.

"Over time, to my complete surprise, I felt, 'I am a Muslim.' It was a big surprise to me. I hadn't previously been able to embrace a religion."

Islam, however, offered Ingrid a path to the ethical life she had always wanted to lead.

Those feelings only intensified in the summer of 1987 when she took on a tree-planting job in British Columbia and read Fazlur Rahman's *Islam* as she traveled across the Canadian prairies. She became so immersed in his descriptions of Islamic theology and law, she wrote to Rahman, a professor at the University of Chicago, to ask if she could study with him.

To her surprise, she found a handwritten note from him when she returned home to Ontario, inviting her to Chicago to study with him. Ingrid decided to accept, but she wanted first to spend a year helping Afghan women in refugee camps in Pakistan.

That year turned out to be, she says, "the best time of my life, a great learning experience for me. You go with the idea to help people, but what you find out is that the people help you. Difficult situations bring out the worst in some people, but they also bring out the best." The refugee women, she adds, "taught me a lot about generosity, grace under pressure. They were hospitable, beautiful people."

She also met her future husband there, Amer Aetak, an Egyptian engineer who was helping construct homes and water wells for refugees—a hundred thousand of them—who were stranded in an almost desertlike section of Pakistan with no trees or shelter. They had been living under bleak conditions for years. Amer was like Ingrid: He wanted to make a difference. They fell in love and quietly married (Ingrid didn't have a wedding dress). When the refugee families found out about the marriage they did something that Ingrid remembers to this day.

"They were so sad," she said in an interview with the *Christian Science Monitor*. "They pooled what little money they had and presented me with this outfit of satin pants and a red velveteen dress with pom-poms—it was incredible."

She worked to help educate the women and girls at the camp as well as help set up medical services, women's centers, and work projects. Only a miniscule number at the camp—less than 1 percent—didn't want girls educated, and those were mostly from a tribe whose elder had claimed there was no need to teach females.

After extending her stay, Ingrid decided it was time for her and Amer to go to Chicago. She had already deferred admission to the University of Chicago in order to finish up projects at the refugee camp. Unfortunately, around that time, Professor Rahman had died after undergoing heart surgery. "I found myself there without the mentor I thought I had." Nevertheless, she remains grateful to him, and has written, "It was his book and his encouragement that inspired me to start on the path to scholarship that I had found so rewarding."

At the University of Chicago, Ingrid found the other students welcoming, the classes stimulating, and the faculty distinguished. But life was difficult: She had a daughter in 1989 and a son in 1991. Given the all-consuming demands of graduate school, she had to rely on her husband. He came through, helping take care of the children while working as an engineer, to help free up time for Ingrid to study. "It was a big blur, to be honest," Ingrid remembers. "I didn't get any sleep."

But a reward awaited her: She finished her doctoral course work and was hired at Hartford Seminary's Duncan Black Macdonald Center for the Study of Islam and Christian/Islam Relations. She finished her dissertation as she taught classes. In 1995 she was made an adviser to the Afghan delegation to the United Nations Commission on the Status of Women. This was before the Taliban had taken over and issued draconian restrictions against women.

After 9/11, she found herself swamped with media interviews with journalists who wanted her to discuss Islam. She even joined a CNN.com chat room to discuss Islam a month after the attacks. One participant asked her bluntly: "What possible justification in Islam can there be for the wholesale massacre of civilians?"

Ingrid's answer was equally to the point: "There is no justification. It is prohibited in Islamic law. It is a great sin in Islamic theology. This has been stated before and after September 11 by leading Muslim scholars throughout the world. Osama bin Laden and his group are not considered scholars or legitimate interpreters of religion by the vast majority of Muslims in the world."

She would later tell other interviewers that it was Muslims' responsibility to denounce the terrorist acts. Still, she admits it can be wearying for Muslims to respond to every action. "It's more than a full-time job," she says.

Although not a Wahhabi follower, she defends it against criticism that it has promoted terrorism. The Wahhabi movement (named after its founder, Muhammad Wahhab) began more than two hundred years ago in Saudi Arabia as a puritanical Sunni sect, Ingrid explains, to rid Islamic societies of cultural practices and rigid interpretations that had been acquired over the centuries. It was analogous to the Protestant Reformation in Europe. She feels it would not be accurate to define the movement as that of an extremely right-wing sect founded and funded by the Saudi royal family and led by Osama bin Laden, as some have alleged. She points out that Saudi scholars who are Wahhabi have denounced terrorism publicly.

In turn, many Muslim feminists in the United States denounce the Wahhabi movement for restricting women. In Saudi Arabia, they still can't vote, drive a car, or go out in public without a veil.

But Ingrid feels Muslim women continue to make progress—not only in Saudi Arabia where a growing number of women are venturing into the workforce for the first time, but globally. One of her best friends has been fighting for women's rights in Afghanistan for years, receiving death threats during the Taliban reign. Today, under the country's new government, women and girls are being educated, Ingrid says. Women are even being appointed to high government positions.

Here in America, Ingrid sees Muslim women progressing, too. While she is a peaceful person, she says, sometimes there has to be a fight for meaningful change, such as making sure everyone feels welcome into the faith.

Ingrid wants to see no one turned away from Islam. Muslim men and women should both feel equally at home when they worship. That's why she supports reforms within American mosques. "I would never take on being the vice president of the Islamic Society of North America were I not willing to be an advocate."

❧ 39 ❧

SARWAT: SPREADING THE WORD

SARWAT HUSAIN thought they were teenagers. She ignored their cat-calls as she proceeded to drive home from a conference wearing her newly acquired *hijab*. "Each time I stopped at a light, they would pull up next to me and call me all sorts of names," says Sarwat, a business-woman and community activist.

She ignored them, but they continued to follow her home, coming into her driveway, screaming names at her. At this point, Sarwat had had enough. She was going to give them a stern motherly lecture about how they had taken their prank too far. She marched over to their car, but then abruptly stopped.

"They were very scary-looking big men, about three of them in the car. I turned around very fast to get in the house. They started shoot-ing at me. I thought it was a real gun. I managed to get in the house and I turned all the lights off. My husband was in his office doing some work. I did not tell him anything, thinking he might go out and they would take a shot at him, too. I waited for about half an hour and it was all quiet. I looked to make sure it was safe before I went outside to get my stuff from the car. But as soon as I opened the door of the car, they appeared again. And again they started shooting. I barely missed one shot. I ran back in the house, called nine-one-one, told my husband what was happening."

Police came and discovered the men *had* been shooting a gun, al-beit one that shot paint balls.

"They shot at my car and it was covered with paint," Sarwat says. "Our lawn was full of paint. Police made the report and said it was hate related."

The officers never found the perpetrators but that hasn't stopped Sarwat from wearing a scarf. Before 9/11, she had never worn the *hijab* in public. But after the terrorist attacks, in an atmosphere of rising anti-Muslim sentiment, many of her veiled friends were harassed. Sarwat says she decided to wear one in solidarity. She thought it would help educate Americans to see a career woman wearing a *hijab*, that it might help change the stereotype of Muslim women being, as she put it, "backward, dominated, and uneducated."

What she wasn't prepared for was how *she* would be educated. She learned what it is like to be stared at and to be sneered at in malls and other public places. And that, one night in her car, she would get the scare of her life. Today, though, Sarwat keeps it all in perspective.

"That incident made me even stronger, *Alhumdolillah* [by the Grace of God]," she says. "Now I am used to covering my hair and I feel most comfortable. It makes me feel very secure." In addition, she doesn't have to spend time explaining who she is: The scarf identifies her as a *Muslimah*.

But she is not from where most people think: the Middle East. Nor is she an Arab. She grew up in Karachi, the largest city in Pakistan, an urban center Sarwat describes as "very cosmopolitan."

Her family was close but her father traveled a lot and was not home very much. Sarwat's mother was left in charge.

"My mother and my older sisters kept a very close eye on me, as well as my brother who is eleven months younger than me," Sarwat remembers. "We were brought up strictly in the Muslim way. As a child I was very inquisitive by nature, so when it came to practicing religion I was always asking questions with lots of whys, whats and why nots. For example, I asked why we have to pray five times daily in a certain way? Why can't we pray in our own space at our own times? To tell you the truth, many times I felt I was forced into following a religion, that I did things because everybody else was doing it. Only after coming to the States, when I was left alone to choose, without being forced to even by my husband, I began studying Islam in depth, as well as Christianity and Judaism."

Today she is proud to say she is not only a born Muslim but a Muslim by choice.

She had wanted to study in the United States but her parents didn't want her to go to a strange country by herself. Sarwat kept insisting. They kept refusing. Finally, they gave her an ultimatum: She could go—but only if she had a husband to protect her.

"Without thinking twice," she says, "I agreed to get married."

In Pakistan, arranged marriages are a purely cultural tradition and have been part of the country's heritage for hundreds of years. Sarwat's future husband had come back to Pakistan on vacation to get married. He had been working and studying for a doctorate in the United States.

"Our parents were introduced by a mutual friend," Sarwat says. "We had not met each other before we were married."

In arranged marriages in Pakistan, she adds, it becomes the parents' responsibility to find the right mate for their children. So they consider many aspects of the prospective couple, their education, maturity level, and temperament, even their personal likes and dislikes.

"Since the marriages are not based on infatuation, looks or money, the divorce rate is very low in that part of the world," Sarwat says. "It turned out that my husband and I were a good match. I call myself a hyperactive person, and my husband is very calm and mature. He has always been there to listen to me and he has encouraged me to do what I wanted to do."

After they married in Pakistan, they moved to Eau Claire, Wisconsin, where her husband was an assistant professor at the University of Wisconsin. He was also finishing his Ph.D. at the University of North Texas in Denton.

"Eau Claire was, in those days, white middle-class society where you would not even see an African American or Latin American anywhere in the city," Sarwat remembers. "When we first arrived there were a couple of Muslim students at the university. After a few years some Muslim doctors moved in. We were only about seven or eight families for the next eighteen years. There was no masjid [mosque] but we met regularly, first in our homes and later at one of the technical colleges. The Muslim families started a small Sunday school for our kids."

By then, Sarwat and her husband had a son and daughter. She was busy taking care of their children and going to school. Although she missed Pakistan and her family, many at the university were kind and "always tried their best to make me feel at home. Some of them sort of adopted me."

Sarwat found raising children in the United States a challenge. She remembers the first day at her daughter's school in Eau Claire, when she went to pick her up. "The bell rang and all the kids started running out of their classrooms, screaming and yelling, without any respect to their teachers or to their principal, who were standing there in the hallway." Such behavior shocked Sarwat. She was used to a more structured dismissal. Pakistani school children would quietly line up and say good-bye to all the teachers as they left. It was considered respectful. So she decided her children would be better off not going to American public schools. Instead, she enrolled them in Catholic schools, where, Sarwat says, morals and values were taught similar to those in Islamic-based schools. She and her husband also taught their faith to their children at home. On Sundays, they took them to Muslim school in nearby Minneapolis.

"The Twin Cities were about a hundred miles from Eau Claire, but no matter what, we were on the road every weekend. We wanted our children to have a chance to meet other Muslim kids and to be able to learn religion in a school environment."

During those years, it was "very lonesome" for Sarwat at Christmas time, with so few Muslim families in Eau Claire. All the streets seemed deserted and most of the people stayed home after they had gone to church. Sarwat and her family often used the Christmas break as a time to travel. But before they left, they always gave a Christmas party for the faculty and others.

Despite a busy schedule, Sarwat saw to it the party was held every year. She wanted to share in the American Christmas tradition, and it wasn't hard: Sarwat describes herself as a "born activist," who needed to have a lot of balls to juggle.

"Probably I am a restless person, who has to have something to do. In addition to working, I've always had hobbies—reading, writing, speaking, cooking, sewing, painting, sculpture, decorating, music, and entertaining. Twenty-four hours in the day are never enough. I need more work than there is time to do it in!"

After finishing college in Wisconsin, she juggled work with taking care of her children. She became a nutritional consultant to nine area nursing homes. "This was the first time I was exposed to the institutionalized elderly. In our culture respect for your elders is inherent. In Islam your parents are your responsibility and it is a form of worship to take good care of them. For me to see all these beautiful but helpless elderly being warehoused, either because their children could not or would not keep them, was unimaginable to me. While working for those places I felt the need to create group homes where I could at least give them a more homelike environment. I told my husband about my plan and he backed me up a hundred percent. In those days no such group homes or alternate care facilities existed for the elderly. We opened three, one after another. Although I ran those facilities for many years, I had one question in my mind that always made me feel very uneasy: How could children leave their own parents in institutions?"

Nevertheless, she found working with American seniors "very rewarding—I felt I was making a difference."

In 1989 Sarwat's in-laws moved from Pakistan to Texas. As their other three children were already in the Lone Star State, they wanted their entire family to be reunited in Texas. It was a hard decision for Sarwat and her husband, as they had been in Wisconsin for years. Her husband was offered a teaching position at Sul Ross State University in Uvalde, Texas. He was to be a professor and chairman of the Business Department.

Sarwat found Uvalde "nice" but too small. After living there for two years, they moved to San Antonio, where they eventually bought a child development center.

"I was happy running the center while my husband was doing consulting for small businesses." Sarwat's life and career remained stable—until 9/11.

"That moment just turned me around," Sarwat remembers. "My first feeling was, How dare anybody do something like this in our country! I felt a very strong sense of responsibility, an urge to do something more than what I was already doing as an American and as a Muslim to build bridges, to show how alike we all are."

She also wanted to dispel stereotypes about Muslim women. Even before 9/11, she had written occasional op-ed pieces for the local newspaper and talked about Islam at churches, schools, universities, and other organizations. After 9/11 she decided this was not enough.

"I wanted to provide an alternative to the day-in, day-out bashing of Islam and Muslims in the U.S. media. It may have boosted ratings, but it also hurt Americans who happen to be Muslims and divided our beautiful country."

Meanwhile, she adds, the number of hate crimes against Muslims kept increasing, locally and across the nation, no matter how she stepped up her writing or public appearances. She decided to try something new: She started publishing her own newspaper, *Al-Ittihaad Monthly*, which means "Unity." In the beginning it circulated only in San Antonio, but within two months it was distributed throughout Texas.

"We have a huge non-Muslim readership. I think my newspaper is popular because Muslims need to have their own voice and many non-Muslims are hungry to find out more about Islam and Muslims. The timing for the paper was just right."

In Texas, she points out, there are other Muslim newspapers, but they all are rather specialized. "There are Arab newspapers for Arabs, Pakistani newspapers for Pakistani readers, or small newspapers intended for local areas." Sarwat wanted to publish a newspaper for *everyone*. It is free. "We try to cover the cost through advertisements as much as possible. First it was tabloid size, but now it is full size."

The paper has been in operation more than two years and went nationwide in September 2004, thanks to subscriptions and distribution by mosques and other Islamic organizations.

"My vision for *Al-Ittihaad* is to rebuild the broken bridges among American Muslims and non-Muslims. When I started the paper, I mainly dealt with religious topics. But then I felt the need to report the other side of the stories that were being aired from the perspective of American media or the government. We write about Islamic events or issues that you would not see anywhere else, such as Muslims' involvement in politics, civil rights, and human rights. We cover stories about

Muslim children, discrimination, and detentions of innocent Muslims taking place all over the country. We publish anything that needs to be said that isn't being voiced elsewhere. It has become my life's mission!"

Sarwat also has worked with others to start a San Antonio chapter of the Council on American-Islamic Relations, the largest Muslim civil rights and advocacy group in the United States, and she has become its chairwoman. She also works with Hispanics and other groups to make sure immigrants are treated fairly. Of course, she is continuing to help educate non-Muslim Americans about the Islamic faith.

Sarwat feels deeply that she is now part of both cultures, proud to be a Muslim and an American. Her loyalties and responsibilities are to both, she says. "America is my home and whatever I can do to serve this 'land of the free and home of the brave,' I will do."

LAILA'S HEAVY CASELOAD:
AN M.D. WITH A CAUSE

RIGHT NOW, DR. LAILA AL-MARAYATI, a board-certified obstetrician/gynecologist, is worried about one of her patients, a young woman in Los Angeles who has developed complications while pregnant. Hers is a high-risk pregnancy, but she has no support system. Her boyfriend is overseas in the U.S. military and he can't obtain leave to help her because they are not married.

These are the things that drive Laila crazy—rules that keep people from getting the help they need. But it is not only the American healthcare system that this forty-two-year-old doctor is concerned about. Laila, an international human rights activist and former presidential appointee, worries that the United States is increasingly limiting the rights of Arab Americans and others who have been unfairly tarnished on account of their faith or where they're from.

Laila is American-born. Her mother is an American who married a Palestinian doctor who became a naturalized citizen. Even though Laila is not a first-generation Palestinian immigrant, she says she faces obstacles that other Americans do not. When traveling, she is not free to go anywhere she wants. In 2004, Israel refused to allow her to enter at the Jordanian border to visit family members living in the Gaza Strip. She had made the trip with her sister specifically to see a sick uncle, a Palestinian now living in Jordan. For Americans it is normally not a problem to go between Israel and Jordan. Many American tourists want to visit both countries, if only to see the ancient religious and historical sites there.

But the Israelis at the border crossing wouldn't let her in. "They would not tell us why. They sent us back to Jordan. It was a big shock—I couldn't even see my family. The Israeli border patrol officer was yelling at us. He was so angry and mean."

She is not sure when she will venture back again. She wants to see her family but on the other hand, doesn't want to go all that way only to be turned back at the Israeli airport, as have other Palestinian Americans in recent years.

"My relatives are in the Gaza Strip, rather than in the West Bank, and the Gaza Strip is much harder to go to."

Although her father's family in Gaza goes back generations, they have lost a lot of property over the years. "Since the end of the Six Day War in 1967," Laila explains, "it's been increasingly difficult."

Most Americans aren't aware of such complications, she says. Nor are they aware that if she speaks publicly in defense of her ancestry or on behalf of other Palestinians or Muslims, she will likely be branded an "extremist" and "anti-Israel." She says she is neither. "Some of the things that have been said about me are ugly, really ugly. It is something I don't understand."

When in 1999 President Clinton named Laila to the State Department's United States Commission on International Religious Freedom, she was immediately attacked. The Zionist Organization of America, for example, issued a press release that called her a "Muslim extremist with ties to Israel-haters." The group did not quote Laila as saying anything anti-Semitic or anything anti-Israel. What was used against her were remarks she made in 1997, from a speech delivered as a Muslim member of the State Department's Advisory Committee on Religious Freedom Abroad. In that address, she wanted to introduce a "sense of balance" so that all religious persecution could be looked at. The Zionist Organization also took her to task for claiming that Israelis had denied Palestinian Muslims and Christians access to their places of worship, which the Zionist Organization denounced as "lies." Nevertheless, despite the outcry, President Clinton did not back down and Laila went on to serve two years on the Commission. (The Zionist Organization cooled its rhetoric against Laila but in 2001 urged the Bush administration to replace her with someone "who is not filled with wild hatred of America's ally, Israel.")

Laila's Iraqi-born husband, Salam Al-Marayati, has not been as lucky. A former engineer, he is now executive director of the Muslim Public Affairs Council in Los Angeles. When in 1999 then U.S. Congressman Dick Gephardt appointed Salam—who at that time was serving on the Los Angeles' human relations commission and who played a role in national interfaith efforts—as a member of the National Commission on Terrorism, an outcry arose from certain Jewish American groups, including the Zionist Organization. Gephardt quickly dropped Salam, citing as his excuse the long time it would take him to obtain security clearance as an Iraqi national. (Salam left Baghdad as a preschooler.) Gephardt's back-sliding outraged even some Jewish leaders, one of whom, a Los Angeles rabbi, calling it an act of "appalling ignorance."

Laila later told a PBS reporter, "I think what we're seeing is an unwillingness to listen to the opposite point of view. It's easy to have conversations with people we agree with and it's difficult to sit and listen to somebody who has a different opinion. But unless we can do that, we will never get any closer to understanding each other."

All the stress from taking an ethical but controversial stand, she says, can make people physically ill and not want to go public. "It is something that creates anxiety, depression and maybe even fear."

The discord Laila has experienced is unlike the warm and nurturing southern California home that she grew up in. She was born into a close family in Los Angeles. As she recalls, her late father was very active at the Islamic Center in southern California. "He wanted to make sure it was a place to go, although ours was not a religious family." Her mother remained a Christian until Laila went to college. Then she had a spiritual awakening and converted to Islam.

To this day, Laila remains close to her family. She goes on trips with her siblings and can depend on them to help take care of her two sons and her daughter if she gets tied up. Her widowed mother now lives with Laila and her family, and Laila is grateful for her mother's help. When she gets stressed and might start to take it out on the kids, her mother intervenes to soften and resolve the situation.

Although she has tried to slow down, Laila is a busy woman. At one time, she maintained her own practice while teaching med students as a clinical associate professor for the University of Southern

California. She has since become a part-time doctor, has set hours at two clinics, and is on duty only once or twice a weekend to deliver babies.

Still, she would not think of quitting: She knows she is needed. Over the years, she has delivered hundreds if not thousands of babies, practicing what has become a high-risk—and increasingly vacant— medical field. Other "baby" doctors in southern California are abandoning the field and new med-school graduates aren't taking their place. Laila reports that 60 percent of ob/gyn positions remain unfilled.

For her work, Laila speaks fluent Spanish to help her non-English speaking patients. She is amused that as an Arab American she doesn't know how to speak Arabic but can readily converse with Latin American immigrants.

Laila's time is also taken up in her role as spokesperson for the Muslim Women's League, based in Los Angeles, and her other humanitarian volunteer work. She helped found the league and has served as its president.

For years, in conjunction with her League work, she has researched and written about Islam and women, as well as human rights violations and religious persecution. Her essays have covered such topics as polygamy, women's dress, sexuality, and motherhood. As an activist, she has helped persuade more than twenty religious and civic groups to start the Women's Coalition against Ethnic Cleansing, to help Muslims in war-torn Bosnia. In 1993, Laila led a Coalition delegation to Zagreb, Croatia, to help determine the best way to help rape survivors and other refugees fleeing Bosnia. Two years later, she served on the United States delegation to the United Nations' Fourth World Conference on Women in Beijing, China. Then, in 1997, she testified before a U.S. Senate Committee on religious intolerance in Europe that targeted Muslims, doing so as a member of the State Department's Advisory Committee on Religious Freedom Abroad.

Closer to home, she helped start a sports camp for Muslim girls and developed a sex education curriculum for all Muslim children.

All of this can be exhausting for even a Super Woman, and Laila has learned to set priorities. So, while she is sympathetic to women wanting equal treatment at mosques, Laila says she must concentrate

on larger issues. Many Muslim women around the world are still denied basic rights. If their husband leaves them, they are left illiterate,
unprepared to earn a living, and they face abuse. Laila has treated
African Muslim refugee women who developed medical complications
from their tribes' primitive operations to circumcise them as young
girls—a procedure that is now called female genital mutilation. Then
there are the honor killings, committed when a patriarch feels he must
kill a daughter or other relative whom he feels has brought disgrace to
the family by being sexually active outside of marriage. "Fortunately,
we don't have that in the United States," Laila says, "but it does occur
elsewhere."

Laila's extensive activism would be impossible if it weren't for her
family and her husband, she says. She met Salam as a teenager during
a class at the Islamic Center of Southern California. He also became
interested in activism, so much so that he switched careers after studying to become an engineer. They married after she graduated from
UCLA.

What saved the marriage, she now jokes, is that she hired a housekeeper to help clean their house. "Salam's idea of a clean house is really
different than mine. I brought in a housekeeper who had worked for
my parents. It was hard on the budget but that has helped us a lot."
The housekeeper is still with the family today.

Laila appreciates how her husband helped her get through med
school and training. Whenever, as a resident, she had to work all night,
Salam was there to take care of their first child. "It was just him and
the baby," she says.

They are still sharing chores—"the drudgery of life" she calls such
tasks as paying bills. "We just figure it out. We have been blessed with
a positive and open attitude."

She wishes the rest of the country had a similar attitude. To her
mind, the U.S. government does not treat all people—or all nations—
equally. Predominantly Muslim countries and their Muslim nationals,
are judged more harshly, in her opinion. Nor do most Americans realize how she and other Muslim Americans have felt unwanted, even endangered, in their own country, long before 9/11.

Laila offers her experience with wearing a *hijab*. Laila once wore a
scarf covering her hair. This was during the 1980s when it was mostly

stay-at-home Muslim moms who donned the *hijab*. As a med student, Laila was unprepared for the backlash that her simple head-covering raised. Most med students took one look at her and shunned her. Others, including doctors and professors whom she revered, made crass remarks, such as: What are you hiding under all that? It only makes you sexier.

"I was getting tired of attracting attention. It was making me an angry person. Even people on the elevator would comment. I found myself explaining myself all the time. I felt so vulnerable."

So she took off her scarf—and was rewarded soon afterward by the reaction of other students, who approached her to say that they had been afraid to speak with her when she was wearing her *hijab*. She became close friends with many of them. She also learned a valuable lesson about fitting in: Despite America's professed craze for individuality, most people want their friends to be just like them—a fact of life Laila calls "really sad."

Although times are changing, and so many more Muslim women are wearing the *hijab* that it's no longer considered such an oddity, Laila is not thinking about putting one on again. Nevertheless, she does consider herself "very observant." She dresses modestly, prays five times a day, and fasts during Ramadan. And she follows the Quran's instructions to be generous to the poor. With so much need still in the world, she feels that there is much to accomplish.

"You have to keep trying," she adds, "to be a positive force."

❧ 41 ❧

AFEEFA'S PASSIONS:
POLITICS AND EDUCATION

SHE SAYS SHE WAS WARNED: As a Muslim woman who wears a *hijab* she'd get doors slammed in her face. Afeefa Syeed decided to run for office anyway.

As a long-time resident of Virginia's Loudoun County, one of the fastest growing areas in the nation, Afeefa was tired of the sprawl, the increasing congestion, the overcrowded schools. She wanted to make her community more livable. As she told the *Washington Post,* "I'm a Muslim, but my issues are American."

So, at the last minute, she threw her hat in the ring to be a candidate for the Loudoun County Board of Supervisors from the Potomac District. Although she won a surprise victory in the Democratic primary in June 2003, outpolling the party pols' choice, a lobbyist and a former legislative assistant, ultimately she lost to her Republican challenger. As an exurbia county near Washington, D.C., Loudoun County is a heavily Republican stronghold. The whole election "was a bad day for Democrats," she quips.

It was also a beginning for local Muslims to become more politically active. Afeefa says she was recruited to run by a newly formed political action committee, the Platform for Active Civil Empowerment, which helped her win her surprising primary victory over the lobbyist. The committee was started after several Muslim homes and businesses were raided in 2002 for having suspected financial ties to terrorists, though no arrests were made. One committee founder, Mukit Hossain, felt that Muslims had to become more active in politics to have a say in how the country is run. "If we have a voice, maybe people will understand a little better about Islam and Muslims," a Muslim woman told a reporter at the time.

Afeefa says the race invigorated her and has encouraged other Muslims to run. Still, she wants to emphasize that hers was a race about issues that affect everybody, not just Muslims. The experience taught her that a Muslim woman *can* be taken seriously when she talks about issues. Even wearing her *hijab,* she says she received none of the harassment or threats she had been warned about.

She had been anticipating some incidents when she began campaigning door to door. She feared the worst might happen on one occasion when a tattooed man answered her knock. Looking into his living room, she could see he had hung a Confederate flag, and he had a big, barking German shepherd. Afeefa assumed that the owner would be just as aggressive as his dog. "I was worried that he was going to cuss me out," she recalls.

Nevertheless, when she told him she was running for county supervisor and asked what his concerns were, instead of slamming the door, he took her question seriously and demanded to know what she was going to do about the Potomac River. The stretch of it nearby was so polluted, he complained, he couldn't fish in it.

"That's one of my issues," she answered happily. She, too, wanted to make the river cleaner for everyone to use. That exchange confirmed to her that issues would trump any prejudices people might have.

Afeefa has brought that same can-do attitude into the educational system. Wanting her three sons to have an Islamic education, although there wasn't a Muslim school nearby, she helped start one. "We wanted to create a place to nurture the children," she says. And so Afeefa is the founding director of Al Fatih Academy, which currently has ninety-five pupils from preschool to fifth grade. (The school is adding a grade every year.)

Around the same time, she also started the Peace Leaders Program, which teaches children ages three and up about resolving conflicts peacefully. It is specifically aimed at working around cultural differences. "Sometimes, the programs we have in schools don't take diversity into account."

Afeefa describes Al Fatih as an amazingly diverse school, where the children or their parents hail from all parts of the world. "We have children who had families living in Iraq during the war, and those who had family members in the U.S. military fighting over there."

She tries to emphasize to the children the concept of giving. To do so, the school teamed up with local churches to send care packages to Iraqis. And she started Kids Giving Salaam to foster the love of community service in children.

Afeefa is a second-generation Indian. Her parents are from the politically torn state of Kashmir. Pakistan and India have fought two wars over the area and a separatist movement started fifteen years ago for Kashmir to become independent. Afeefa's father had been jailed in India as a political prisoner. Later, when he and Afeefa's mother came to the United States to study for their doctorates, they decided to stay.

Afeefa grew up in the heartland; her parents both attended Indiana University in Bloomington. They later moved to Virginia where Afeefa's father is now secretary general of the Islamic Society of North America. Afeefa went to high school and college in Virginia, earning a master's degree in anthropology.

Her interest in cultures has motivated her to teach others about Islam and Muslim. As a diversity consultant and multicultural trainer, she has appeared on a PBS program discussing Islamic teachings and such holidays as Ramadan. She also has gone into public schools to educate students about her faith, an activity that at times has sparked controversy.

In a magazine article, a writer claimed that Afeefa's teaching about Ramadan and Islam in public schools was an example of the "spread of Islamic propaganda in American public schools." The writer told of how Afeefa carried in a globe "to point out the areas of the world lived in by Muslims—which is almost every area of the world, given their propensity to emigrate from their native countries." She added that Afeefa brought with her Muslim children with prayer mats to further talk about Islam.

In a letter to the editor Afeefa later protested that the whole exercise was innocent of propagandistic intent. She was invited by teachers to educate children who might not know much about Islam. "The presentations are celebratory about cultural traditions and are aimed at highlighting the commonness among us all," she tried to explain. "No one is told that Islam is a better religion; no one is asked to accept Islam as the 'true path.' "

She pointed out that she goes only where she is invited, and went on to elaborate: "As a parent of three boys, I know the value of having my children understand the worldviews of others from the others' standpoint, not just from mine."

Despite the controversy, she is upbeat about the progress Muslims are making in American politics. More are running for office, including those whom Afeefa has encouraged locally. "We decided we could make a difference."

⸎ 42 ⸎

CLAREEN AT THE FRONT

WHEN CLAREEN MENZIES was recently interviewing for a job at Islamic Relief USA, she made two requests: that she be able to hire more women, and that her fundraising would help establish more programs set up by women to help women. Both requests were readily agreed to, and she was hired.

Now Clareen divides her time between her longtime home in the Minneapolis–St. Paul area and the Los Angeles area where Islamic Relief USA has its headquarters. It was important to her that she keep her midwestern roots: She is an Islamic leader in the Minneapolis–St. Paul area and was the first woman to serve among all men at the Muslim Organizations of Minnesota. She was also an officer at a mosque and on the board of Tarek ibn Ziyad Academy, a charter school that serves predominantly Muslim students. She serves on another board of a social services group that offers counseling and is establishing a program for Muslims to become foster parents to Muslim children in state care. And in 1999, Clareen founded Sisters Need a Place (SNAP), a nonprofit group that helps midwestern Muslim women faced with domestic abuse, or problems with housing, employment, transportation, child custody, and divorce. SNAP is an all-volunteer effort: Clareen, for example, helps five women in need while other volunteers handle the cases of abused or needy women. As a former battered woman, Clareen knows firsthand how a little kindness can help victims turn their lives around.

"We have learned a lot in order to serve women," she says. "We have made many friends in both the Muslim community and the community at large."

Anisah David (see Chapter 27), who sits on Clareen's SNAP board, calls her a "Muslim powerhouse" who has helped other Muslim women throughout the Midwest. "She has long been a fixture of the human services industry (such as charities and foundations) and her story illustrates how Islam plays a role in the lives of Americans," Anisah says. "I think of her as a role model."

Clareen was one of the first white women to become a Muslim in Minnesota in the mid-1970s. She became interested in Islam when a new family moved into the house in back of hers. They turned out to be Muslims practicing their faith secretly. "They were from Uganda and had left when Idi Amin took power," she says. The infamous dictator Amin, who had been responsible for as many as 400,000 murdered or missing in his country, issued an ultimatum to Asian property-owners living in Uganda: Leave or be slaughtered. That was sufficient reason for Clareen's neighbors Roshan and Abdul Osman to flee. They eventually settled in the Minneapolis–St. Paul area, with a church as their sponsor.

"To have a sponsor they had to be Christian, so they pretended to be, going to the church on Sunday," Clareen says. "Then they had Muslim services in secret at their home." When Clareen's daughter Naomi became friends with her neighbors' daughter, Tasneem, she got to know her parents—and Islam.

"I was having trouble rationalizing my Lutheran upbringing," Clareen explains. "The questions I asked were causing me trouble. I asked my neighbors questions about Islam and they answered them all."

But she was an unlikely candidate for Islam. At that time most converts to Islam were African Americans, especially prison inmates who had been attracted to the faith by the Nation of Islam. A blue-eyed redhead, Clareen was a secretary who was raising a daughter on her own. Her parents had seen to it that she had had a religious background as a mainstream Protestant. All the same, Clareen felt more comfortable with Islam. It seemed to her to make more sense. Islam, she says, "has accepted my intelligence, taught me discipline, and made me curious."

As a Christian child, Clareen remembers being lonely. As an

observant Lutheran she was expected to quietly stay at home after church on Sundays and spend the rest of the day with her family. "But I had no sisters or brothers," she says. "I had no one to play with."

She became a Muslim at age twenty-eight in a July 15, 1977, ceremony in which she simply repeated the words, "There is no God but God and Muhammad is the Prophet."

Clareen's early years as a Muslim weren't easy. There were only two mosques in the entire state of Minnesota—both in Minneapolis—and she didn't feel comfortable at either. One was for African Americans who at the time didn't exactly welcome white people at their services. The other was attended mostly by immigrants who were born into the faith. "Few spoke English," she says, so there was trouble communicating. "I didn't fit in," Clareen concludes.

But she kept studying Islam. After all, she was used to being different. Even before she became a Muslim, Clareen was a nonconformist and a risk-taker, despite the difficulties that caused.

As a young woman who had just graduated from high school in the late 1960s, she began dating a black man—a scandalous development to her parents. Clareen's family wasn't prepared to accept a black man into the family. They threatened to disown her if she persisted in seeing him—and they did.

"Here's how the story goes," Clareen says dryly, "I was fired from my job on Thursday, got disowned from my family on Friday, and got pregnant on Sunday."

What followed was almost material for a sitcom: Her mother would visit her and urge her not to tell her father. Then her dad would stop by and warn her not to tell her mom. Both blamed the disowning on the other's more conservative, and scandalized, relatives.

As a single mother at age nineteen, Clareen was urged to give up Naomi, her biracial baby girl. Adoption is better for her, everyone agreed. "I was under big pressure to place her," she remembers. But Clareen resisted and kept her daughter. She knew that she faced years of struggle, of juggling work and going to college at night, but Clareen couldn't give up her daughter. Naomi's father supported them off and on, though he and Clareen never married. At times he could be violent and hit Clareen. Clareen and Naomi made peace with him before he died.

The man Clareen did marry was another African American whom she met while going to night school for her bachelor's degree in humanities and community organization. He was part of a program to help rehabilitate ex-offenders through education. While in prison, he had become a member of a blacks-only Muslim group called the Moors Science. Clareen knew about his Muslim faith but wasn't encouraged to learn about it.

He also turned out to be batterer—"a very violent man," in Clareen's words—and she left him after twelve years of marriage. Most of those years, she adds, "he was in prison. He was home with me for only twenty-two months." He too is now deceased.

She met a third man whom she thought was "the one" but he also began to hit her. Clareen threw him out after three years.

By then she was sick at heart. What was there about her that attracted these men, the worst kind? She had been a devout Muslim for years and it bothered her that she couldn't find a man to share her faith and treat her as she deserved to be treated.

A dear friend, another battered woman whom she lovingly calls a "radical Baptist," told Clareen something she remembers to this day: Clareen wasn't facing reality. She had stayed with one abusive husband for twelve years, but stuck it out for only three years with the next one.

"You *are* getting better," the friend insisted.

That epiphany helped keep Clareen on the right track and she never again became involved with another abuser.

In retrospect, she says, she and her "radical Baptist" friend had, at least in the early days, fooled themselves into thinking they could reform "bad boys." As she now admits, "All women think they can change bad boys. When you get to be fifty, you want to find someone who doesn't need changing."

After they wised up, the two women relied on each other for reality checks on prospective men. "We wormed our way out of self-deception and settling for something less than we deserved."

At the same time, Clareen was thriving professionally. She has been a development executive, planning fundraising drives for various charities, for the last twenty years. It all started when Clareen got laid off from her job as a secretary in a Minneapolis company that had eliminated her department. She soon found a job as an administrative assistant with the Minnesota Women's Fund, one of the first foundations for women in the country. "I was there about twenty minutes — and I was writing a grant," she remembers. She eventually became its development director.

"It was set up brilliantly," she recalls. If the group wanted to solicit a wealthy woman for a donation, they sent another well-off woman to plead its case. The same formula was used for women executives, African Americans, Native Americans and others. It was the new girl's club, and it attracted big donors, one of whom later joked, "I decided to give $1 million and I was going to ask my husband, but then I thought, what the heck, it's my money!"

It turned out that fundraising was something Clareen had a knack for, as well as the passion. She helped raise millions of dollars for the Fund while overseeing more than five hundred volunteers.

Eventually, though, she became "sick of the politics of women's organizations" and abruptly quit one day.

Within hours after learning that Clareen had resigned, a Native American woman persuaded her to raise money for Indians. She believed that Clareen understood native culture, and could communicate it to potential funders in a way they could understand. The woman had thought it down to the last detail.

The strategy worked. "We never got a no," Clareen says.

After that experience, Clareen went freelance, serving as a consultant to such groups.

"I was just crazy," she says. "I can remember going to bed and setting the alarm for four A.M. because I had to put together ten proposals for the Minneapolis Foundation by four p.m. I would get it done by noon, take a shower, and then go to present them."

She also ended up being recruited to work part-time for the Minnesota Department of Corrections planning committee for women offenders. One of her assignments: Find out why so many black women prisoners were ending up in isolation in much higher numbers than their white counterparts.

"I told them, You can't send a white woman inside to find out what's happening. I was told, No, just shut up and go."

Clareen did and, as usual, upset some of the prison officials by her nonconformist ways: She asked a recently released prisoner to dine with her—breaking the rule against fraternizing with inmates. But, Clareen protested, how could she find out what was wrong if she couldn't have heart-to-hearts with the women who knew best about the different treatment?

She ended up concluding that blacks and whites were treated differently because the guards tended to believe what the white prisoners told them. As a result, white inmates tended to receive more privileges and less punishment than their African American counterparts.

"If you were black and you committed an offense, you went to the hole," she says. "If you were black you *may* see your kids during visiting hours while whites *automatically* got to see theirs."

Clareen did have success with helping some women prisoners. One Native American woman who was finally paroled after being convicted of feeding rat poison to an abusive husband, called her up later to thank her. She proudly told of how she had completed her education and had now attained her dream job: decorating homes. Clareen later passed on the good news to the late Senator Paul Wellstone, who had helped the woman with her appeals and parole hearings.

Soon afterward, Clareen went to work for City Inc., a nonprofit group in Minneapolis that offers family outreach and advocacy programs in an alternative junior and senior high school. She came on board first as a consultant and later as its director of development. She has now been with this agency for six years. "That's too long. I've got to go," she says with a deadpan expression.

She was joking—but it wasn't long before Islamic Relief USA began wooing her.

Clareen has also remarried, this time to a gentle Muslim man who pursued her until she decided to take the chance. Like her, he's a convert to Islam, becoming a Muslim only a few months before Clareen did. They live in a quiet St. Paul neighborhood.

However, when he first proposed to Clareen, he was married to another woman. Clareen wasn't about to tolerate polygamy, no matter that Islam condones it. She told him bluntly, "I am an only child and I never learned to share," and forgot about him.

"He would write cards every week," she says. "I threw them all away."

He didn't give up and divorced his wife. Once more, he asked Clareen to marry him. This time, friends urged her to consider it. One reminded her, "You've been hurt by men who hurt you. Why not try someone who will love you?"

So Clareen cornered him. Why, she demanded, do you want to marry me?

"I want to marry you," he replied, "because I love you and want to care for you—and because I want to be entertained for the rest of my life."

How could she resist such an answer? "He is hilarious," Clareen says. "He's one of the funniest human beings who has ever lived."

But Clareen has her own sense of fun. For her *mahr*—what Muslim men give to their new wives as a sign of lifelong commitment— Clareen asked for twenty pounds of green coffee beans. As it turns out, Clareen loves her coffee—and this man in her life.

Life has indeed turned out well for Clareen, the pioneering Muslimah. She says she received tremendous support from her friends, family and co-workers after 9/11. They are as fiercely protective of her as they are of her faith. As she puts it, "Before 9/11 people loved me in spite of Islam; now they love me because of it."

With her new career, she had to resign from being part of Muslim leadership in Minnesota—including the Imams who head the mosques. As the group's secretary, she was one woman among twenty-nine men. "Once a month I took the notes" of the meeting, she says. She was awed by how they treat her—with respect and deference. (Clareen is modest about her own accomplishments.)

She attends a mosque where men and women are on different floors. The women listen to the service through a speaker (translation from Arabic is done through headsets). At other mosques in the area men and women are in the same room but separated, or the men are on the main floor and women in the balcony.

At the present time, Clareen is glad that she will be able to make a difference for women at Islamic Relief. She's also glad that other Muslim women are joining SNAP to reach out to their sisters in trouble. They are realizing that domestic abuse exists in all cultures. A preliminary study shows that Muslim households in the United States have the same rate of domestic abuse as non-Muslims: 12 percent. Such abuse can come in different forms. One woman she is helping is an African refugee who was being treated as a virtual servant by her husband and mother-in-law.

Her volunteering is all part of a day's work, which can include accompanying other Muslims to the FBI office in Minnesota to demand they quit singling out Muslims for extra scrutiny as potential terrorists. It can also include demonstrations to the curious of how she winds her *hijab* around her head. In the Minneapolis–St. Paul area, Clareen is known as the woman with fifty *hijabs*. She likes to color-coordinate her head coverings with her other clothes. Sometimes people want to try one on. And Clareen, ever the friendly and helpful nonconformist, promptly obliges by taking it off and handing it to them.

"Knock yourself out," she says.

❧ 43 ❧

W. L. CATI'S MISSION: SAVING
ABUSED MUSLIM WOMEN

NEED AN ESCAPE PLAN? W. L. Cati has one listed on her website, www.ZennahMinistries.com.

While she would never say every Muslim male is a wife-beater, she knows firsthand that abuse does occur and she has dedicated her life to helping other Muslim women escape it.

W.L. has gone full-circle: Once a veiled *Muslimah,* she has returned to Christianity, and as an author and evangelist her mission is focused on abused Muslim women.

"The life I was living was not worth anything," she says. "Literally, I walked out of my marriage with nothing."

She did leave with something, however: Bleeding ulcers. "Everything escalated—it was just too intense. Nothing was ever good enough."

W.L. gets e-mails from grateful women thanking her for giving them the strength to leave. She also gets her share of hate mail from Muslims who think she is blaspheming their religion. One was so angry that the writer's message lacked capitalization, proper spelling or even coherence: "Shame on you so called followers of christ. If jesus came back today and see you getting worldly gain by selling dirty doctrin, he would tell you that you have nothing to do with that he convey long time ago. i will invite you in the name of allah to study one true way of life which is islam, so you can go by his mersy go to heaven."

W.L. patiently replies to each e-mail or letter, no matter how nasty. She tries to persuade them with logic and knowledge.

"I was a Muslim for many years," W.L. wrote in one message. "I know as much if not more about Islam than the average Muslim."

Indeed, there was a time when W.L. lived in a seven-bedroom house in suburban Atlanta, had two vacation homes in Florida, and jetted off to Egypt for Nile cruises—all courtesy of her husband's million-dollar annual income from a chain of twenty furniture stores throughout Georgia and Florida. Birthday bashes included limousine rides to a favorite Indian restaurant, closed for the day to accommodate W.L.'s celebration with family and friends.

She seemed to have it all spiritually, too. She was a devout Muslim convert who gladly donned a *hijab*, attended Quran classes, and traveled to the Middle East to officially declare her conversion at the mosque of her husband's family.

But behind all that glitter and piety was misery. Her charming, worldly husband Muhammed could turn violent; her volcanic mother-in-law would erupt into rages in which she spit on W.L. and violently pushed and pulled her. And W.L. felt violated and humiliated when her husband kept asking her to accept polygamy. Although she refused, he still womanized and was away from home most of the time with his business and girlfriends. (His brother did, in fact, marry two women in the United States.)

W.L. might have put up with all this were it not for an event that occurred at the birthday party of a niece. She wanted to take their toddler twins home to rest. It was a simple request and W.L. asked her husband, as she had been taught that a good Muslim wife does. But her husband erupted in anger. "You will stay here," he ordered, as the children began crying.

That did it. W.L. rebelled. As she got up to leave, she saw her enraged husband, his face almost beet-red, lunging at her. The next thing she knew she woke up from a blackout. She was in the backseat of their car with their four children.

This, she decided, was rock-bottom. She decided to leave him despite tremendous fear and uncertainty. How would she support their children? How would she live without a man she had thought was her soul mate? How could she turn her back on Islam which she had so eagerly embraced?

She can now say ruefully, it *has* been a long, arduous journey. It took her five years merely to get a divorce. During those years there have been tearful reunions, passionate promises to reform—and more abuse.

Today, her life of luxury is gone. She's now living in an 1,800-square-foot duplex and driving an old van. But, she says, she has something much more enriching: her freedom and her faith. She's back to her childhood Christianity. She's an ordained minister who has written a book, *Married to Muhammed*. She has set up Zennah Ministries to help other abused Muslim women.

"God bless them, but there are a lot of them out there," she says.

W.L. Cati is her pen name; she asked that her real name not be used. She regularly receives threats because her book criticizes what she considers encouragement of the abuse of women within Islamic culture and by the Quran. The book's chapter titles plainly state her revulsion for such conduct: "His Before Yours", "The Husband's Right to Beat The Wife", and "Polygamy", in which she quotes the Quran— "Marry women of your choice, two, three, or four (Surah 4:3)."

W.L. says she knows that there are many Muslim women in America who thrive in Islam and are treated well by their husbands. On the other hand, many Muslim women in the United States eagerly want to taste what other American women take for granted: going where they want, wearing what they want, and not fearing an abusive husband.

"In no way do I hold Islam responsible for the actions of my husband," she writes on her Zennah Ministries website. "I do not believe that all Muslim men beat, abuse, or mistreat their wives, that all Christian and Jewish men treat their wives with love the way they should."

Still, she is concerned that abusive, controlling men use the Quran to justify abusing their wives, mentally and physically.

That's why www.ZennahMinistries.com lists abuse escape plans.

She named her ministries after her own adopted Muslim name— Zennah. It is also the name of her firstborn daughter. *Zennah* is Arabic for "perfect" or "fine." In Farsi it means "beautification, arranging or setting in order to look better." Ironically, it was to please her husband that W.L. took Zennah as her new name and in countless other ways tried to become the ideal Muslim wife.

Those efforts took her far from her family and home in Alabama.

She had been born into a warm and loving family. "I had led a very sheltered life," she says. Her family was not serious about religion, though they dutifully showed up in the pews at Easter and Christmas—until W.L.'s mother started going to services regularly. W.L. was impressed at her mother's transformation. "I saw such a change in her over a short period of time that I had to go to church just to see what it was about."

W.L. was a pert, pretty teenager who modeled and won beauty pageants, including Miss Alabama Hemisphere. With her pastor watching over her, W.L. settled down to an early marriage at age seventeen with a twenty-two-year-old churchgoer. W.L. discovered that they couldn't have children so they quickly adopted three children, including a child from Brazil. Her life would have seemed set and, indeed, it was for a dozen years. She continued to win beauty pageants as a Mrs. contestant, but W.L. couldn't get over the yearning to give birth to her own child. Her marriage floundered, and she had just won the Mrs. Alabama pageant when she and her husband divorced. She headed to Atlanta to start over and, as she now says with a laugh, "to seek my fame and fortune." She quickly found modeling jobs and one night went to a new nightclub with a friend and fellow model who was helping promote its opening. It was W.L.'s first time in a nightclub, and it was where she met Muhammed.

He walked up to her and asked her to dance. He was charming, and he was quite the dancer. They whirled around the dance floor and then talked.

"He didn't tell me he was an Arab. He said he was Italian. He told me his name was Jamie. But something was not setting right and as we continued talking I asked him again where he was from. He broke down and said he was from Syria. At the time I didn't know where that was. He told me he was a Muslim. I had no clue what that was. I thought it was something like being a Methodist or Baptist. He told me it was just another religion—we all believed in one God. Other than that, we didn't talk about religion. He swept me off my feet. I had never met anybody like him before—he was so handsome."

She had been divorced for six weeks. As it turned out, his wife had just left him. He, in fact, had been married twice. His first marriage, which his mother had helped arrange, had been to an older woman so he could get a green card to permanently stay in the United States. He was eighteen. He later married a girl his own age but he told W.L. that she turned out to be a drug addict and had just skipped town with his car.

At age twenty-two he was available. So was W.L., who was in her late twenties. Despite the age difference they clicked and married a year later. "We had some wonderful times," she remembers.

Muhammed, who had gone to college to become an engineer, was good at sales so both he and W.L. went into selling commercial real estate. Seeing the influx of people flocking to the Sunbelt, Muhammed bought a mattress store franchise, which soon grew into a chain of furniture stores, along with his own factory and warehouse.

W. L. concedes that it was a rags-to-riches story. W. L. worked in one of the stores until their second child was born, after which she stayed home. She took her children and spent long periods in the Middle East living with her husband's family and learning Arabic and about Islam. On her third visit, she converted while in Syria. She became immersed in Quran study, holding small groups at her Atlanta home. She became active at the mosque and helped welcome new converts into the faith. But at the same time she knew something wasn't right in her marriage. The business was consuming Muhammed. "There was so much to manage. He started drinking heavily. He had always gone out at night but that escalated."

She discovered he had phone numbers from other women. "When I confronted him, he beat me up," W. L. says. "I called the police."

Muhammed apologized and promised it would never happen again. W. L. believed him. The violence, however, didn't end. Perhaps a month or so would go by peacefully, but then something would upset him and he would fly into rages.

"He said I made him do it," W.L. remembers, "that it was my fault that he hit me."

Again there would be tearful reunions, his promises to reform, and on one occasion a nine-karat diamond tennis bracelet.

W. L. also had to put up with Muhammed's suggestion that he should take another wife. "Throughout our marriage, the topic would come up. He would ask me how I felt about this. He would say it was legal and part of his customs. Of course, I said no—it was *not* part of my customs."

In retrospect, W.L. says she should have noticed the danger signals within Muhammed's family. The entire clan had trouble controlling their anger. Fights would break out at family get-togethers. Muhammed's mother thought of herself as a matriarch and eventually moved from Syria into W.L.'s home. "She felt everything I had was hers. She could take anything she wanted because her son was the provider. She would even tell me that I had no right to anything—everything goes to the mother."

Mother and son would also clash. One time, they began arguing in the kitchen while standing next to a coffeemaker. "She took the hot coffee and scalded him," W. L. recalls. "Then he got her by the throat and I tried to get in the middle to break it up. It was not fun."

By the time of that fateful birthday party, W. L. also was beginning to have doubts about Islam. How could a peaceful religion create such havoc? She could take no more of it.

When her husband had gone to work on the Monday after beating her at the party, she sprung into action, got the locks changed at her house and emptied money from their bank accounts. A sympathetic judge gave her a restraining order. He also ordered Muhammed to pay for her and the children's support. "The judge gave me everything." When Muhammed returned from his business trip he found he had no home and no cash.

But that was not the end. More reconciliations would follow, then more fights. When W.L. decided she was going back to Christianity, her husband became furious and uttered three times, "I divorce you." W.L. believed that to be an Islamic requirement for her husband to divorce her. After seemingly endless messy court battles, her marriage was dissolved.

Since becoming a Christian again, with its philosophy of forgiveness, she prays for her ex-husband and has visited him in the hospital when he has suffered from heart problems. She has since remarried and continued with her Christian studies. And she has her website to maintain. W.L. also speaks at meetings held in mosques where she talks about her experiences. She lets people ask her questions. Most, she says, are taken aback by her courage. "A lot of Islam," she believes, "thrives on fear."

❧ 44 ❧

ANEESAH: SCHOLAR AND
SOCIAL WORKER

GOD KNOWS THE STRUGGLES—and triumphs—of Aneesah Nadir. She is first in her family to earn a doctorate while working, raising a family, helping out in the community, and serving as president of the Islamic Social Services Association. She knew she *shouldn't* do it all— but she did anyway. Her frenetic schedule went on for seven years. Last year, at age forty-eight, after more than two decades of going to school off and on, she finally got her Ph.D. Today she is on the tenure track at Arizona State University in Phoenix while leading efforts na- tionwide to help bring needed social services to the growing Muslim population in the United States.

"I've got to say, faith is the foundation. None of this would have happened without God's grace," she asserts. "There were lots of times I didn't think I could make it, and He would carry me through."

Aneesah certainly wasn't the typical doctoral candidate. She was a working mom wearing a brightly colored *hijab*. She didn't come from a family of scholars; no one in her family had ever dreamed of such ed- ucational possibilities. Her parents had to struggle just to put food on the table.

"Growing up in inner-city New York," she told an interviewer for the Muslim website soundvision.com, "I saw the disparity between the haves and the have-nots and I felt that it was somehow important to be involved in making a difference and making a change, so there would be a greater degree of social justice for everyone involved."

Her parents also encouraged her. They may have come from

humble backgrounds but they wanted their children to achieve and have a better life. "I can remember vividly my mom taking me to the public library in Queens and getting me tons of books. She couldn't help me with my homework but she was there to encourage me."

Her family also saw to it that she got religion. She went to church regularly. However, it was her time at Adelphi University, where she earned her bachelor's degree in social work in 1978, that changed her forever: Classmates at the university introduced her to the Nation of Islam, which promoted black nationalism, spiritual development, and empowerment.

Aneesah felt drawn to Islam, and has never regretted it. She is now a member of a mosque in suburban Phoenix that is made up primarily of immigrant Muslims.

"Having grown up Christian, I felt Islam was the rest of the story," she says. "Islam has given me a framework for living, a clarity of purpose, a connection. I would say it has also given me a strong family life. Islam has provided me with moral meaning in my life."

Her family was not immediately thrilled by her conversion, especially her father. "My dad worried about me because of how Islam was portrayed in the media." Now, after decades of seeing how Islam has strengthened his daughter, he supports her.

Aneesah has had to rely on that strength to get through some difficult times.

Take her move to Arizona in 1981. "It was a cultural shock to me," she now says, laughing. "I came as an African American to a part of the country where there are very few African Americans—only 3 to 5 percent of the population—with the number of Muslims even smaller. I was still a very young woman with two children. Moving was a big step for me."

Her first conclusion after settling into the Phoenix area: "I can't stay here." But she stuck it out. She enrolled in a master's degree program for social work at Arizona State in nearby Tempe and, as she puts it, "I made connections." She adjusted to Arizona but faced daunting challenges at school. "The social work program was very rigorous. The required internships were like going to work. At the same time I was raising a family."

The stresses from juggling home and school caused a strain in her marriage. ("We learned; we both matured," she now says.) Because of her early marital problems, Aneesah knows from experience the stresses that confront so many American couples these days. She believes that all couples should get some counseling before they marry, and Muslims are no exception. Like other Americans they have a high rate of divorce. One estimate has it that in the United States over 40 percent of Muslims' marriages end in divorce. Premarital counseling would help couples determine whether they are compatible and help them weather the inevitable difficulties.

"Being married is one of the most important things we'll do, developing and establishing a family. It's also one of the least prepared things we will ever get to do. Most of us aren't really prepared to be a husband or a wife, and eventually a parent.

"But Allah and his Messenger (peace and blessings be upon him) have placed before us guidelines, lessons, and teachings that will help us to be well prepared. Unfortunately, many of us aren't seeking that guidance. I think it's important that those who are getting married — be they young or old — should prepare and understand their rights and roles and responsibilities. We call these the three Rs."

Having a sense of faith greatly helps in a marriage, she adds. Islam emphasizes marriage and family, and marriage is a way of serving God. Indeed, Imams can help promote strong healthy marriages by discussing this and offering premarital sessions and other counseling. In the past, though, Imams haven't been trained to counsel, especially if they are immigrants. Many Imams are beginning to realize the value of counseling, and are increasingly reaching out to Muslims, many of whom are coping with life in a strange land and face a weakening of familial bonds as their children gravitate to their new American — and non-Muslim — friends. Throughout the country, some Muslims are fighting substance abuse although Islam forbids the consumption of alcohol or drugs. Some are grappling with domestic violence in their homes, with many women afraid to say anything.

For some time, Muslims would not even discuss domestic violence. The assumption was, Aneesah says, "That's a tragedy that doesn't affect Muslim families. But it does affect Muslims just as it affects Christians, Jews, and other religious and cultural groups."

Aneesah has been trying to spread the word in the American

Muslim community that families can get help and that physical and mental abuse need not be tolerated. She refers to Islamic teachings that condemn domestic abuse: "Prophet Muhammad (peace and blessings be upon him) instructed Muslims regarding women: 'I command you to be kind to women.' He said also, 'The best of you is the best to his family.' "

When she helped start the Islamic Social Services Association in the United States and its sister organization in Canada, she intended it to serve as a network for discussion about social service concerns and to provide education and training to social workers to help them reach Muslims. Every year the association has a conference to update professionals about the latest trends and the best practices in providing social and mental health services to Muslims.

The group's affiliate in Canada produced a public education manual, "Muslims and their faith and culture," which was revised for the United States with grants from the National Conference for Community Justice and Chevron Texaco. The manuals seek to educate police officers, social workers, journalists, and school administrators about Muslims.

It's particularly needed now. Since 9/11, Muslims around the country have been targeted for vandalism and even worse violence. Ten minutes away from Aneesah's home, a man reacting hysterically to that day's terrorist attacks, shot to death Balbir Singh Sodhi, a Sikh gasoline station owner who was mistaken for a Muslim because he wore a turban. In 2004, Aneesah's mosque was defaced with a spray-painted swastika. Another mosque in nearby Glendale, she says, was set on fire.

Nevertheless, where some see problems, Aneesah sees opportunities to reach out. "I see myself as a bridge builder."

To Aneesah, she is only doing what other Muslim women have done. "The history of early Islam," she says, "was filled with strong women—women who were scholars, who were courageous, and were agents of change. They were not afraid to speak out." Nor is she.

❦ 45 ❧

MASTER ZAKIA MAHASA:
COURT IS IN SESSION!

A TEENAGER WAS APPEARING in juvenile court before Master Zakia Mahasa. *"I don't want to see you again, you hear?"* she said.

In the nearly eight years since Master Mahasa was appointed to the Baltimore bench, she has been on a mission not only to serve justice, but to make sure kids don't get caught up in the system again. She is a Master in Chancery in the Family Division of the Baltimore City Circuit Court.

Master Mahasa is believed to be the first Muslim woman judicial appointee in America. She believes that her faith helped her get where she is today, and that it soothes the stress of handling the enormous number of cases that appear before her in her court.

In just forty minutes during one afternoon court session, she presided over five cases. In one of them, she gave a year's probation to a convicted first-time drug offender, a boy whose mother died of cancer and who has now been taken into the home of an older brother. She also assigned him a mentor and directed he be given other social services to try to turn his life around. The state had actually been willing to settle for six months' probation but Master Mahasa was concerned that the boy should have enough time for an effective rehabilitation. She was also worried about him talking back and not being respectful enough to the brother who was financially supporting him. "He is your father-brother," the judge told the boy sternly, demanding that he wipe the grin from his face. She wanted him to realize the seriousness of his condition: "He didn't have to take you in. Be a benefit, not a burden." The boy, serious now, assured the judge he would be.

In another case, she meted out probation to a first offender, a thirteen-year-old boy whose mother advised the judge that she thought her son had been caught selling crack cocaine because he was trying to raise money to run away to his grandmother's. Again, Master Mahasa assigned a mentor and other social service programs to turn around the boy's attitude. She wanted him in school—on time, every day—and the mother said he was already going regularly.

Master Mahasa recalls that when she first graduated from law school in the 1980s, she could count on one hand the number of Muslim women attorneys in the United States—and she would have most of her fingers left over. "I knew of only two," she says.

Today, the Muslim community has come a long way, something Master Mashasa sees firsthand: Her son, a second-generation Muslim, is now a criminal defense lawyer, practicing in Baltimore. There are also many more young Muslim women attorneys throughout the United States. She wants to be a role model to them—to set an example as an American Muslim woman who can wear a scarf and still succeed at her work. While sitting on the bench one day, she wore a smartly wound black scarf around her hair that matched her tailored skirt and jacket. "There are different ways of doing it," she points out. "You can be stylish."

Master Mahasa hasn't been hurt professionally by wearing the *hijab*, although her family once worried she would be. She has found that because she is proud of her faith and apparel, she is respected by others.

"You can still ascend the career ladder," she says. "It has not been as difficult as one would have thought."

She has also managed to decorate her judge's chamber in a style that makes her comfortable. She lights scented candles while she works. Her crystal paperweights and globes—she collects them as a hobby—glitter on a counter by the window. She has artwork, stained-glass lamps, and a Persian rug, too.

Master Mahasa wants a younger generation to know that a woman can balance work and family, career and community service. Despite being a working mom, she has managed to fit in years of volunteering. She is currently chairperson of the Michigan-based Mercy USA, a predominantly Muslim charity organization that makes contributions to underdeveloped countries to help people become self-sufficient, regardless of their religion. (Mercy helped the earthquake and tsunami victims in South Asia, for example.)

Master Mahasa is glad to be a part of it.

She also has given back to the community by serving on a state-wide court improvement committee on foster care that finds methods to improve foster children's stays in the system. In this and other ways, judges can have a profound influence, from placing children in the most appropriate foster care to determining when parents are ready to get their kids back. From her extensive experience presiding in family court, Master Mahasa knows how crucial it is to improve foster care.

She is also aware that it is not a simple matter for women to juggle everything. She herself struggled for years as a divorced single mom, working full-time at the Social Security Administration's office in Baltimore while studying and taking care of a small son. Sometimes she hated her work; processing disability claims, she says, was the worst. But she is grateful to the agency, which paid for most of her college education.

She needed whatever help she could get. She was a mom at age seventeen—a teenager who had dreamed ever since she was four years old of being an attorney. But there she was—a girl herself with a baby. Even then she had a steely focus: She proceeded to college, then law school. Goals, she says, "keep you focused and *InshaAllah* it will work out."

It did work out, but it took eleven years. During those years, she says, she "never missed a PTA meeting and I went to all his school and sports activities. I was on autopilot. I just did it."

She was blessed, she adds, that her parents pitched in and watched over her son while she had to be at work or class. Thanks to them, she never had to have a babysitter.

It was while she was a young mother with a toddler that she began thinking about a new faith. Her family was Christian, but, she says, "I didn't believe in the Holy Trinity." She felt she needed a faith that made sense to her. "I realized I was a spiritual person."

She didn't agree with the philosophy of the black nationalist Nation of Islam, but she kept coming back to the more orthodox Islam. This was something with which she felt at peace, and it answered her questions. "It was intellectually stimulating," she remembers.

It also gave her a sense of assurance: with Allah in control of the world, things would work out. "Nothing is ever going to be safe or easy," she observes, but she knows that with a higher being in charge, she does have a destiny, a reason for being here. "It's made me want to be the best I can be."

When she was considering converting to Islam, she pondered for a long time and finally asked God to give a sign that He favored her becoming a Muslim. Just as she was walking across the street, she saw a beam of light flash upon something shining. Curious, she walked toward the illuminated object. She was stunned: It turned out to be her own missing earring, a birthday present that she had lost exactly a year earlier, on the day before her birthday. The judge took that as a sign of affirmation that she had found her faith.

The mysterious light would appear to her again more than twenty years later when she went on the Hajj, the yearly pilgrimage to Mecca. She joined the tens of thousands walking or taking a bus. "All these people were going for the same thing," she marvels. "You had this feeling that Allah was with you. It was a very palatable feeling, of being protected by Allah."

After a lot of walking, she would get tired, but when she would see people in wheelchairs pushing on the sight galvanized her. Then she climbed up Mount Arafat to pray. As she began reciting her prayer she suddenly felt a beam of sunlight directed right at her. It flashed before her, just as the light had appeared years ago when she found her earring. There, on the Saudi mountain, she began to weep.

"This light opened me up. I had a sense of my powerlessness and of providence. I had this sense of His magnificence, of His awesome power. I just started crying."

Afterward, she felt the same intimation of divine power that she had experienced so many years before.

She has never regretted her move to Islam. Her parents, however, were particularly skeptical about her change of name. In Arabic, Mahasa means "to examine closely," or "to be just," and Zakia signifies purity. She loves her name—and what it means.

She accepts Islam's rules, including that she must marry another Muslim. So far, though, she has stayed single after her divorce. She likes to joke that she has had many opportunities but no real choices.

Other experiences have beckoned, though, such as travel to South Africa, Kenya, and Egypt. And, of course, there is her work. After she finished law school, she opened a general legal practice, taking everything from divorce cases to personal injury lawsuits. She did that for two years before joining the Legal Aid Bureau to represent abused or neglected children. At last, she had found her niche. Later, she also served as legal counsel to a nonprofit organization that worked with abused women and their children, eventually becoming managing attorney in its legal clinic before being appointed a Master in Chancery.

"I love helping juveniles. It's been very rewarding."

She requires many of the youngsters who come before her to write a letter about what services they need and, more important, what *they* feel they must do in order to stay out of trouble. They're also directed to write about their future career plans. It's the first thing she asks for and usually she insists it be finished within two weeks of the youngster's court appearance.

"I don't care about spelling or punctuation," she recently told one of the youngsters. "But I do care about the thought."

If there isn't enough of the latter, she will order it redone. Or, as she told one juvenile, "If I don't think you have thought about it enough, you'll be writing another letter."

The letters, she adds, are the first things she looks for when she goes to work.

She wishes many of the youngsters who pass through her courtroom received better guidance. Too many are growing up without any at all. They lack parameters and rules that a structured way of life provides.

"There has to be a guiding force," she adds. For herself, she feels Islam has helped her with "a sense of commitment and of keeping my priorities straight."

ᦉ 46 ᦂ

AZIZAH AL-HIBRI: CHAMPION
OF HUMAN RIGHTS

IN THE FALL OF 2002, Azizah al-Hibri, a former philosophy student who had once been asked by her American professors why she was bothering with graduate school, was seated on a podium next to one of the most powerful women in America, then National Security Advisor Condoleezza Rice. Dr. al-Hibri had toughed it out during the days when women grad students were looked down on, and had gone on to distinguish herself in her adopted country, as a philosophy professor, feminist editor, Wall Street lawyer, law professor, and an international advocate for human rights. As the founder of Karamah, a Washington-based group of Muslim women lawyers for human rights, she is now considered one of the go-to Muslim leaders in the United States. She has appeared with Supreme Court Justice Sandra Day O'Connor at a forum to discuss women's issues. And she has advised President George W. Bush on the matter of how best to protect American Muslims from persecution after 9/11 and how to draw up guidelines so that Muslims in the United States could contribute to charities without being wrongly linked to terrorists.

Condoleeza has praised Dr. al-Hibri and Karamah for their essential work. "Let us work for a world where all women and all girls, from Kansas to Kandahar, can pursue their dreams and live up to their potential," Rice said. "Remember, democracy is a journey, not a destination. It is something that you get up and you build day by day, brick by brick."

That is a message Dr. al-Hibri takes to heart. From her own difficult journey toward secularism and her return to an enthusiastic embrace of Islam, she has come to see Islam as a powerful force to help women and bring peace to a troubled, embittered world.

As she has said, "God gave Muslim women all the rights, it is only the *Jahiliyyah* [patriarchal thinking] of others that has restricted them."

When Dr. al-Hibri came from her native Lebanon to study in the United States in the early 1970s, she was ready for feminism. She was tired of the patriarchal traditions she had encountered in her country, traditions that favored men. Then she got the shock of her life: Her American male professors were *worse*. They would pelt her with questions: "Why am I going to school when a guy could have my place so he could support his family? Why don't I go home and be a good homemaker?" They did not take her seriously. "In my own country I was given a lot more respect," she says. But Azizah believed in herself, and as the women's movement gathered strength Dr. al-Hibri became a part of it. It changed her life.

She became friends with other American feminists, women who still keep in touch decades later. They were idealists intent on bettering conditions for all women, including the religious ones who were trying to meld their feminism with their spiritual beliefs in spite of what feminists viewed as centuries of discrimination imposed on women by religious leaders, be they Christian, Jewish, or Muslim. Some feminists were openly hostile to religion. Nevertheless, Dr. al-Hibri says, "We wanted to make room for those religious women. I learned to be inclusive."

Azizah earned her Ph.D. from the University of Pennsylvania in 1975. At a time when colleges were beginning to cut back on hiring liberal arts professors, she found a tenure-track position at Texas A & M University. While teaching, she published in academic journals, even starting one herself—*Hypatia: A Journal of Feminist Philosophy*. She was soon highly respected in her field.

Her personal life was also flourishing. Friends had introduced her to a Saudi graduate student, who courted Azizah for five years. She is grateful he was persistent. "We have been happily married for twenty years," she says.

Despite her personal and academic successes, she felt restless. She wanted to act on her beliefs, to further pursue shattering glass ceilings for women. "At one point, I thought I would like to bring about change rather than *write* about it," she says. She decided to give up teaching and take up a completely new career: law. She was accepted at the law school of the University of Pennsylvania, and back to Philadelphia she went.

"I left a very nice teaching job," she says. "It was the hardest thing I have ever done in my life."

Law, she felt, was one of the last frontiers for women, particularly the formerly all-male preserve of corporate law. She set her sights on Wall Street. Although she briefly returned to academia as a visiting scholar at the Harvard Divinity School and the Center for the Study of World Religion, by 1986 she was firmly ensconced as an associate in a New York law firm and, later, as a Wall Street attorney specializing in securities regulation. She exuded polish and confidence as she began working the required marathon hours the job demanded. She again found emotional support from other Muslim women lawyers trying to achieve in a male preserve. Life was good, but Dr. al-Hibri kept asking herself: Is this all there is? After all, she wasn't doing it for the money. After six years on Wall Street, she discovered she missed teaching and researching. In 1992 she got a chance to go back to teaching, this time law, and accepted a position as an associate professor at the T. C. Williams School of Law at the University of Richmond in Virginia and later became a full professor there. It was at Richmond that she rekindled her passion for Islamic law and women's rights.

In 1992, she broke ground in a new academic field, writing an article about Islam and democracy for a scholarly journal. "They said, You must write about it," she remembers. "But I had no idea what to say. No one had examined the topic so basically I had to invent the wheel." She delved into Arabic texts, hundreds of years old. What she came up stunned many in the academic community. It turned out that early Islam leaders had emphasized free thought and movement, what today is considered essential in a democratic society. "The first thing that the Prophet did was to put together a bill of rights. He had a charter between him as the head of the city, and the people—the Muslims and Jews." All were to be treated with respect, given individual rights, and expected to defend their city. The charter, she says, is remarkably similar to the United States Constitution. At the same time, it is at odds with the policies of the authoritarian regimes in the Middle East and of other Muslim-dominant countries in Asia and Africa. Dr. al-Hibri believes that the powerful corrupted the faith, and that many clerics — who themselves were not well-versed in Islamic scripture — helped perpetuate for centuries a status quo that was not based on Quranic teachings. This wrongful use of scripture, she points out, served to justify the repression.

Her article showed how early Islam promoted democracy. What she had to say on the subject was, she says, "so unusual and so fresh, it created quite a stir." Her article was widely read, although some scholars found it hard to believe that Islam was ever as she described it. However, she adds, "In the Muslim community, it was a huge success."

Other scholars followed Dr. al-Hibri's lead, writing many other articles and books on the issue. "And now everybody thinks of Islam and democracy as compatible." She says, adding with a laugh, "I had to do the hard work."

In her next article, she discovered her passion for analyzing the status of women as set forth in Islamic family laws. Again, she says, "that was a very new topic."

Writing gave Azizah pause to reflect on her own life, to review Islam, and to welcome it back more deeply into her life. By then, she had been reading the Quran on a daily basis and found it empowering. She realized that the Prophet Mohammed had been ahead of his time in promoting the treatment of women, quite the opposite of many male religious leaders who misinterpreted the Quran intentionally in order to shore up their power and keep women subservient.

Human rights, Dr. al-Hibri says, "flow from God and no individual or government can take them away from us." In that light, she named her human rights group Karamah, after an Arabic reference to a Quranic verse that means, "We have given dignity to the children of Adam."

She is keenly aware, though, that change does not come quickly. "What was really hard while growing up was the interpretation of Islam I was receiving in my society."

Reading the Quran changed her. "I found out that I have all the rights I ever wanted. There was no reason for alienation; there was no reason at all to think that the Quran gives women a subordinate place in society."

Azizah acknowledged that her newfound knowledge of Islam empowering women surprised her. It also caused her to reflect more favorably on her own upbringing—how her family had pushed her to become a highly educated woman in a male-dominant society. "Islamic culture," she adds, "was patriarchal but supportive. Otherwise, I wouldn't be where I am today."

She was born into a distinguished family in Beirut, where her grandfather was widely esteemed by other Lebanese religious leaders there. He and her father emphasized education and saw to it that Azizah went to Lebanon's finest schools. "I was very young, about three years old, when I first went to school," she says. She spent two years of preschool and kindergarten at a French-run school, but when her father decided she must learn English rather than French, he transferred her to the American School for Girls. "I had a great time there for twelve years," she says. She would later graduate from the American University in Beirut with a bachelor's degree in philosophy.

At the same time, she was being educated about Islam at home. She was her grandfather's pet and he confided in her about his religious thoughts, and the result was that she, as a young girl, became more knowledgeable about Islam than some poorly educated Imams. This knowledge would come in handy with her academic research in the United States. But her family gave her more than scriptural instruction. They also emphasized a life of service, of helping others and acting on their Muslim faith. Growing up, she was very active in charitable work and social work.

She recognizes that today many Muslim women do not receive the same encouragement as she did. This perception has been supported by her travels throughout the Muslim world, where she has seen the differences in how women are treated.

Nevertheless, she is optimistic that Muslim women will be granted more rights—through working within the cultures of their own countries. For example, she's been a consultant to the Supreme Council for Family Affairs in Qatar to develop a draft family code. However, she is mindful that what works in, say, Jordan, may not be suitable in more conservative countries such as Saudi Arabia. But change will come. Already in many Middle East countries including hyperconservative Iran—more women are occupying more college classrooms than men.

In Dr. al-Hibri's opinion, American feminists mean well in their efforts to aid women around the world, trying to end genital mutilation in sub-Saharan Africa, for example. But they have to realize that women in Muslim countries have their own priorities which may be different from those attributed to them by American feminists. Women in Muslim countries, she says, are first and foremost concerned about their families' well-being. In her article, "Introduction to Muslim Women's Rights," she has stated, "Although gradual change is frustrating, it is, nevertheless, more stable and less destructive of society than a radical coercive change."

And, she says, it's not just in the Middle East or Africa where the potential of Muslim women is being suppressed. In the United States, some women are held back because they're ignorant of their rights. Separated from their families and not always able to speak English, they can be abused by husbands, Dr. al-Hibri says. Indeed, one of Karamah's missions is to help Muslim women in the United States become educated about their rights.

"There is a real need among the American Muslims to develop what we call legal literacy," she told a seminar about the challenges American Muslim women face. "There is really not much knowledge among the Muslim population in the United States about the law in the United States. And, as a result of that, very often unfair situations could have been avoided had the person known about American law."

She cites the example of a Muslim woman who decided to divorce her husband under Islamic law—but decided she couldn't afford to get a divorce in U.S. civil courts. According to her reasoning, she was divorced in the eyes of God and later she remarried in an Islamic ceremony. But, of course, this was not a legal union, as she was still married to her first husband. Dr. al-Hibri points out that later, when the second union fell apart, the woman couldn't ask for any assets or "enforce her rights in court because she was not legally married in the United States. She could have avoided all that by simply finding a way, through Legal Aid or some other community resource, to finalize her civil divorce. There is no reason why she should have disadvantaged herself."

Some immigrant Muslim women may also endure abuse unnecessarily because their husband tells them they have no rights in the United States, and they believe it. Some husbands are so underhanded they obtain permanent residence and citizenship for themselves and their children, but not their wives. These men tell their wives that they must obey them or risk being deported. Sometimes they divorce their immigrant wife and claim she is not entitled to any of the family's assets. They may try to obtain custody of their children. Often their ex-wives are left destitute, without money or work skills, forced to rely on family in the United States or assistance from a charitable group. That, Azizah says, is an injustice that can be remedied in the courts. Immigrant women are entitled to the same divorce protection laws as are American-born women. They can also apply for legal residence on the basis of being abused by their husbands.

U.S. courts have not always been protective of Muslim women, particularly if they are immigrants who married in their native country. When they divorce in the United States, the courts may not always give them what they are entitled to, such as their delayed dowry, called a *mahr*, that has been agreed upon before the wedding as part of the *kitab*, the Muslim marriage contract. In Muslim countries, the delayed *mahr*—usually cash or property—is automatically given to the wife in cases of divorce (unless, as the Prophetic precedent shows, the woman sought the divorce for no reason other than that she dislikes her husband and fears certain ethical and religious consequences as a result). However, Dr. al-Hibri explains, some U.S. courts, relying on inaccurate expert testimony, have been reluctant to give the woman this settlement. In one case, the judge was told by "experts" that a woman loses her dowry if she initiates the divorce—something Dr. al-Hibri refutes. The rule is more complicated than that. Unfortunately, the woman in this case ended up losing her *mahr*, and was compelled to suffer the court's moralizing that any Muslim marriage contract in which it is specified a woman receives her *mahr* upon divorce is "designed to facilitate divorce" and is rendered "void as against public policy."

"In other words," Dr. al-Hibri says in disbelief, "if you have an agreement which encourages you to divorce, that's against public policy. The court says that a *kitab*, an Islamic marriage contract, encourages the woman to divorce. Why? Because the *kitab* says that if she divorces she gets money. So, in other words, to get money, she will be motivated to divorce. I would argue that by their logic, a *kitab* also encourages a woman to murder, because she will also get money upon the death of her husband—if she is not discovered. This is ridiculous."

In its efforts to protect Muslim women, Karamah has started summer seminars at the University of Richmond to educate Muslim women community leaders about American law, particularly those on divorce and immigration. Dr. al-Hibri herself lectures widely to better educate American legal scholars and practitioners. She is also working to show how the Quran can be used to resolve disputes peacefully. In many passages, it promotes peace through problem-solving and dialog, she says. She has been using these passages when she lobbies for human rights.

And her message is heard. She has been impressed that some American leaders have responded sensitively when she and other Muslim leaders asked for help to safeguard the rights of Muslims during the tense time after 9/11. "Dialog works," she concludes.

She is also ready to talk with Christian and Jewish groups about the origins their religions share with Islam.

"Let me tell you about our religion and yours," she offers. "For you, too, come from an Abrahamic religion, which believes in loving even your enemies."

Throughout her commitment to promoting human rights in the Muslim world, she has rediscovered her homeland and her faith. And she has found that time marches on. She is an American now—enriched by her Lebanese culture and Muslim faith, but an American, nonetheless.

She takes care to point out, though, that her "Americanization" was gradual.

"When I first came to study here, I did not want to become an American. I thought, I'm Lebanese. I'm going to study and go back home to Lebanon. What you soon find out is that your perception of the United States is changing, and that you too are becoming an American."

❧ 47 ❧

DEEDRA'S DUTY

DEEDRA ABBOUD, glowing and gracious as she makes the rounds, meets with business and political leaders in the Phoenix area, greeting people by name in her soft Southern accent. She's wearing a smartly cut business suit with her trademark *hijab*—elegant, but down to earth. She wants people to feel comfortable around her, and they do.

Her ongoing mission is to bring Islam and its followers into mainstream America. Until recently, she did so as the director of the Arizona chapter of the Council on American-Islamic Relations, the largest Muslim human rights group in the United States. Now she serves as the Arizona director of the Muslim American Society's Freedom Foundation, a national grassroots religious, social, and educational organization.

Most Muslim immigrants in the United States are already in the mainstream, Deedra says. They have adapted to American ways and, if necessary, have changed some of their habits. Take shaking hands between the sexes. In the West, it's taken for granted as a friendly gesture or a way of cementing a business relationship. Muslims, however—especially newly arrived immigrants or exchange students— believe they are not to touch members of the opposite sex except their family members. Deedra assures them that it is okay even necessary, to shake hands, to limit misunderstandings. She's observed that Muslim men especially don't want to look chauvinistic by refusing to shake the hand of a female colleague, customer, or business acquaintance. In this regard, Muslim women are on safer ground, as etiquette books in the West say it is a woman who has the choice of extending her hand. Indeed, some Muslim women do not want to shake hands with strangers. Personally, Deedra believes firmly that *she* must and she does: she wants to give a good impression as a leader in the Arizona Muslim community.

She also wants to project a self-assured image to the public. She believes Islam has deepened the feminism first nurtured in her by her mother, one of the first women in Arkansas to become a law enforcement officer.

Born in Pine Bluff, Arkansas, Deedra, now thirty-three, grew up mostly in the Little Rock area. "My mother got married when she was pretty young—eighteen. I was the youngest of four girls. My dad was abusive and he was also a cheater. We grew up in a chauvinistic society and family."

Her mother was expected to ignore her husband's transgressions— the womanizing, the fits of rage, even the beatings. Calls to police about domestic abuse sometimes went unanswered. Finally her mother gathered her courage and left her husband, despite her family's disapproval. "I was two," Deedra remembers. "I really didn't miss him but my sisters did." Although her mother obtained a divorce and won child support, there was no enforcement. Her mother had to assume responsibility for the girls.

That's what pushed her to become a deputy sheriff in the Little Rock area. It was not only the good, steady pay; she felt she could make a difference and help make changes to benefit other divorced women and their children. Deedra's mother spearheaded a state policy of garnishing the wages of noncustodial parents who failed to pay child support.

"My mom raised us to be very independent," Deedra says. "She would tell us *not* to look for the guy on the white horse. He's not coming."

Instead, her mother promoted feminism. She urged her daughters to work together and help each other out. As a result, they were close as children, and remain close as adults.

Deedra's introduction to Islam was not a good experience. Her sixth-grade textbook, discussing Islam in the context of the Middle East, mentioned the low status of women, and how wives were beaten by their husbands. "It made me angry to read how they were treated," Deedra remembers.

As a deputy sheriff, her mother had her own stories about Muslims, of black inmates who became part of the Nation of Islam while in prison. They were violent, anger-filled men, her mother believed—dangerous to be around. She did not see anything positive in what she considered a strange religion. Neither did Deedra.

School reinforced that impression, Deedra says. In seventh grade, one text referred to Islam as "Mohammedism" and described how adherents worshipped the Prophet and that women were forced to wear black and walk one step behind men. Her teacher warned that such people "were going to hell." Deedra believed her.

During her senior year of high school, while still going to her traditional Pentecostal church, Deedra got to know some Malaysian students who were Muslim. She would try to "help" them by explaining how their religion was bad.

"I used to go up to them and argue they were going to hell, that the women had been treated so badly. They would say, 'No, Islam doesn't treat women badly. Maybe individuals do but they are not practicing Islam.'"

Deedra began soul searching, bought a book about Islam, then a copy of the Quran itself. To her surprise, she found she liked the faith and what it stood for.

She knew she wanted to become a Muslim but couldn't see herself doing so in Arkansas. For one, she didn't see how she could hold a job and wear a *hijab*. Through a fortunate turn of events, her mother invited her to accompany her to a convention in Phoenix—and Deedra fell in love with the Southwest. She felt she could move there and start over, that this was a place where she could become a practicing Muslim and comfortably wear the traditional scarf and clothes. In 1998 she packed all her things in a car and drove with a girlfriend and her older sister to Phoenix. She got a job immediately as a collections clerk. Soon she found herself a mosque, after it had held an open house to dispel anti-Arab stereotypes shown in a movie called *The Siege*.

There, Deedra met Yuko Davis (see chapter 25) who became her best friend. That year, Deedra formally became a Muslim, going through the Shahada ceremony. She began going to mosque regularly and wore the traditional clothes on more occasions.

"I wore a *hijab*, but not to work. Everywhere else but there," she added.

When she was laid off, she told Yuko it was actually an opportunity to find a company where she could feel comfortable wearing a *hijab*. Coincidentally, a Muslim family-owned construction company needed a secretary. The owners, two brothers, preferred a woman who wore the *hijab*. Deedra was interviewed, and the job was offered to her.

She started work with one of the brothers, Ali Asim Abboud Al-Janabi, who was polite but distant. He spoke very little to Deedra, but that was okay with her. She liked her job, and the quiet office enabled her to get more things done. She thought of Ali as a nice family man — he had pictures of children on his desk.

"He was so respectful, I was clueless," Deedra says.

But Ali had taken a fancy to the tall, blue-eyed Deedra. It turned out he was single: The pictures on his desk were of his brother's children.

He went to Yuko's husband for advice on courting Deedra, and was advised to do it the traditional way: Get to know her in a chaperoned setting. Yuko and her husband invited him to meet Deedra at their house. Meanwhile, Ali's family was encouraging the would-be romance. His sister-in-law described what a great guy Ali was. Deedra listened politely. "I wasn't getting it," she now chuckles. "You would think I would put two and two together."

When, finally, Yuko clued her in — within minutes before Ali was supposed to come and "meet" Deedra outside the workplace — Deedra flew into a panic. She had shown up at Yuko's house wearing sweatpants, assuming she was only going to see her friend. But Yuko lent her proper clothing and Deedra met Ali as planned. She also began to view him in a new way — as a potential husband. They hit it off during their first chat but something occurred to Deedra. Ali was kind and amiable, but he was a secular Muslim, not a religious one. Like many born to the faith, he didn't practice Islam. Nor did he pray.

Deedra was tactful, but she was also blunt: She couldn't marry a nonpracticing Muslim. The Quran forbade it. She immediately gave up the idea of a courtship.

Later the next evening, Ali called her at home, to tell her he had prayed for the first time. Their relationship took off. In the end, it transformed both of them. Ali, for one, discovered Islam and began practicing it with the zeal of a convert. ("He definitely has surpassed me in piety," Deedra now says.) As for Deedra, after their marriage, she began to feel the need for a job separate from her husband and his family. At the time she was helping start an Arizona chapter of the Council of American-Islamic Relations, serving on its board of directors. When the group decided to hire staff, Deedra applied and became its director.

Although Deedra believes Arizona is a good home for Muslims, it has been a hotspot of sporadic violence against Muslims after 9/11. Tensions continued to escalate following the wars in Afghanistan and Iraq.

In 2003, Deedra wrote to Arizona governor Janet Napolitano, asking her to "denounce all types of stereotyping, racial slurs, discriminations, violence, loss of life, loss of property, hate crime and other forms of intimidation." The letter turned out to be eerily prescient: The day it was delivered to the governor's office, four dry ice explosives were tossed into the backyard of an Iraqi family in Phoenix. Local police investigated it as a possible hate crime and the governor did denounce the attack. More incidents have occurred, including the spray-painting of a swastika and a thunderbolt-shaped "SS," among other Nazi symbols, on a Tempe mosque. Deedra appeared at a press conference with other Muslims and Tempe police chief Ralph Tranter to protest the vandalism. Soon afterward, police arrested a suspect with a rap sheet who was picked up near the mosque, and conclusively linked him to the crime.

Chief Tranter praised Deedra for working with police while she worked hard to educate the public about Muslims. Nevertheless, Deedra says, her office continues to get hate mail.

But she sees the better side of America, and that's what keeps her going. In her new job, she is encouraging Muslims to become more involved in American government and charity groups. It's important, she believes, that Muslims become part of the system. "I'm out there meeting new people every day and I find those who hate are the minority."

ᘛ 48 ᘚ

DALIA: STRUGGLING FOR
CIVIL RIGHTS

MOST AMERICANS have either forgotten—or never knew—that in late
2002 hundreds of Middle Eastern men and boys in Southern California were arrested by federal immigration agents in one sweep. But not
twenty-nine-year-old attorney Dalia Hashad, who grew up in California and is now the New York-based national advocate for Arabs, Muslims, and South Asians for the American Civil Liberties Union. The
memory of those who were arrested haunts her, as does the thought of
thousands of others who've been arrested, deported, or had their
homes or businesses searched since the USA Patriot Act enabled
heightened security policies and practices.

"It has happened to a lot of people," she says. "Countless Muslims
are quietly suffering."

She doesn't believe we are safer for the crackdown. Rather, Dalia
believes, America is the weaker for it, thanks to an increase in racial
and ethnic unease. "This dragnet technique used by the FBI is simple
racial profiling and it violates our most cherished fundamental
freedoms."

ACLU executives hired Dalia to help fight what they believe are
attacks on freedoms most Americans take for granted. Dalia lauds the
organization's new national director, Anthony Romero, under whom
she works, for aggressively fighting restrictive policies at a time when
dissent is often characterized as unpatriotic.

Dalia has been traveling around the country directing the ACLU's
national campaign against racial profiling and responding to the post

9/11 backlash against Muslims, Arabs, and South Asians. From coast to coast she addresses audiences on the dangers of newly enacted policies and practices, including the Patriot Act, that encourage negative treatment of Middle Eastern ethnic groups. She also helps recruit and train attorneys to provide pro bono legal services to those caught up in federal investigations.

"This is a huge problem and it is not just happening to the man from Jordan working at Dunkin' Donuts on a tourist visa," she says. "It is the idea that we can solve crime by going after people because of their ethnicity or religion."

Her job as advocate is to make sure that Arabs, Muslims, and South Asians have the same rights as anyone else in the United States. However, not everyone supports Dalia's efforts or agrees with the ACLU's new emphasis on protecting immigrants and second-generation Muslims. In a 2003 article titled "The ACLU's War on Homeland Security," the conservative magazine *Front Page* said "many of these 'unaccounted for' visitors were already in violation of their immigration status when the [U.S. government's] registration drives were launched." Nor, it goes on to say, is the ACLU "interested in informing its followers that many of the Muslims and Middle Easterners it insists the government is targeting due to their race, religion or ethnicity were deported by the government as part of a year-old crackdown on at least 5,900 illegal aliens from countries where al-Qaeda is active. Most were targeted because they ignored deportation orders. . . . Thus, as realties demonstrate, federal agents fighting terrorism must now also fight the ACLU every step of the way."

Dalia believes the U.S. government would be more effective in ferreting out terrorists if it didn't throw out such a broad dragnet, which ensnares many innocent people whose cases clog up the system.

Racial profiling, she adds, is worse than ever. People's fears after 9/11 only added to an increasingly unhealthy climate. In Dalia's opinion, racism is still with us—only more subtle. The United States Senate no longer has the likes of the late Strom Thurmond thundering for segregation anymore, but many Americans now distrust numerous entire groups of people. "The discrimination against Muslims is intense," she says. "I see it every day."

As the daughter of Egyptian immigrants, Dalia considers herself a "brown" American. She grew up in California, living at times in the San Francisco Bay and Orange County areas. Her mother is a nurse; her father an engineer. They met in Kuwait, married, and emigrated to New York before moving to California.

"My parents never tried to shield me from ideas," she remembers. "My sister and I grew up in an extremely political household where we watched and discussed the news every night. I remember being the only kid in my seventh-grade class who knew who the secretary of state was. As small children, my sister and I were sat down in front of the TV to watch programs about the famine in Ethiopia. We were raised to know about the world around us and to feel that we were required to help."

She calls her father the "most informed individual I know" and her mother "the friendliest and most clever. When I was growing up, I thought how, of all the Muslim kids I knew, I had the coolest parents."

She and her father, early on, were politicos. She jokes her father would be attending a city council meeting for one issue—say, a gasoline station being proposed too near a residential area—while she was going to the next meeting when an environmental issue was on the agenda.

As befitting a California liberal, she went to UC Berkeley as an undergrad and found herself elected as chairperson of the California Public Interest Research Group, a 60,000-member nonprofit grassroots environmental and consumer-advocacy organization. During one summer, she worked eighty hours a week to fund-raise for the campaign to "Stop the Rollback" by the U.S. Congress of environmental and public health laws.

Several years later she was off to law school at New York University, another bastion of liberal values. Berkeley, she jokes, is a top supplier of students to NYU's law school.

With her typical energy she signed up for a summer internship in the West Bank after her freshman year at law school: It was to be one of her most memorable experiences. She went as part of the Palestine Peace Project, a team of lawyers, law students, and professors, and became involved in researching and writing about the controversial program by which the Israeli government reassigned Palestinian homes to Jewish residents. "It was heart-breaking, that summer," she recalls.

Dalia remembers going to visit a family who had been evicted from *part* of their house—including the kitchen—which had been taken over by an American-born Jewish family. When Dalia, along with about seventy others who were nearby to attend an academic conference, went to pay their condolences to the Palestinian family, they were met outside the home by the Jewish family, who were toting guns.

"They pointed their rifles right at us," Dalia says.

She was standing near one of the young men brandishing a weapon and she saw in his eyes a fierce determination. She remembers thinking, "Oh, my God, he really will shoot us."

But she was grateful for her Islam. She found herself calm and composed. She was confident she wasn't doing anything wrong, that to console the other family who had lost part of their home was the right thing to do. Despite the guns, she calmly and patiently sat down on the home's unpaved driveway.

"With Islam, you do what is right," she says. "It allows you the freedom from worrying about the consequences."

The Israeli Defense Force arrived, as did television crews from the international media. Suddenly the event became high-profile, the Defense Force acting quickly to disarm the Israelis. They then turned their focus on the visitors, becoming violent in their efforts to remove them from the scene. "Three men shook one poor woman around like a rag doll," she remembers. "They started dragging people away."

One of the key speakers at the conference, a Jewish American professor, suffered a broken ankle. Others had severe bruises, lacerations, and sprains. Dalia herself was approached by an Israeli soldier who spoke to her first in Hebrew. The trilingual Dalia speaks French and Arabic, but not Hebrew. "Okay," he said, exasperated. "I'll give it to you in English. We don't want to hurt you. Just get up and leave."

When Dalia didn't move, she found herself gently lifted and carried away from the house. Later, she learned that the incident had been broadcast on TV—and pretty accurately, she adds.

After the West Bank, she went on to another—safer—internship in New York City, graduated from NYU, and worked for a time as an associate at a law firm in Los Angeles, although she realized she wanted a job that involved advocacy law. The job opening at the ACLU fit the bill. Already, she feels she has made a difference.

Her boss there also gave her a priceless and unforeseen reward: He introduced her to her future husband, a Moroccan who came to the United States as a ten-year-old. He, too, works for a nonprofit agency. And, yes, he is a Muslim.

Dalia remembers one of her male friends becoming upset when she once said she could only marry a Muslim, a notion he thought too restrictive. He himself was marrying out of his faith: He's Jewish, his bride Christian. Although Dalia thinks that is fine for him, she can't imagine not marrying within her faith. Not only does Islam require her to marry a Muslim but she feels it is important for her.

"Being a Muslim—I don't think of it as a religion," she says. "It is a way of thinking, a way of life."

She wanted a soul mate to feel the same way—and she feels blessed that she got one. "Islam," she adds, "has created the best part of who I am."

OKOLO'S ODYSSEY: STARTING THE FIRST U.S. MUSLIM MUSEUM

OKOLO RASHID IS THE CO-FOUNDER and executive director of the first Muslim museum in America, the International Museum of Muslim Cultures in Jackson, Mississippi. She tells the story of how this came to pass:

"I had my own private consulting business in Jackson, Mississippi, promoting community development and historic preservation projects, when I heard that a huge, $10 million exhibition, called "The Majesty of Spain," would be presented at a local museum. Some of the artifacts to be displayed had never left Spain before and many were lent by the royal palace. In fact the king and queen of Spain planned to attend the opening.

"This was exciting news—until I learned that the exhibition would ignore Spain's almost one thousand years of Moorish rule, that it would depict only *Christian* Spain. It was then that I decided that a companion show should be mounted to depict the history of Islamic Spain.

"My partner, Emad Al-Turk, who was then a board member of our mosque and the chairman of its economic development team, became excited about the idea, as did the rest of the Muslim community. We wanted the exhibition to show how under Muslim rule Spain was for centuries a peaceful oasis for all religious and ethnic groups. Most people don't know that when we use the term "Moor," we're talking about African people. The exhibition would be about how Africans and Arabs ruled a European country.

"We decided to call it 'Islamic Moorish Spain—Its Legacy to Europe and the West.' Initially, we thought we could create a modest show for about $30,000 to $40,000. But in the end, despite considerable volunteer labor, it turned out to be a half-million-dollar project, presented at a building near the other Spanish exhibition.

"We got a lot of help. One of our key supporters was Don Simmons, then a deputy director at the Mississippi Humanities Council. As he had done his doctoral dissertation on the Iberian Peninsula and knew its history, he was upset that 'The Majesty of Spain' wasn't even going to mention the country's Islamic legacy. 'They can't talk about Spain without acknowledging this influence,' he said at our first meeting. 'We have to do this.'

"Don helped us get our first federal grant. We were able to open our exhibition in about four months—we call it a miracle project. That show became today's Museum of Muslim Cultures, which opened in April 2001 and drew about 25,000 visitors in its first year. Mississippi's then-governor, two former governors, and Jackson's mayor, Harvey Johnson paid visits. We've had international guests from some forty-five countries. The federal government uses the museum as a cultural stop—Muslims and non-Muslims from around the world come here as guests of the U.S. government to learn more about the United States' religious tolerance and Muslim culture. There are articles about the museum on the websites of U.S. embassies in such countries as Nigeria and Indonesia.

"Although the exhibition was a great success, it would have closed, as scheduled, on October 31, 2001. However, sometime after 9/11, someone threw a brick through the museum's plate-glass front window. When we saw the vandalism the next morning, we began to worry. The exhibit still had six weeks to run, and we had planned a much-needed corporate fundraiser that was being hosted by the mayor and other supporters. Former Governor Ray Mabus was to be the guest speaker. Both he and the mayor expressed reservations about the wisdom of going forward with the fundraiser. We, however, stressed that it was important we come together to support community education and multiculturalism at a time when it was most needed. They agreed, and the event moved forward.

"During this same time, people from all faiths, showed up in support, encouraging us to keep our doors open, that the museum was needed in Jackson. So we did, and the museum is now thriving.

"We have been surprised at the support—about 80 percent of our guests are Christians. So I guess an Islamic institution *can* thrive in the Bible Belt. It's been my experience that Americans are curious and eager to learn, especially when they are challenged, as they were after 9/11.

"Of course, I have also seen Mississippi at its worst. Mississippi was justifiably an embarrassment to the rest of the country, among the last states to give up its Jim Crow laws. It was as bad as movies and books show—and probably worse.

"I was born in 1949 into a poor sharecropping family in a small town called Flora, about twenty miles outside Jackson. I was the fifth out of eleven children—that is, eleven children who *lived*. Four were stillborn. My mother had a baby every year at a time when there was no birth control, as such. Babies' deaths were a sad part of life back then, especially for African American sharecroppers. My mother grieved for her lost children but tried to do her best for those of us who lived.

"My mother worked very hard. I consider her a smart woman, but with a limited education. She is also a very spiritual person. Her mother was very religious. In fact, she was a pillar of her community because of her strong religious convictions and character.

"My father, on the other hand, was not spiritual at all, and I do not mean to say that in a negative way. He had a very difficult childhood, with an abusive father of his own. He ran away at an early age, became a functioning alcoholic, and was, in turn, physically abusive to my mother.

"Interestingly, however, when my father was not drinking he was an entirely different person. I remember my father as a man with integrity. He was honest, had a strong work ethic, and insisted on the same from his children. He was highly respected both by whites and African Americans. He worked as a long-distance truck driver for a rich white family in Flora at a time when very few African American men had that kind of job. Although he made pretty good money, the family didn't see much of it because he would go out on weekends and come back home with nothing.

"My parents also sharecropped. As kids we had no choice but to help out in the fields, even when we were little and supposed to be in school. We would work through Christmas and go to school in January. That meant we hardly—if ever—went to school. My mom hated that. It was my father's decision, not hers.

"This was one of the main reasons why my mom left my father, taking the nine children who were still at home. She worked two jobs in Jackson to provide for us. She would always say she wanted her children to get an education.

"I was ten years old and in fourth grade when we moved. Even though we missed out on a lot of school, I didn't fail a grade. But I have to say, I carried scars from my learning disadvantages. I struggled through my elementary school years, but began to improve significantly when I went to high school. I became an honors student. I was motivated: I finally had the chance to go to school all year. I never missed a day of school from the fourth grade through the twelfth.

"My father later joined us in Jackson and he and my mom got back together. To be with us, my father had to quit his job as a trucker. He couldn't find a similar position—or anything else that paid as well. He was limited to menial jobs, such as working at a service station, and he hated that. He began drinking again. To this day I think of how sad his situation was and how segregation really hurt him. It wasn't easy to see my dad transformed from a very strong man with a firm work ethic to a man hating to go to work—feeling humiliated, and with no other choice. It was all he could do to help us scrape by. When I reflect back, I realize how difficult it was for me as a child to see so proud a man reduced by such daily humiliations. After a few more years together, my father and mother divorced.

"As my father got older, he quit drinking and told us how he regretted his mistakes. He died in his late sixties under my mother's care, whom he praised for her hard work, good character, and devotion to her family.

"I finished high school in 1968, at the height of the civil rights movement. I became involved in the movement as I worked to integrate Mississippi's major junior college, now called Hinds Community College. It was just a handful of us—seven or eight African Americans—who elected to enroll at Hinds.

"After I graduated from Hinds with a degree in secretarial science, I went to work for several years, still living with and helping my mom. Eventually, I started working at Tougaloo College, a private, four-year liberal arts college, historically black. It is known nationally as the "cradle" of the civil rights movement in Mississippi and has been ranked among the top U.S. colleges. Tougaloo was great for me because I could work there full-time as a secretary and go to school tuition-free.

"The mid-1970s were important years for me; I got married and both my husband, Sababu, and I became Muslim. Sababu was a civil rights activist, and was involved in the movement long before I was. He was one of those students who marched for civil rights with Medgar Evers. He got arrested—the dogs were set upon them and he was loaded with the other protesters into garbage trucks to be taken to jail for booking.

"One thing that has been the guiding force in our life and has kept us united, is Islam. Islam has kept us strong as a couple and as parents. The basic moral teachings of Islam and its pragmatic approach to life, such as kindness and dignity for all, have strengthened our relationship.

"Our earliest experience of Islam was through Elijah Muhammad's Nation of Islam. Our involvement, however, came about as a result of our study of the teachings of Elijah Muhammad's son, Imam Warith Deen Mohammed. The Nation was established on a sound moral base and we felt comfortable in it. We were also attracted to Imam Mohammed's perspective on Islam. He presented Islam as emphasizing a strong sense of dignity for all human beings, and that Muslim Americans should see themselves united with Muslims around the world. The basic principle of Islam is the oneness of God and the oneness of humanity, all men and women are afforded individual freedom and equality under God. These ideas were very appealing to me and Sababu. It is that very spirit of universal brotherhood that informs Sababu's and my work to build a more diverse Islamic community in the Jackson area.

"Another thing I love about Islam is how it promotes learning. I want to always learn, to contemplate, and to pass on my knowledge to others. This propels me to be a better person. To be honest, I don't see myself as serving as executive director of the museum indefinitely, but rather becoming a full-time lecturer. (As executive director, I have already given a lot of talks.) To that end, I want to become more fluent in Arabic and to travel more to Islamic countries in Asia, Africa, and the Middle East to share with others what I have learned. Giving and caring about others is crucial.

"After all, God came to Mohammad not for his brain but for his heart."

❧ 50 ❧

RIFFAT: LIFE WITH A PURPOSE

AT AGE SIXTY-ONE, DR. RIFFAT HASSAN could be excused for slowing down. A pioneer in Islamic feminist theology research, she had been teaching for decades at two major Kentucky institutions, the University of Louisville and the Louisville Presbyterian Theological Seminary.

Instead, she is busier than ever, recently squeezing in a telephone interview before she flew to lead a Middle Eastern tour of somewhat apprehensive U.S. scholars. (By the end of the trip, she predicts, they will be relaxed and glad they went on the fact-finding trip that, with any luck will also be a goodwill mission.) As founder of the International Network for the Rights of Female Victims of Violence in Pakistan, she also finds time to defend women against honor killings, a "tradition" she abhors with a passion.

"I work eighteen hours out of twenty-four—there is so much work to do," Riffat says.

The Muslim world is familiar ground for Riffat. She was born into an upper-class family in Pakistan, her grandfather a well-known scholar and writer. Her father, however, was traditional in his views. He loved his daughters and felt it best that they marry at age sixteen, their marriages arranged by family. Two of Riffat's older sisters were, indeed, married as teens. "My father was a very kind man but he was part of a patriarchal society," Riffat says. She would have shared the same fate had she not rebelled. Her mother, a feminist in her own right, supported her.

After she finished high school at an Anglican school in Pakistan, Riffat was off to study at the University of Durham in England. She earned her doctorate by age twenty-four, was teaching at the University of Punjab in Pakistan in the mid-1960s—a career that would have been unusual even for a woman in the United States—and she married. "My choice," she points out.

She and her husband had a daughter and came to the United States in the early 1970s, but making a living was tough. Riffat found herself doing any work to survive, including ringing up groceries at a supermarket. That didn't last long—a day. But eventually she got lucky and learned of an opening at the University of Oklahoma, where she taught for two years before going to the University of Louisville.

By then her marriage was breaking up, having lasted only a few years. "I knew so little of myself and my culture, there was no chance it would work," she reflects. "There is no point in staying in a bad marriage." In any case, she says, "Your family doesn't necessarily have to have a man."

She is, however, grateful that this brief marriage gave her a daughter. There were, though, rough times ahead as a single mom. She followed a route familiar to many American working women: babysitters when her daughter was young, followed by day-care centers and preschools. By evening she was exhausted. "I think ultimately it made me stronger. It made my daughter stronger, too. But it was very difficult in the beginning. I made so little money."

Mother and daughter were close and remain so today even though they are often thousands of miles apart. Her daughter is now an actress with a career in India and Pakistan. (Riffat herself owns a home in Pakistan.)

Meanwhile, she had found her life's work—feminist theory and Islam. "That has been my major work as a theologian for more than thirty years," she says. "I came to feel that on the basis of my research the Quran does not discriminate, that the majority of the Muslim women lack religious education. The tradition has always been interpreted for women by men. The major mission of my work is to educate women."

She disputes some translated passages in the Quran's text that denigrate women. One, Surah 4, speaks of men as the "managers of the affairs of women" and says that women must be "obedient." Reading the same passage in Arabic, Riffat discovers that linguistically *qawwamun* has been misinterpreted. To her tutored eye, it refers to "those who provide a means of support or livelihood." Accordingly, Riffat sees this verse as an exhortation to men to financially support their wives who will bear their children.

She compares this misinterpretation to how Paul's admonishments to women in the Bible's New Testament have been mischaracterized by generations of Christian leaders to promote a patriarchal point of view.

More than ever before, Riffat believes, Muslim women must educate themselves about their faith. "In my judgment, the importance of developing what the West calls 'feminist theology' is paramount today, not only for Muslim women but also Muslim men. Unjust social structures and systems of thought make a peer relationship between men and women impossible. It is extremely important for Muslim women activists to realize that in the contemporary Muslim world, laws instituted in the name of Islam cannot be overturned by means of political action alone, but through the use of better arguments."

To make her points, Riffat speaks directly. Today's average Muslim woman is "poor, illiterate, and she lives in a rural environment." To reach her, Riffat believes lofty talk about human rights is not the answer. The better way is to remind her "that God is just and merciful" and that as a creation of this Supreme Being she is entitled to being treated with justice and dignity. "I have seen the eyes of many Muslim women light up when they realize what possibilities for development exist for them within the framework of the beliefs which define their world."

She is just as honest about how her belief in Islam has propelled her forward. "My whole life has been full of struggle and if I didn't have faith I don't know what I would have done."

She also believes that knowledge of the Quran can help Muslims counter the extreme right-wing or anti-religious groups who have "hijacked" Islam in many Muslim countries. Such people do not represent "the vast majority of Muslims who are religious without being fanatic, narrow-minded, or inclined toward violence and terrorism."

Riffat saw what she calls the "Islamization of Muslim societies" spread "from country to country in the late 1970s and 1980s." From Iran to Afghanistan, these extremists came with patriarchal baggage. "It was very detrimental to women. I began to see how people were going to misuse religion against women."

Education is the key to stop this abuse of Islam and to promote peace. In that spirit, Riffat worked hard to help the University of Louisville win a State Department grant to educate professors from the Muslim world about the United States and American Muslims. As part of what the grant supports, she will also take American professors to Pakistan and other Muslim countries for similarly instructional visits.

At first, the program was met with a lot of skepticism, she admits. American scholars didn't want to go to the Middle East. "They were so scared," she says. But those who did make the trip were transformed after they returned, having seen for themselves that most people in Muslim countries aren't extremists.

The scholars from South Asian Muslim countries have been equally surprised by their visits to the United States. As Riffat explains, "Since 9/11, America has been perceived as being very much against Islam, and in Muslim countries one finds a lot of anger against the war in Iraq."

But Pakistani scholars soon discover that Americans "are just like themselves," as Riffat puts it. "They find kind people, good people. They make a lot of friends."

And they discover that American Muslims are diverse. When they visit some American mosques, they find people from twenty nationalities praying together. "This is an experience they would never have in their country. They find the diversity quite astonishing, just as they do the openness of Americans."

In 1999, Riffat took up the fight against honor killings when she was asked by the television program *Nightline* to offer commentary on a BBC documentary that graphically showed teenage girls or women being burned or mutilated by their own male family members in Pakistan to restore "honor" to the family. Many of the women had done nothing to deserve such brutal punishment. Riffat says it is a centuries-old tribal custom that is being carried on today by impoverished and uneducated rural villagers. Among them are even some women who think that their daughters or daughters-in-law should be killed if they are found to be adulterers or caught looking at another man. Even more horrible is the fact that some men may fabricate evidence so they can get rid of a wife, sister, or daughter they no longer want.

"After I was on *Nightline,* I received e-mail from around the world from people asking how they could help stop these crimes," Riffat says. "We began an international network and support group, the major objective of which is to highlight the nature of these crimes. Pakistanis were in a state of denial."

Since then, she says, her group has documented thousands of cases. She met with Pakistani president Musharraf and found him sympathetic to helping end honor killings. He began denouncing the practice publicly and in January 2005 signed a law to outlaw honor killings, making the crime punishable by death.

Still, Riffat remarks, "Domestic violence is a problem around the world, including this country. Many people place very little value on the lives of women."

The solution, she says, is empower the victims. And that is why Riffat, entering her seventh decade, isn't thinking of retiring to a simpler, easier life. No, she is on a flight to Pakistan or teaching a new generation in Louisville, as her faith leads her to work as hard as she did as a young scholar.

"Faith gives you a certain structure and meaning to your life. There is a purpose for human life. This is serious business."

EPILOGUE

Muslimah have already changed America. They are running for political office, leading mosque reform movements, and advocating for social change. They are a young generation on the move. A Cornell University study in 2002 found that sixty percent of Muslims in America are age thirty or younger. Arizona State law student Zarinah Nadir in chapter 1 describes this confident young generation. She sees herself and her friends as go-getters, poised to achieve in America while retaining their faith. "The sky is the limit," Zarinah concludes. "We are coming of age."

America is beginning to notice. Newspapers across the country have covered the quest of Ferial Masry, a Saudi emigrant, for the California State Assembly as a Democrat in a predominantly Republican district in suburban Los Angeles. Other Muslim women are making headlines, starting prayer sessions on Capitol Hill and helping to make federal policy as congressional aides. The start of their own sorority by *Muslimah* college students has received national coverage. One of Gamma Gamma Chi's founders told *USA Today* that she wanted to belong to a sorority where she felt comfortable without compromising her Islamic beliefs. "I don't wear short sleeves," Imani Abdul-Haqq told the reporter. "I wear my hair covered."

Other Muslim women are asking for—and getting—things that would have been unheard of even a decade ago. Increasingly, both local governments and private companies are arranging for traditional *Muslimah* to play sports without allowing men to watch. (If men were present, they would have to wear their hijabs, pants, and long sleeves.) The city of North Seattle granted a request from Muslim women to have a time at a public pool when men are not allowed. In Lincoln Park, Michigan, Fitness USA agreed to wall off an area in its aerobic center so that *Muslimah* can work out without men being able to watch.

Of course, this segregation is controversial. Muslim women who want separate facilities must persuade other Americans that their position is based on religion. And they have to show that non-Muslims won't be adversely affected.

Some Muslim women are adapting to a coed America. Teenager Aseel Abdallah in chapter 6 sees nothing wrong or embarrassing about donning pants and a hijab to play soccer at her public high school if men will be present. Neither do her Muslim classmates—they want to play sports at their school. And, of course, most Muslim women in the United States do not wear any kind of veil. At one of my book discussions in North Miami, a woman in a T-shirt and jeans stood up to announce to a mostly Jewish and Christian audience, "You may not believe this, but I am a Muslim. My family is from Palestine." Not even her neighbors realize she is a Muslim, yet she credits her faith in Islam with guiding her to become a teacher.

Muslimah are among the most educated women in the United States. The push to educate a new generation remains fierce. Even desperately poor refugee women, arriving illiterate in America, want their children to achieve in school, urging their kids to bring home top grades so that they can win scholarships. One Muslim refugee woman agreed to tell her story for this book on one condition: that I advise her daughter on getting into college. In their own country, she told me, her children would never have had the chance to attend a university. But in America she is more than willing to work two jobs to help her kids get a higher education.

Women converting to Islam credit the faith's emphasis on education for motivating them to achieve in the classroom. Aisha Musa grew up in the West and converted to Islam as an adult, becoming so immersed in her faith that she worked her way to a master's degree in Islamic studies. When she applied for doctoral programs, she was stunned to find herself accepted at Harvard. Today Dr. Musa is helping set up South Florida's first Islamic studies program as an assistant professor at Florida International University in Miami.

This push for education has helped many *Muslimah* achieve the American Dream. While many are homemakers, content simply to live in peace with their families, especially if they came from wartorn countries, many others have become professors, lawyers, doctors, engineers, pharmacists, and computer techs, like the professionals portrayed in this book. Setting aside the recent influx of impoverished refugees, Muslim women tend to better educated than the average American woman. Like other well-educated women in the United States, many have opted to stay in the workforce. In an opinion column for the *Detroit Free Press*, I noted that the book's Shahida Shakir should be a "red, white, and blue" success story. An immigrant, she worked her way through medical school and now directs the laboratories of two Florida hospitals. She passed her drive on to her daughters: one graduated from law school; the other was an investigator for the Miami-Dade State Attorney's office before she married.

Muslim women are among the most accomplished women in the United States. They lead worldwide humanitarian groups in Washington, preside over juvenile court in Baltimore, deliver babies in Los Angeles, teach in Miami, and help the homeless in Las Vegas. Just like other American women, the *Muslimah* have made startling progress in the workplace in the last thirty years.

They are far from the stereotype of the secluded or downtrodden Muslim woman. Even so, a Washington Post/ABC poll in spring 2006 showed that nearly half of Americans have a negative view of Islam. In a poll conducted for the Council of American-Islamic Relations, most people also said that they would feel less negative if they thought Islam treated women better.

The evidence to the contrary is in our own backyard: Unlike the poor North African Muslims who went to Europe for a better life, Muslim immigrants to America have been given more opportunities to better themselves, and have become part of the national fabric. Again unlike their European counterparts, Muslims in America don't limit themselves to particular parts of the country or even neighborhoods. In Nashville, Zainab Elberry found the courtly manners and the good ol' boy ways of doing business similar to what she knew growing up in Egypt and has thrived, becoming a success in insurance and a civic and political leader.

Interestingly, many Muslims have settled in the Bible Belt. Quietly, hundreds of thousands of Muslims have moved to the South in the last three decades, buying homes, opening businesses, starting mosques, and becoming community activists. Muslims have moved for the same reasons as other Americans: the jobs and the weather. Dr. Haq (chapter 9), for example, was thrilled that she and her husband could move their his-and-her medical practice from Chicago to the Fort Lauderdale area because subtropical South Florida reminds her of her native India.

Everywhere they live, Muslim women have increasingly demanded that mosques provide them the same services men receive. Around the country, mosques are trying to make Muslim women feel at home. Does more need to be done? Yes, judging from several Muslim women who have approached me to complain about their own mosques' inadequacies. One young woman, a convert, asked me at a book signing in Northern Virginia if mosques would really ever offer women equal opportunities. She loves her faith, she told me. But she has been disappointed to find that women are relegated to smaller worship areas, some of them dirty. I told her that many women were committed to improving conditions. The problems stem in part from immigrant mosque leaders who are not used to the American way. Not simply resistant to change, they appear genuinely perplexed as to why American women view separate quarters as discrimination. American converts to Islam are asking other Muslims to consider how they treat the newest members to the faith. Otherwise, they say, Islam will risk losing these women. Aishah Schwartz, who became a Muslim in 2002, formed an e group, Sisters4Dawah, to provide an outlet where converts could discuss frankly the often cold treatment they receive from other Muslims. "Today, the group has 229 members, attesting to the fact that a serious problem continues to linger within the Muslim *ummah* [community]," Aisha e-mailed me in April 2006.

Women continue to Americanize the mosque. They bring in Brownie troops, self-help sessions, and Quran study—just as they promote equal treatment. In May 2006 the Islamic Foundation in Villa Park, Illinois, held a workshop to address the fact that about 60 percent of converts go back to their original faith. Some converts discovered they couldn't understand their local imam, who only spoke Arabic or another language. Others become disillusioned with the lack of welcome at the mosque; some felt rejected outright. One woman complained to Aisha, "The biggest challenge I faced as a new *Muslimah* . . . was the discrimination from other *Muslimah*. I didn't cover as they did, so when I gave them salaam, they never salaamed me back. It was very hurtful." New *Muslimah* need to be embraced, nurtured, and integrated "without fear of chastisement or ridicule for their minor imperfections or what they haven't learned yet," Aishah concluded.

"Muslims need to be a little less self-centered," she added in an e-mail to me. "If some of the time spent crying about being misunderstood and expecting the rest of the world to respect their religion was spent actually practicing the teachings of Islam outlined in the Quran, Sunnah, and Hadith, they wouldn't be spending so much time and energy feeling the need to defend themselves."

Still, American Muslims are united on their faith's basic teachings. In particular, Muslims value family life, and children are a priority. Two of the women profiled in *The Face Behind the Veil* gave birth since the hardcover edition was published. Muslims will become a force in America because they are a relatively young population with a high birthrate. Even when trained as professionals, Muslim women tend to have at least two children; many have three or more. Like other American mothers, they balance work and family.

Before they leave their teens, Muslim girls are trying to figure out how to have both a challenging career and children. One Muslim teenager followed me out to my car after a lecture to ask how the successful women in the book had managed it. I told her that many had married at an early age, stayed at home until their children went to school, and only then started careers. The young girl nodded: That was exactly how she planned to do it, she told me. I was amazed that a girl 13 or 14 would be making such detailed plans—but she is far from alone.

Two of the women in *The Face Behind the Veil* find motherhood bittersweet. Cassy David couldn't bear not seeing her daughter after an American judge gave custody of the toddler to Cassy's more educated ex-husband, who had moved back to Egypt to teach at a university. Cassy didn't see her daughter for months until she, too, flew to Egypt. Now she works at an English school and sees her daughter at least once a week. Samirah bint Jackie Todd, living in Philadelphia, still hasn't been able to see her estranged older daughter, nor has she seen her younger daughter since a judge granted custody to the father, who then disappeared with the child. Many *Muslimah* activists believe they need to help women like Samirah and Cassy win in the American courts because, they say, some judges misunderstand Islam and discriminate against *Muslimah*.

In their personal lives, American Muslim women will continue to grapple with how to follow traditional Islam while fitting in with the rest of American society. The American *Muslimah* are divided over interpretations of their faith. The veil is often the center of raging arguments. Although a growing number of Muslim women are returning to more traditional dress, most want to decide for themselves how they will interpret the Islamic mandate of modesty. In America, they can. Whether they will be accepted by more conservative Muslims remains a question. One veil-less woman told me she feared the reaction of the audience if she went on camera on a predominantly Muslim cable channel in America.

Ironically, Edina Lekovic in chapter 10 had the opposite problem. A secular television station told her she would never get on air wearing her scarf. A newspaper reporter, interviewing me after the book came out, questioned why Edina would ever think she could be accepted on TV. The broadcast media has always had only beautiful people and even most non-Muslims cannot expect to face television cameras, the reporter argued. Still, a new generation of veiled Muslim women remains committed to breaking into this world. Just wait and see, they told me.

They are, indeed, a reflection of the new generation of American *Muslimah*: optimistic and focused.

Glossary

HERE ARE SOME WORDS, mostly Arabic, that are commonly used in connection with American Islam and the *Muslimah*. Please note that many of the words' spelling can vary.

Abaya — A Muslim woman's outer garment or gown that is long, loose and modest.

Allah — God in Arabic

Burqa — A severe head-to-toe outer garment that completely covers a woman except for her eyes.

Chador — A Muslim woman's covering, what some refugees calls a scarf but what others consider a cloak-like garment that is not as severe as a burqa.

Co-wife — A Muslim woman in the United States who shares a husband with another woman (or up to two others). Islam allows a man to have up to four wives provided that he can provide for all of them and provide for them equally.

Deen — Way of life, destiny

Eid — Refers to two Islamic festivals: Eid ul-Fitr, which marks the end of Ramadan and Eid ul-Adha, which celebrates Prophet Ibrahim's willingness to sacrifice his son Ishmael for Allah.

Hadith — A collection of the teaching of the Prophet Muhammad

Haram — What is unlawful, prohibited in Islam

Hijab — The veil or the covering of a Muslim woman's head, with usually the hair completely hidden. Some sort of head covering is required at prayer services but many women also say it is mandated that they wear a covering over their head when in public where there will be men.

Imam — Has different meanings in various Islamic groups but generally is known as the congregational leader of a mosque who advises members on religious matters and leads Friday prayers.

Imamah—A female leader of prayers, especially for an all-women gathering. But it is a term not generally recognized as men have been thought to be the only ones to become Imams.

Jilbaab—Loose outer garment like a coat or cloak that covers the entire body except for eyes.

Khimar—Arabic for covering. Can be dress, shawl, blouse, or other apparel that covers the bosom as mandated by the Quran. Also can mean a head covering.

Khutba—Central sermon at Friday prayers.

Masjid—An Islamic house of worship, a mosque where Friday prayers are conducted.

Mosque—An Islamic house of worship where Friday prayers are conducted. In the United States many mosques are becoming like churches, hosting classes and other activities. Some predominantly African American congregations may meet on Sunday for classes in addition to Friday prayers.

Muslimah—A woman who is a Muslim; an adherent to Islam.

Niqaab—Saudi Arabian–style burqa that completely covers a woman from head to toe.

Prophet Muhammad—Considered the "founder" of Islam; Allah came to him with the Islamic teachings.

Quran—The holy book of Islam, revealed by the Prophet.

Revert—A person who converts to Islam. Called a revert because Muslims believe all people are born Muslim although their parents may raise them in a different faith.

Salat—Ritual prayer or divine service.

Shahada—Ceremony when usually new converts give their declaration of faith to Islam.

Resources

YOU CAN RESEARCH more about Muslim women by going online or contacting refugee, civil rights, and immigration groups around the nation. Here is a sampling:

American Civil Liberties Union
(It has staff that works on
   Muslim civil rights issues.)
125 Broad Street, 18th Floor
New York, NY 10004
www.aclu.org

Arab American Institute
(Group committed to civic and
   political empowerment of
   Arab Americans)
(202) 429-9210
www.aaiusa.org

Arizona Refugee Community
   Center
(Works with many *Muslimah*
   refugees)
P.O. Box 40482
Phoenix, AZ 85067
www.arizonarefugee.org

Council on American-Islamic
   Relations
(Largest advocacy group for
   Muslims)
453 New Jersey Avenue, S.E.
Washington, DC 20003
(202) 488-8787
www.cair-net.org

International Institute of Erie
(Works with *Muslimah* refugees)
517 E. 26th Street
Erie, PA 16504
www.interinsterie.org

Islamic Society of North America
(Largest Islamic group on the
   continent)
P.O. Box 38
Plainfield, IN 46168
(317) 839-8157
www.isna.net

Karamah: Muslim Women
   Lawyers for Human Rights
(202) 234-7302
www.karamah.org

Muslim Public Affairs Council
(Advocacy group with offices in
   Washington and Los Angeles)
3010 Wilshire Boulevard,
   Suite 217
Los Angeles, CA 90010
(213) 383-3443
www.mpac.org

Muslim Wake Up
(Progressive online Muslim
   magazine)
P.O. Box 196
Pleasantville, NY 10570
www.muslimwakeup.com

Muslim Women's League
(Works to help Muslim women
   around the world)
3010 Wilshire Boulevard,
   Suite 519
Los Angeles, CA 90010
(626) 358-0335
www.mwlusa.org

Progressive Muslim Union of
   North America
(646) 485-1163
www.pmuna.org

Tahirih Justice Center
(Promotes justice for women
   and girls worldwide)
6066 Leesburg Pike, Suite 220
Falls Church, VA 22041
(703) 575-0070
www.tahirih.org

Vital Voices
(A women's international
   advocacy group)
1050 Connecticut Avenue, N.W.,
   10th Floor
Washington, DC 20036
(202) 772-4162
www.vitalvoices.org